Beachcomber's Guide to

MARINE LIFE
of the
PACIFIC NORTHWEST

THINGS TO PACK FOR TIDEPOOL
- HAND LENS ON CORD
- SMALL SHOVEL
- COLEMAN COLLAPSABLE STOOL
- WINTER BOOTS
- SKI SWEATER
- BOOT SOCKS
- BIRDING HAT
- FOUL WEATHER PARKA
- PROBABLY THE CANON SX50
- BOAT SHOES

Gulf Publishing Company
Houston, Texas

Beachcomber's Guide to

Marine Life

of the Pacific Northwest

Includes Vancouver, Washington, Oregon, and Northern California

Color Photography by Thomas M. Niesen

Black-and-White Photography by
Michael E. Kunz and Thomas M. Niesen

Line Drawings by David I. Wood

THOMAS M. NIESEN

To Peter Frank, Lynn and Jerry Rudy,
Nora and Bob Terwilliger, Bayard McConnaughey,
and Eugene Kozloff, marine biologists who taught me and
shared their love of the Pacific Northwest with me.

Beachcomber's Guide to
Marine Life of the Pacific Northwest

Copyright © 1997 by Gulf Publishing Company. All rights reserved.
This book, or parts thereof, may not be reproduced in any form without
permission of the publisher.

Gulf Publishing Company
Book Division
P.O. Box 2608 ☐ Houston, Texas 77252-2608

10 9 8 7 6 5 4 3 2 1

Library of Congress Cataloging-in-Publication Data

Niesen, Thomas M.
    Beachcomber's guide to marine life of the Pacific Northwest / by
Thomas M. Niesen ; color photography by T. Niesen ; black & white
photography by Michael E. Kunz & T. Niesen ; line drawings by
David I. Wood.
        p.   cm.
    Includes bibliographical references and index.
    ISBN 0-88415-132-8
    1. Marine organisms—Northwest, Pacific.   2. Coastal animals—
Northwest, Pacific.   3. Coastal plants—Northwest, Pacific.
4. Beachcombing—Northwest, Pacific.   I. Title.
QH104.5.N6N53   1997
578.77'09795—dc21   97-54
                                                                  CIP

Printed in the United States of America

CONTENTS

ACKNOWLEDGMENTS

To me, living in the Pacific Northwest was time spent in paradise. I moved to Oregon in 1969 to attend graduate school at the University of Oregon. Although I moved back to California four years later, I still consider myself a displaced Oregonian. For a marine biologist, nothing compares to the rugged yet diverse marine environment of the Pacific Northwest. In this book I hope to introduce the beachcomber to this beauty and variety.

I was shown great kindness by many people who helped in the preparation of this book. During my nostalgic trek through the Pacific Northwest, I benefited from the warm hospitality of Marcy Frank and Kevin O'Connor, Jim and Celeste Niesen, Bill and Nancy Edger, Lynda Shapiro, Nora Terwilliger, Lynn and Charlie Hunter, Diana and Mert Harris and their llamas, and especially, Jack and Mary Norman.

My knowledge of the Pacific Northwest was significantly enhanced by suggestions and conversations with Tony Roth and Anne Shaffer, and Drs. Jim Carlton, David Cowles, Megan Dethier, Jeff Goddard, and Charlie Hunter. These scientists shared their intimate knowledge of the Pacific Northwest marine environment with me, and I hope I have passed at least some of it on to you. Dr. Ray E. Wells of the United States Geological Survey was of great assistance in helping me understand the dynamic nature of the marine geology of the Pacific Northwest.

A special note of thanks goes to my dear friend Matt Luerken. Matt was my lab partner in my first college zoology class and has remained a partner in discovery ever since. Matt spent two weeks with me along the Oregon coast, assisting me in every aspect of this project. Unfortunately, an untimely injury sustained while experimenting with aging and gravity forced his premature departure from the trip. He has since fully recovered and gone on to contribute some excellent line drawings to this text.

In more direct relation to the technical preparation of this beachcomber's guide, I want to single out Michael Kunz for his extraordinary patience and consummate skill in black-and-white photography. Many of the black-and-white photos within are his, with an occasional "lucky" shot of my own. I would also like to thank David Wood for his expertise as an illustrator and biologist, and Linda Johnson for all the logistic support. The many line drawings David prepared for this book and for my previous *Beachcomber's Guide to California Marine Life,* particularly those in Chapters 2, 3, 4, 5, and 8, are exceptional. Matt Luerken rendered the drawings of the crabs *Oregonia gracilis, Oedignathus inermis, Telmessus cheiragonus,* and *Pinnixa faba.* My dear friend and longtime collaborator Suzanne Offutt Pouty provided the line drawings of the sea urchin and encrusting bryozoan used in Chapter 3.

Monique Fountain prepared most of the technical figures used in Chapters 1 through 4. Dr. Edward Lyke provided carte blanche access and borrowing privileges to his excellent dry shell collection which was the source of many of the shell illustrations in the book.

I would especially like to thank computer graphic artist Diane Fenster for all her time, help, and patience as I blundered into the realm of multimedia.

My wife, Anne Niesen, worked diligently to support us while I was on sabbatical leave writing this book. My daughter Amy, freshly graduated with honors from college, patiently read and corrected several drafts of the text, always with good humor, excellent suggestions, and much-appreciated encouragement. Thank you both.

At Gulf Publishing Company I'd like to thank Mr. Timothy Calk who supported the idea of this book from the beginning and helped in many ways to see it through. My special thanks go to my editor, Mrs. Toni King, who was a delightful partner to work with. I thank her very much for her kindness, patience, and professionalism.

1
INTRODUCING THE PACIFIC NORTHWEST

THE PACIFIC NORTHWEST COASTLINE

The Pacific Northwest conjures up different images for different people. To me, it is craggy sea stacks rising defiantly out of the ocean (Figure 1-1). To others, it is tall coniferous forests marching down to the ocean's edge or the majestic fin of a killer whale breaking the mirrored, quiet surface of a San Juan Island strait.

Whatever image comes to mind, one thing is clear: This region of breathtaking beauty does not correspond to any state or national boundaries. Most would delineate Oregon, Washington, and British Columbia as the Pacific Northwest, and some would include southern Alaska as well. However, for the beachcomber, the flora and fauna that characterize the Pacific Northwest region really begin in earnest in northern California as far south as Monterey Bay.

Anyone exploring the coastline of the Pacific Northwest quickly becomes aware of its beauty and diversity. Beyond the next curve in the coastal highway may lurk

Figure 1-1. The coastline of the Pacific Northwest. Ageless sea stacks rise defiantly from Rialto Beach, Washington.

a long sandy beach, a towering coastal headland, or a picturesque cove. Although these habitats may appear to pop up randomly along the coastline, there is a pattern to their distribution, and a brief consideration of the geology of the Pacific Northwest is helpful in understanding this pattern.

The Pacific Northwest sits along the eastern side of the Pacific Ocean and forms part of the Pacific Rim. The western side of the Pacific Rim consists of the Asian mainland and the Japanese and Philippine islands. The Pacific Rim is also called the Ring of Fire because of the numerous active volcanoes that are present along it. Recall the fury of Washington's Mt. St. Helens captured on film to understand the awesome power these volcanoes possess when they erupt. The flows of molten rock from the frequent eruptions of these volcanoes provided the erosion-resistant igneous rock characteristic of much of the Pacific Northwest. The volcanoes, along with the frequent earthquakes, are all manifestations of very active geological processes that are characteristic of the Pacific Rim.

The surface of our earth is not a continuous sheet, but is divided into a series of crustal plates. These plates float on the earth's molten core like a cracked but intact eggshell would sit on the surface of a hard-boiled egg. These plates are not static, but are in motion. On the deep sea floor along ridges where two oceanic plates join, molten rock (magma) wells up from below and adds new material to the edges of the plates, increasing their size. This causes the sea floor to spread and pushes the oceanic plates against the plates that make up the continents.

The Pacific Northwest consists of a number of plates butting up against one another (Figure 1-2). As the sea floor spreads actively along the Juan de Fuca and Gorda ridges in the deep Pacific Ocean immediately to the west of the Pacific Northwest, the oceanic plates

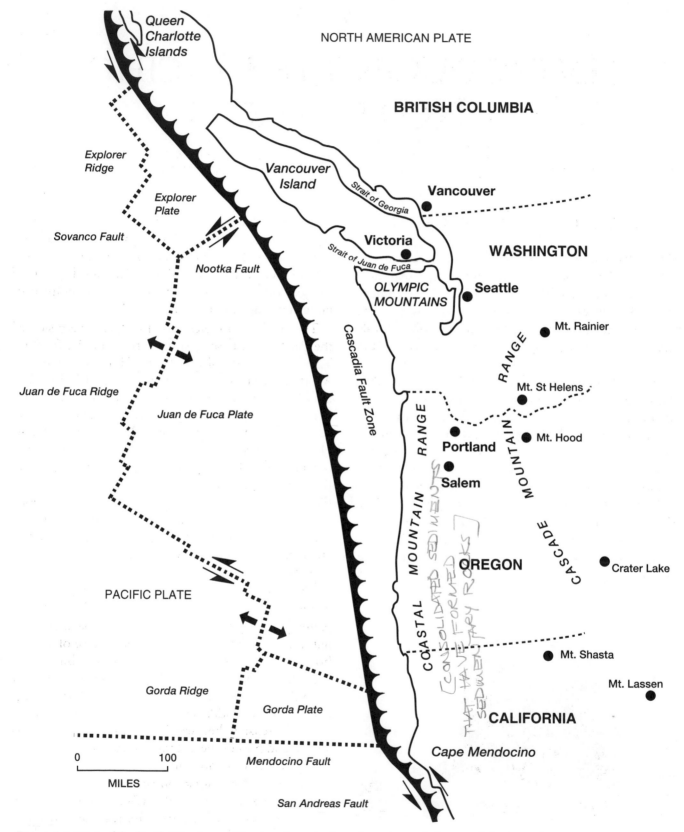

Figure 1-2. Map of the Pacific Northwest showing the oceanic and continental plates and the Cascadia Fault Zone. The Cascade, Olympic, and Coastal Mountain Ranges are also indicated.

SUBDUCTION (PUSHING)

(Juan de Fuca and Gorda plates) push eastward against the North American Continental Plate, and they buckle and jostle one another. The oceanic plates are made of heavier rocks than the continental plate, so the heavier oceanic plates slip underneath the continental plate in a process known as *subduction*.

The subduction process is not always a smooth one. For example, as the Juan de Fuca oceanic plate is subducted beneath the continental plate, the two plates do not slide past one another smoothly. Instead, tremendous friction develops along the plates' margins and they temporarily stick or lock. Geologists refer to this interface between plates as a *fault zone* and have named this region the Cascadia Fault Zone (Figure 1-2). Because the plates are temporarily unable to move, stress builds up along the fault zone, buckling the continental plate. The plates along a fault zone do not remain permanently locked. The mounting pressure caused by the continued growth and spreading of the oceanic plate overcomes the friction along the fault zone. The result is a sudden release of the locked plates which slide violently past one another, causing an *earthquake*.

Scientists have recently determined that the strain along the locked plates of the Cascadia Fault Zone builds to a point where it overcomes the friction causing the lock on an average of every 500 years [1]. This sudden release of built-up stress along the fault zone results in a catastrophic earthquake and a tidal wave called a *tsunami*. The last such earthquake and tsunami probably occurred in 1700, before white settlers had reached the Pacific Northwest.

As the oceanic plate is pushed down under the continental plate into the earth's mantle, its leading edge comes closer to the earth's molten core and is heated. As the edge of the plate is heated, volatile elements in its rocks and sediments are released, and the heat melts the mantle rock nearby. This molten mantle rock then rises up through fissures in the continental plate to manifest itself explosively on the surface as lava flows from volcanoes. Over millions of years of geological time, this process has provided the erosion-resistant igneous rocks (basalts and others) that were uplifted to form the present Olympic Mountain Range and inland Cascade Mountain Range (Figure 1-2). The deep fold that formed between these ranges became the Puget Sound basin in Washington and the Strait of Georgia to the north, and the Willamette Valley in Oregon to the south. The Olympic Range now forms the formidable coastline of northern Washington. The Cascade Range provides us with vivid reminders of the mountains' volcanic origins by the towering presence of such volcanic peaks as Washington's Mt. Rainier and Mt. St. Helens, Oregon's Mt. Hood and Crater Lake, and California's Mt. Shasta and Mt. Lassen.

Another geological process related to sea floor spreading—the addition or accretion of sediment—has also contributed to the coastline of the Pacific Northwest. Remember, as the sea floor spreads offshore along the deep sea rift zone, it pushes (subducts) the oceanic plate under the North American continental plate. In southern Washington and Oregon, the edge of the continental plate acts like a gigantic bulldozer blade and scrapes rocks and marine sediments off the oceanic plate as it is subducted beneath the continental plate. Over millions of years, these oceanic rocks and sediments piled up against the continental plate's edge and added to its margin. Today, these consolidated sediments form the sedimentary rocks that make up the low-lying coastal hills and mountains we see in Oregon and southern Washington, known collectively as the Coastal Range.

Thus, we see that sea floor spreading and the related processes of subduction, volcano formation, and continent building by sediment accretion have contributed to a dramatic and varied coastline available for the beachcomber to explore.

In the more recent past, the Pacific Northwest has been influenced by the last ice age. About 12–15 thousand years ago, much of the northern hemisphere was covered by a thick ice sheet. This ice sheet spread as far south as Puget Sound. The water contained in the ice sheet caused sea level to drop 400 feet. This exposed much of the shallow continental shelf along the coast. As the ice sheet melted and sea level rose, many changes were wrought along the coast. The advancing water weathered the soft sedimentary rocks of the Coastal Range, cutting flat marine terraces that typify the southern portion of the Pacific Northwest and providing much of the sediment that formed many of our sandy beaches and sand dune systems. Harder basaltic rocks that had been formed by volcanic processes and intruded into the sedimentary rock of the Coastal Range resisted erosion and became sea stacks and coastal headlands such as Oregon's Cape Foulweather and Otter Crest [2]. Coastal river valleys were flooded with the rising seawater. As sediment washed down from the mountains, it became trapped in these *[handwritten margin note, top: INTERTIDAL ZONE [LITTORAL ZONE] — WHERE OCEAN MEETS LAND]*

[handwritten margin note, left side, vertical: (3) DEGREE OF TIDAL EXPOSURE TO AIR | (2) TYPE OF BOTTOM SUBSTRATE | (1) WAVE ACTION]

drowned river mouths to form estuaries such as Coos Bay and Willapa Bay. Similarly, the San Juan Island Archipelago and Canadian Gulf Islands represent the tops of drowned mountain ranges. Finally, deep troughs caused by metamorphic folding or gouged by glaciers were flooded to become Puget Sound and the fjords of Washington, British Columbia, and Alaska.

PHYSICAL FACTORS INFLUENCING MARINE ORGANISMS

The beachcomber's domain—where the ocean meets the land—is known as the *intertidal zone* or *littoral zone*. Wave action is one of three major physical factors which influence what the beachcomber will discover in any given marine habitat. The other two factors are the type of bottom substrate and the degree of tidal exposure to air. The amount of wave exposure a given habitat receives is due to a combination of the proximity of offshore protection, the direction of the prevailing waves, and the geographic orientation of the habitat. For example, along the Oregon and Washington coast there are no large islands and few offshore submarine banks to intercept waves. Waves approach the shoreline primarily from the northwest in the summer and the west and southwest in the winter. Therefore, a rocky headland facing to the west will experience the full brunt of the heavy Pacific waves. The only organisms capable of living here will have to be able to attach and grow under the onslaught of the pounding waves. Behind the headland, a small sheltered cove that faces southeast will experience decidedly less wave action, and many fragile organisms may survive and flourish here.

Rocky substrate habitats provide many places for organisms to live. Depending on the nature of the rock and how it weathers, rocky areas can have considerable topographic relief. Broad rocky reefs with ledges, crevices, outcroppings, boulder fields, and tidepools provide a myriad of niches for organisms to occupy. Soft substrates, such as the sand on a sandy beach or the mud of an estuarine mud flat, provide many fewer sites for organisms. Because the surface of a soft substrate provides no fixed sites for attachment and is usually quite flat and exposed, the only place to live is beneath the substrate surface. As a general rule, the marine community living in a soft substrate habitat will have a relatively low diversity of organisms but can have very high numbers of individual species. Hard substrate communities tend to be highly diverse, with smaller numbers of individual organisms.

The final physical factor that influences what a beachcomber will encounter is the degree of tidal exposure a habitat receives. The higher an organism is located relative to the low tide mark, the longer it will be exposed to air. Most marine organisms must remain moist in order to breathe, and exposure to air dries them out. So not surprisingly, the only organisms a beachcomber will find in the highest tidal zone will be those that have special adaptations or behaviors to avoid drying out. As you move lower into the intertidal zone, the degree of exposure an organism encounters is reduced and more diversity will be discovered, with the most diverse areas occurring at tidal levels exposed by only the lowest tides. This effect is especially noticeable in rocky substrate habitats where organisms are attached to the rocks and directly exposed to air. The effect of tidal position can be somewhat reduced for organisms living in soft substrate habitats if the substrate remains saturated with water at low tide.

WHY IS THE WATER SO COLD?

Why is the water so cold? A visitor to the Pacific Northwest is sure to pose this question if he or she attempts to swim in the ocean. This is especially true if the beachcomber is from the East Coast and used to the warm water of summer that occurs there.

Why does this happen? In the ocean basins of the northern hemisphere, surface water circulates as a broad current in a large clockwise eddy or spiral. In the Pacific, the water warms at the equator, and the warm current flows northward along the coastline of Asia and then west in the chilly northern latitudes. When the water begins its southward flow along our coastline, all the heat that was captured at the equator has been released to the air. What we experience is the cold water that is flowing south back towards the equator to begin the cycle all over again. This southerly flowing cold water is known as the California Current. If you lived on the east coast of the United States, however, you would experience the warm water of the Gulf Stream, the surface current that flows north near shore in the summer bringing warm water up from the equator and the Gulf of Mexico.

The cold California Current is not the only factor in our cold water puzzle. Another is *upwelling*. Upwelling is a process that occurs when the wind blows along the shoreline, pushing the upper surface layer of water off-shore and allowing the colder water from below to well up in its place (Figure 1-3). This process occurs all along the West Coast; however, it occurs later in the season and much more strongly in central and northern California and southern Oregon than in southern California. By late spring, the winds that produce upwelling have pretty much abated in southern California, allowing the nearshore surface water to stay in place and be warmed by the increasing spring and summer sunshine. In central and northern California and Oregon, however, the northwesterly winds that produce upwelling are just beginning in the spring and will persist well into summer and sometimes into fall. Upwelling also occurs in Washington and British Columbia, but it is not as vigorous or persistent as seen in southern Oregon. These more northern latitudes are strongly influenced by the cold California Current and the water never warms much beyond the 50s.

Thus, cold water near shore is typical for the Pacific Northwest. And there is a bonus: As the air comes in contact with the ocean surface, it becomes saturated with water vapor. The air is cooled when it comes in contact with the cold upwelled water, and the water vapor condenses and produces that summer staple of the open coast of the Pacific Northwest—fog. As hot air rises from the summer-warmed interior valleys, it pulls the fog onshore where it sometimes remains on the open coast of Oregon and Washington for weeks at a time. Farther north where the coastline of Washington makes an abrupt turn east up the Strait of Juan de Fuca (Figure 1-2), you leave the consistent fog for the warm shadow of the Olympic Peninsula that gives the Puget

Sound region its mild winters and relatively fog-free summers.

Before you feel too sorry for the fog-bound beach-combers of the open coast, a few other facts need to be made apparent. Upwelling allows water loaded with plant nutrients to enter the upper sunlit portion of the ocean, which fosters a tremendous level of photosynthesis in the single-celled marine plants called *phytoplankton*. This high level of plant production that persists through the spring and into the summer enriches the food chain greatly and produces one of the richest marine environments in the world. To the beach-comber, this means a lot more diversity to discover and simply a greater abundance of marine life in general. Secondly, the spring and summer fogs influenced primarily by upwelling tend to occur most persistently in the early mornings. During these months, the lowest low tides also occur in the early mornings. Therefore, during the period when the fragile, low intertidal organisms of rocky habitats are liable to their most severe exposure to air, they are typically swathed in a cool blanket of moist, sun-blocking fog.

THE MARINE FLORA AND FAUNA OF THE PACIFIC NORTHWEST

Initially, the beachcomber who comes to the Pacific Northwest for the first time may feel that there are really two distinct marine environments: first, the exposed open coast of Oregon, Washington, British Columbia, and the west coast of Vancouver Island; and second, the protected inland waters of Puget Sound and the nestled islands of the San Juan Archipelago and British Columbia (Figure 1-4). However, with some exceptions that will be pointed out, these two areas share a similar suite of habitats and organisms that can be treated together.

Another complicating factor is that not all organisms are distributed continuously throughout the Pacific Northwest region. To explain this, one must understand that the primary physical feature that influences the geographic range of a marine organism appears to be water temperature. Water temperatures vary from north to south along the Pacific Northwest, and members of most groups including fishes, snails, and crabs may have their northern or southern distribution terminate midway along the extensive stretch of coast that encompasses this region. However, it should also be pointed out that many of the intertidal zone organisms

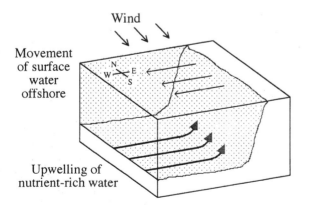

Figure 1-3. The upwelling process. Northwest winds blowing along the coast move surface water offshore, and cold, deep water replaces it.

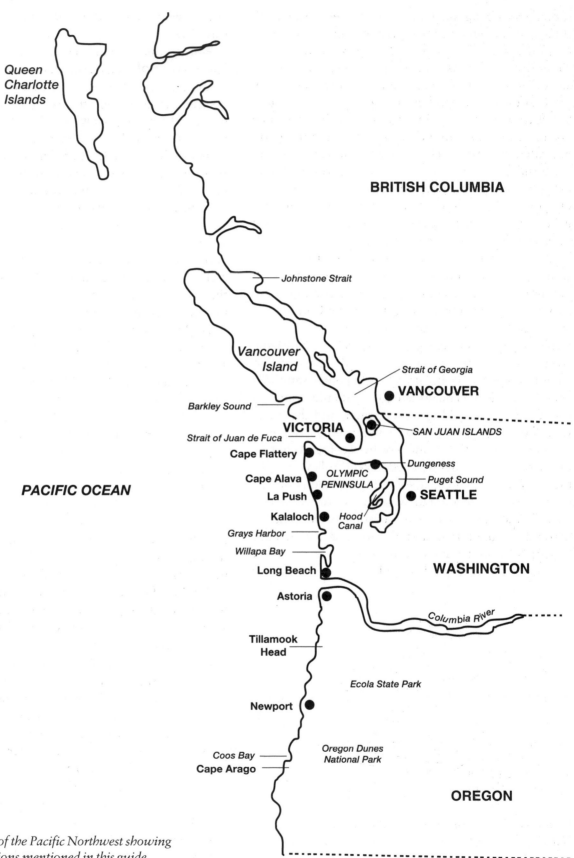

Figure 1-4. Map of the Pacific Northwest showing geographic locations mentioned in this guide.

BIOGEOGRAPHY — SCIENTIFIC STUDY OF DISTRIBUTION OF ORGANISMS

that a beachcomber will encounter are distributed continuously from Alaska to Baja California.

Origin of Marine Organisms of the Pacific Northwest

The scientific study of the distribution of organisms is known as *biogeography*. Marine biogeographers look at the geographic distributions of all the members of a group and, based on the pattern of overlap and co-occurrence they see, designate biogeographic provinces. Marine plants, especially the large seaweeds, essentially occur all along the coast without distinct, recognizable provinces. For marine animals, the biogeographers recognize a distinct cold water province that includes much of Alaska and a warm water province that includes the Gulf of California and the tip of Baja California. In between these two is a province referred to as a cold temperate region, and British Columbia, Washington, Oregon, and most of California fall into this province.

Over geological time, water temperatures have fluctuated along our coast. During periods of warmer water, elements of the tropical fauna to the south have migrated northward. Conversely, when the water cooled down, elements of the Arctic fauna moved southward. When the sea water temperature began to change, these animals either adjusted to the new water temperature, retreated back to their respective provinces, or evolved into new species capable of existing with the new seawater temperature.

What does all this mean to a beachcomber? Basically, it means that when you explore a habitat in the southern end of the Pacific Northwest you will encounter some animals that have the majority of their close relatives in the warm-water province to the south. These animals usually also have a distinct northern limit to their distribution along the open coast. An example of this would be the green-lined shore crab, *Pachygrapsus crassipes*. This crab is common in California and southern Oregon and has a majority of its relatives living in warm water [3]. However, along with these restricted warm-water species, you will find a much larger group of organisms distributed along the entire coast of the Pacific Northwest. Exploring a similar habitat farther north in the Pacific Northwest will reveal a certain portion of the organisms with affinities to cold-water relatives and distinct southern limits to their distribution. An example of this is the hairy crab, *Hapalogaster mertensii,* which is rarely found south of Puget Sound [3]. These animals with northern affinities will occur along with essentially the same batch of hardy critters you saw in the southern Pacific Northwest.

The types of marine habitats that the beachcomber will encounter in the Pacific Northwest are frequently much more influenced by the prevailing, unique conditions of the specific habitat rather than some overriding geographic condition. Likewise, the fact that the majority of the flora and fauna of these habitats is broadly distributed allows this beachcomber's guide to be organized into distinct habitat types that recur throughout the entire Pacific Northwest.

In this presentation, I will introduce those organisms with the broadest distributions as well as point out species that are present only in the open coast or the protected regions of the Pacific Northwest. I have followed a common, though not geographically correct, practice and arbitrarily lumped Puget Sound together with the inland waters to the north (technically, Washington Sound) as the "greater Puget Sound region" and will refer to them collectively as Puget Sound throughout this book.

Finally, it should be stressed that the organization of this book into distinct marine habitats is necessarily arbitrary. Most marine habitats are bordered by or merge with others, and likewise the organisms found therein frequently overlap. Always be prepared for a surprise, and don't hesitate to flip through the text to discover the identity of some creature that has the audacity to occur "out of place."

REFERENCES

1. Hyndman, R. D., "Giant Earthquakes of the Pacific Northwest," *Scientific American,* December 1995, pp. 68–75.
2. Baldwin, E. M., *Geology of Oregon.* Dubuque: Kendall/Hunt Publishing Company, 1976, 147 pp.
3. Jensen, G. C., *Pacific Coast Crabs and Shrimps.* Monterey: Sea Challengers, 1995, 87 pp.

2
KEYS TO SUCCESSFUL BEACHCOMBING

HOW AND WHERE TO LOOK

First of all, I should point out that if you have taken up beachcombing, you're already a success! There is nothing more relaxing than strolling along a broad, sandy beach in any kind of weather, or more exciting than the discovery of a new organism in an old familiar habitat. Here I will propose some helpful hints and suggestions for the beginner.

One of the first things new beachcombers should learn to do is adjust the way they observe the environment. We are preconditioned by our own bulk to look for large organisms and forget that the majority of marine organisms are inches or less in size. Many of the most fascinating organisms will only be discovered when you are anticipating something small. The big things will take care of themselves.

Because many organisms are so small, it is helpful to carry some type of magnifier. Many experienced beachcombers wear small hand lenses on cords around their necks. Others prefer simple magnifying glasses that they can slip into their pockets. Most nature-oriented stores stock a variety of such devices. One of the most ingenious is a plastic magnifier the size of a credit card that fits in your wallet.

Many small animals that become stranded on sandy beaches and some more delicate animals and plants of tidepools are more clearly viewed and appreciated when they are under water. Short of sticking your head in a tidepool, carrying a few small resealable plastic bags can be very practical. A word of caution, however: Placing an animal in such a small volume of water and passing it around to be handled by warm human hands can quickly heat up the water. Keep the observation time to a minimum or change the water frequently, every few minutes or so. Be sure to replace the animal where you found it. Don't carry glass containers, especially to rocky sites. Cuts from broken glass can bring a beachcombing outing to a quick and disappointing end.

Where To Look

Virtually any accessible site in the Pacific Northwest can be a rewarding place to beachcomb. However, beachcombers should be aware that beach access rules vary and much of the coastal area is private property. Be mindful of areas that are posted as "off limits" or signed "no trespassers." A good rule of thumb is to check with the local authorities if there is any question about access. Another way to proceed is to limit your beachcombing activities to the many designated sites found throughout the Pacific Northwest. These include national parks, state parks, and regional and county parks. Many beachcombers enjoy combining exploration of the ocean with camping.

The Pacific Northwest is a tourist mecca, and the states and provinces derive a good deal of their revenue from tourists. They eagerly welcome visitors and provide excellent assistance on site, over the phone, and through the mail. For British Columbia, call Super Natural British Columbia at 1-800-663-6000; for Washington, call Washington State Tourism at 1-800-544-1800; and for Oregon, call Oregon Tourism at 1-800-547-7842. I have experienced nothing but total cooperation and friendly, knowledgeable people at these numbers.

As mentioned in the first chapter, rocky intertidal sites tend to have a greater diversity of organisms than do habitats with soft substrates. Sandy beaches tend to be the least diverse, but their exposed nature allows them to collect a continuing parade of interesting wash-ups and occasional visitors. This is especially true after a storm when the bounty of the ocean is sometimes augmented by the folly of human beings. In 1991, 80 thousand pairs of sports shoes were lost overboard off the Oregon coast in a container ship accident. The shoes weren't tied together! Enterprising beachcombers soon organized swap meets to match up pairs of washed-up shoes. The shoes were still wearable after a year at sea.

shovel?

When beachcombing in soft sediment habitats, most discoveries will be made by digging. Sandy beaches have virtually no organisms that normally live exposed on the surface. Protected sand flats and mud flats may have a few hardy species obvious on the surface, but the majority of the organisms will be burrowed beneath the substrate. Carry a small shovel along or even a garden spade that you can stick in your belt or daypack. (Remember to wash these implements off—seawater is very corrosive.) Most organisms will be in the upper six inches of the substrate as they must maintain contact with the oxygenated water above to breathe. Some of the larger clam species in protected embayments may be considerably deeper, and only the most dedicated clammer is going to see them on any given day. Remember the size rule as you dig—many of the most interesting organisms will be quite small. Dig a narrow trench about a foot deep, two feet long, and six inches wide, and then carefully excavate the sediment along the side of the trench. Done with patience, this will reveal the organisms in their natural, burrowed position. When you are finished, cover up your excavation and bury your discoveries under a few inches of sediment—they'll take it from there.

Beachcombing in rocky habitats can be a lifelong adventure with new discoveries almost guaranteed with every trip. It is human nature to be drawn to the large and colorful organisms first. By all means, enjoy them to your heart's content. However, once you've run out of big, obvious organisms, readjust your search pattern and explore the diversity of the smaller, more cryptic organisms. Many small animals seek the shelter of crevices or seaweed, and many live under loose rocks and boulders. Careful searching of any of these niches will be rewarded with new treasures. A word of caution about turning rocks: Animals live attached to the rock's bottom as well as freely underneath it. Be careful when turning the rock not to crush any of the inhabitants. When you've finished exploring, turn the rock back over the way you found it. Place the free-living animals under other rocks or amongst seaweed so they won't dry out. Remember that organisms in the rocky intertidal zone are usually found in fairly specific locations

DIGGING

relative to the tide and exposure. Don't move them out of their preferred locations.

Tidepools are also great places for beginning beachcombers to explore. Take your time. Find a pool a few feet across and about a foot deep. Sit down quietly beside it, hold still, and watch. Soon you'll begin to detect flashes of movement from small tidepool fishes and shrimps. Next, the hermit crabs will poke themselves out of their shells and resume their never-ending search for pieces of food. After several minutes, the entire pool will come alive with the movement of dozens of snails and small crustaceans.

When To Look

Any time is great for beachcombing. Some of the most exciting trips take place at night when many nocturnal creatures are about. However, the serious beachcomber soon realizes that more can be seen during low tide than high, and some places aren't even accessible during high tide. It is necessary to learn about tides and tide tables to guarantee a fruitful beachcombing stint.

Tides are caused by the gravitational attraction of the sun and moon to the earth. The moon is the more powerful force, as it is so much closer to the earth than the sun. The Pacific Northwest coast experiences mixed, semi-diurnal tides. There are two daily high tides (one higher than the other) and two daily low tides (one lower than the other) over a 24-hour and 50-minute lunar day. Besides the daily cycle of tides, there is also a 29.5-day cycle that corresponds to the lunar month, the time it takes the moon to make a complete rotation around the earth. The sun and moon are lined up with one another during the new moon and full moon phases, and their combined attraction for the earth produces the most extreme tides, called *spring tides*. During the first and third quarter moon phases, the sun and moon are at right angles to the earth, and their counteracting attractions produce the smallest tidal variations, known as *neap tides*.

Tidal height on the west coast of the United States is measured from an arbitrary zero point called *mean lower low water* (MLLW). This zero point is the average of all the lower low tides that occur in a year. All tidal levels on the west coast of the United States are given in reference to this arbitrary point. A high tide listed in the tide table as +6.0 feet means the tide at its peak will be six feet above the average level of lower low water. A low tide listed as −1.5 feet means the tide

NEAP TIDES-SMALLEST TIDAL VARIATIONS

will be a foot and a half below this average level. The latter tide is referred to as a "minus tide," and represents the best time to beachcomb as more of the intertidal zone will be exposed.

Tidal height in Canada is not based on the MLLW tidal datum standard used in the western United States. To align Canadian tides with MLLW, beachcombers will need to subtract 2.5 feet from tide levels given for Victoria, and 3.8 feet from tide levels listed for Vancouver. Tide tables for the open coast of Vancouver Island are based on the tidal station at Sitka, Alaska, and are referenced to the MLLW tidal datum point.

Tides are listed in most coastal newspapers and in yearly tables which are available in most tackle shops or where fishing licenses are sold. Some of these tide tables are correct for the local area. More often, the tides listed are given in reference to fixed geographic locations where tidal information has been gathered. Most tide tables provide corrections for points that fall in between the fixed tidal locations. For example, tide levels and times for the Coos Bay, Oregon, area are given based on Humbolt Bay, California. Consulting the tide correction table reveals that the high tide in Coos Bay, which is up the coast from Humboldt Bay, will occur one hour and nineteen minutes later than at the Humboldt Bay tidal reference station.

Tide tables can be made up years in advance because the positions and effects of the sun and moon are highly predictable. However, tide tables cannot anticipate local weather conditions, which can significantly alter the actual tide that occurs on a given day. Large storm waves pushed by strong onshore winds can completely wash out a scheduled low tide and cause a high tide to be several feet above the tide table prediction. Likewise, a strong high-pressure area over the coast can push down on the water, causing the low tides to be lower than predicted and the high tides to fail to reach their predicted heights.

The tidal cycle is just one aspect of local ocean conditions that the beachcomber should be aware of. Periods of low wave action coupled with very low tides can provide the most opportune times for beachcombing, while high waves can prove very dangerous no matter what the tidal level. Never turn your back to the sea. Be very careful that you know whether the tide level is rising or falling. This is especially critical if you are exploring a cove or pocket beach that might get cut off as the tide rises. Similarly, a rocky intertidal area that has low-lying areas between you and the shore might flood as the tide comes in. Be very careful of large floating objects that lodge on the beach. This is especially true on the open coast where large logs often accumulate on open sandy beaches. Never get between a log and the water on a rising tide. Common sense coupled with a knowledge of the local tides and an awareness of local ocean conditions can provide a safe, enjoyable day of beachcombing.

A Note On Tidal Zonation

Beachcombing at low tide is usually best approximately two hours before and two hours after the scheduled low tide. Obviously, the lower the tide, the more area that will be exposed. This is important for rocky habitats as the organisms are distributed in somewhat distinct tidal zones. The lower you go in the rocky intertidal zone, the shorter the time the area is uncovered by the low tides. Thus, these lower zones experience less exposure to drying and are able to harbor a more fragile, diverse community. In this guide, I will present the organisms of the rocky intertidal habitat as they occur in these zones. A good beachcombing method is to explore the lowest exposed tidal zone first and move up into the intertidal as the tide rises. Remember to watch the waves!

Where To Go When It's Raining

When the Pacific Northwest weather is showing its ill temper and beachcombing is not an attractive option, beachcombers still have continued access to marine life. The Oregon Coastal Aquarium in Newport is a delightful place to spend a rainy day, or any day for that matter. In addition to more traditional aquarium displays, beachcombers can observe marine birds and mammals in specially designed outdoor enclosures. The aquarium is adjacent to the public wing of Oregon State University's Mark O. Hatfield Marine Science Center on Marine Science Drive.

The Oregon Coastal Aquarium has gained national recognition as the current home of Keiko, the killer whale star of the "Free Willy" movies. The United Parcel Service (UPS) air-lifted Keiko to Oregon in January 1996 after years in cramped quarters in a Mexico City amusement park. His new one-million-gallon home is ten feet deeper than his previous enclosure and has four times the water volume. Keiko is seen by the public only through huge underwater viewing windows, as there is no ring of spectator bleachers around the top of his tank. He will not be used in any shows or made to do any tricks. The tentative plan is to rehabilitate Keiko in Oregon because he is nearly a ton underweight and has some medical problems. The rehabilitation will last at least two years. If Keiko becomes strong enough to survive in the wild, he will be released back to his home pod in the waters off Iceland.

The Seattle Aquarium is also worth a visit. It sits in a decidedly more urban setting than the Oregon Coastal Aquarium, in the middle of Seattle's busy harbor-side tourist mecca. There is ample, (though expensive) parking, and the famous Pike's Market is right across the street for lunch. The Seattle Aquarium has excellent displays of local fish and invertebrates as well as marine mammal enclosures on the upper level housing sea otters and seals. There are also thoughtful exhibits on the ecology of Puget Sound and how human impact can be moderated.

The Vancouver Public Aquarium, located in Vancouver's Stanley Park, is a truly spectacular setting. The large outdoor marine mammal deck has killer whales, beluga whales (new baby born in July 1995), sea otters, and sea lions. Inside, exotic galleries include re-creations of an Indonesian national park complete with a coral reef and an Amazonian rain forest featuring free-ranging sloths, iguanas, and caiman crocodiles. There is also Rufe Gibbs Hall with native freshwater fishes displayed, and the Sandwell Hall with the marine life of the British Columbia coast displayed. Stanley Park itself is quite lovely, and a picnic lunch seems almost required.

In addition to these large public aquaria, numerous smaller aquaria and marine life exhibits abound in the Pacific Northwest. Check the local tourist literature for these opportunities. There are also several university marine stations throughout the Pacific Northwest, most of which have exhibits and public displays available to the beachcomber. These include Oregon State University's Hatfield Marine Science Center mentioned above; the University of Oregon's Oregon Institute of Marine Biology in Charleston, Oregon; the Friday Harbor Laboratories of the University of Washington on San Juan Island; Western Washington State's Shannon Point Marine Center at Anacortes; Walla Walla College's Biological Station at Rosario Point on Fidalgo Island; and Bamfield Marine Station on Vancouver Island, run by the Western Canadian Universities Marine Biological Society.

GEAR FOR THE COMPLETE BEACHCOMBER

I have already mentioned several pieces of equipment that come in handy for beachcombers. Shovels, hand magnifying lenses, and plastic bags are all simple but very helpful implements. I find it helpful to carry a small daypack to stash my gear so my hands can remain free to explore. If you are beachcombing on a sandy beach in the San Juan Islands on a warm August afternoon, you may wish to wear nothing more than your bathing suit and sunblock. More power to you! However, on that same afternoon in Yaquina Bay or Cape Avala, a down parka and hip waders might be more appropriate for the fog and cold wind that may occur.

A good dress code for beachcombing is that it is always better to overdress (Figure 2-1). You can always take it off if it gets too warm, but if you don't have it along you can get very cold which can ruin your day. Working on the open Oregon coast winter through

Figure 2-1. Beachcombers dressed for the Pacific Northwest.

summer, my standard outfit consists of a faithful pair of jeans, a wool sweater, a wool stocking cap, and a 20-year-old army field jacket that I can't part with. I wear boot socks and a good pair of lined rubber hip waders. I carry a backpack with my camera, a hand lens, some plastic bags, sunblock, waterproof paper and pencils, and a baseball cap to exchange for the wool cap if it warms up. If it looks like rain, I substitute a yellow foul-weather parka for my field jacket or carry a large garbage bag as an emergency poncho. I seldom get too cold, and I can be down to a T-shirt in very short order if the weather calls for it. I also carry a change of clothes in my car for the periodic dunkings I invariably experience.

I'm not trying to create beachcomber clones here, but just make the point that the day goes much more successfully if you are dressed for the weather. One final point is footwear. The classic barefoot beachcomber may be the ideal for the tropics and you may wish to emulate this on sandy beaches. However, you are better off shod when you explore rocky habitats which can have very sharp, slippery rocks. You will get your feet wet. It is required. Knowing this, you should avoid wearing leather shoes. Seawater will ruin even the best oil-treated boots. Wear shoes made of rubber or synthetic materials and rinse them well when you arrive back home. Soles that grip the surface, like the rippled soles on boat shoes, can give you some traction on slippery rocks.

FISH AND GAME REGULATIONS

Some beachcombers like to combine their exploration of the Pacific Northwest coast with some fishing, clamdigging, or crabbing. There are many opportunities for these enterprises, but it is up to the individual to be aware of the sport fishing regulations that apply. In Oregon, clamming and crabbing do not require a fishing license, while in Washington and British Columbia they do. Fishing requires a license in all locales.

Regulations vary for the different species of sport fishes. Some are protected by size limits and closed seasons, and some have specific gear requirements. It is a good idea to check with the local tackle shop for specific regulations. Most will have a brochure that outlines the state game regulations. I have also found these brochures available at the tourist information centers provided at strategic sites by the states of Oregon and Washington and the province of British Columbia.

The rules governing the taking of shellfish are also quite specific and differ among Oregon, Washington, and British Columbia. For certain species of clams, you are required to take the first animals you encounter, while other species have a size limit. Again, it is a good idea to check the sport fishing regulations for the specific location you wish to visit.

In addition to individual fishing regulations, clams, mussels, oysters, scallops, and crabs can experience periodic quarantines in local areas. Shellfish may be contaminated from exposure to bacteria, toxins, viruses, or chemicals. Consumption of contaminated shellfish can pose a health risk to humans. One common toxin occurs when particular plankton undergo growth spurts and cause a condition known as a red tide. The red tide organisms (single-celled, called "dinoflagellates") produce a toxin that is concentrated in the bodies of filter-feeding mollusks like clams and mussels. Eating contaminated shellfish can result in paralytic shellfish poisoning in humans. Severe cases can be fatal. Humans can also contract another illness, amnesic shellfish poisoning, when they eat shellfish that have been filtering a species of diatom (a single-celled phytoplankton organism) that contains a toxin called domic acid.

So be especially alert for posted notices of shellfish quarantines, and if there are any questions call the local health district office or the appropriate state or provincial agency. In Washington, there is a special Department of Health marine toxins hotline, 1-800-562-5632. In Oregon, the Department of Agriculture's Food Safety Division issues public health advisories for shellfish; the number is 503-986-4720. In British Columbia, the shellfish information number is 604-666-3169 and includes red tide updates.

CRABBING IN THE PACIFIC NORTHWEST

A special treat to beachcombers in the Pacific Northwest is crabbing. The Dungeness crab, *Cancer magister,* is the prize catch and can be taken successfully from docks, piers, breakwaters, and jetties in estuaries and embayments throughout the Pacific Northwest. Crabbers typically use crab rings or crab hoops that can be purchased or rented locally. These are usually baited with a fresh fish carcass and tossed over the side to "soak" for ten minutes or so. With great anticipation,

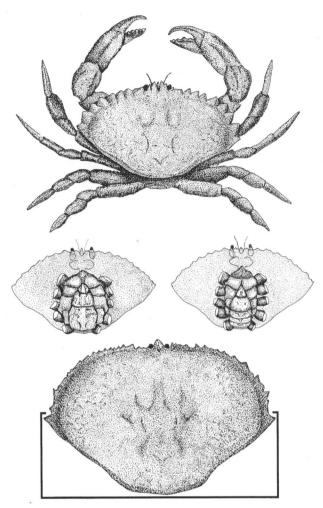

Figure 2-2. Dungeness crab carapace width measurement and male (right) and female bellyflap differences.

the trap is hauled up and the catch evaluated. Only male Dungeness crabs may be taken, and these must be at or over a minimum size. Sex is determined by the width of the bellyflap (abdomen) folded under the crab. Males have a slender flap; females have a wide flap (Figure 2-2). Size is measured across the back of the carapace just in front of the points at the carapace's widest point (Figure 2-2). Legal size varies throughout the Pacific Northwest, so consult local fishing regulations.

Crabbers should make sure that the crab is not soft. Up to half the crabs caught by crabbers have soft shells. Although they may be legal size, they contain only a small amount of watery meat that is hardly worth the trouble of cleaning and cooking. Soft-shelled crabs are not diseased, but have recently molted (see Chapter 9 on the Dungeness crab's life cycle). The new shell is not yet hard and the muscles have not grown to fill up the new, larger skeleton or shell. To determine if your crab is soft-shelled, give it the pinch test. Pinch the large section of one of the walking legs with about the same force you would use to burst a grape. If the shell gives easily, the crab will yield less than 20 percent of its weight in soft, mushy meat according to the Oregon Sea Grant Extension Service. The shell of a hard crab will not give when you pinch it and will yield top-quality meat. If you catch a soft-shelled crab, gently toss it back into the water. In two to three months it will be fully hardened and ready to be caught again, maybe by you!

A NOTE ON CONSERVING MARINE RESOURCES

I wish to conclude this chapter with a plea for conservation of our precious marine resources. Every year the marine habitats of the Pacific Northwest are visited by millions of people seeking recreation, relaxation, and revitalization. Our very presence takes its toll. Mindful of this, each visitor should endeavor to leave the marine environment as intact as he or she found it for the next visitor. Be careful where you walk. Replace marine organisms carefully where you find them. Don't expose delicate marine animals to undue stress. The temptation to take a sea star or hermit crab home ends with the death of the organism and a smelly reminder of your folly. A photograph will last a lot longer and ultimately will be much more satisfying. Treat these marine habitats with the same respect you would the home of a friend, because they are home to lots of friends of yours and mine.

3
SOME QUICK MARINE BIOLOGY*

A NOTE ON SCIENTIFIC NAMES

Traditionally, biologists give all unique living organisms a scientific name that is used to identify a distinct species. The scientific name consists of two words. The first, which is capitalized, is known as the generic name or the name of the genus to which the organism belongs. The second word, which is written in lowercase, is the species or specific name. By convention, the scientific name is either written in italic characters or underlined. As you know, humans are classified as *Homo sapiens*. The common Pacific sea star of the rocky intertidal zone is *Pisaster ochraceus*. It is possible for two species to have the same generic name or the same species name (for example, there is a whole batch of species named *nuttallii,* after the naturalist Nuttall); however, no two species will have both the same genus and species name. Sometimes, there is some uncertainty to the species name of an organism, and it will be represented with its generic name and the abbreviation "sp." (for example, "a new sea star species in the genus *Pisaster* was identified" or "a new *Pisaster* sp. was identified"). Sometimes, more than one species of a genus will be common to an environment, and they will be referred to as a group using the abbreviation "spp." meaning more than one species (for example, "several species of clam in the genus *Macoma* were common" or "several *Macoma* spp. were common").

In this book, I will first give the organism's common name if it has one, and will follow with the scientific name. Common names are easier to remember and often much more descriptive than scientific names, although they tend to vary with locality which can be confusing.

Quick and painless, I hope!

LIFESTYLES OF MARINE ORGANISMS

Unlike our earthbound habitat, the marine environment offers a new dimension for life: the water column. True, we have birds that fly in the air, but water provides buoyancy and effortless transport that simply doesn't have a terrestrial parallel. Marine organisms have evolved into ingenious forms to take advantage of this resource. The organisms most beachcombers will encounter are associated with the bottom and remain in place when the tide goes out. We refer to these bottom-dwelling organisms as *benthic* organisms or simply the benthos (meaning the organisms of the bottom). Animals and plants that use the water column for a home are referred to as *pelagic* organisms. Those pelagic animals and plants that drift passively with the water currents are known as *plankton*. Animal plankton is known as zooplankton, and the single-celled plants (diatoms and dinoflagellates) are called *phytoplankton*. The larger animals that are strong enough to swim free of the currents are called *nekton*. Nektonic animals include most fishes, squid, and marine mammals.

The majority of organisms included in this book are intertidal members of the benthos. Even though they live on or in the bottom and remain behind when the tide recedes, most are very dependent on the water column for one or more of their vital requirements. Obviously, these organisms need water to prevent death from dehydration, but many also use the water column for fertilization of their eggs, for transport of their kind to new environments, and for feeding. Sea urchins and sea stars, many snail species, clams, and a host of other benthic animals release their sperm and eggs into the water, where fertilization occurs. The fertilized eggs typically develop into larval forms that reside in the plankton, developing and feeding, until they mature and settle back to the bottom. More sophisticated animals that have internal fertilization, such as crabs and many bottom-dwelling fishes, still release their young as planktonic larvae.

Besides providing a rich food source for the planktonic larvae of benthic dwellers, the plankton and other organic material suspended and transported by water movement are a food source for a diverse group of benthic animals known as *filter feeders*. Animals such as sponges, clams, barnacles, sea cucumbers, and sea squirts employ an array of intricate filters to trap this rich food source. These animals are found in areas where water movement is relatively continuous, like open sandy beaches and exposed rocky habitats.

When water enters a quiet protected area, like a closed embayment, factors that cause water movement, such as wind and wave action, are reduced. As the water slows down, much of the suspended organic material falls out of the water onto the substrate. Here it is gleaned by a guild of animals known as *deposit feeders*. Deposit feeders include hermit crabs, some species of snails and shrimp, and many different kinds of worms. Some deposit feeders pick up individual deposited particles with specialized appendages and mouth parts. Others simply engulf the substrate wholesale like earthworms, and digest whatever organic matter it contains. Deposit feeders tend to dominate areas of quiet water in bays and estuaries where the bottom is typically soft mud.

Intertidal and nearshore subtidal rocky areas provide the solid substrate necessary for the attachment of large marine plants. These are chiefly the green, red, and brown seaweeds and surfgrass. Seaweeds provide a food source for a large group of invertebrate *herbivores,* such as snails and chitons, that graze directly on the living plants. Pieces of seaweed that are detached by wave action or herbivores provide a source of drifting algae that forms the staple diet of animals like sea urchins and abalone. Finally, the large plants are broken down mechanically by water movement and by decomposers like bacteria into particulate matter that becomes food for filter and deposit feeders.

With all the filter feeders, deposit feeders, and herbivores around, it's not surprising that an array of *carnivorous* species are in place to eat them. Fish and squid move in from the water column, while sea stars, crabs, and some snails and worms search along the various bottom habitats for their prey. Still others sit and wait to ambush their prey, like those deadly flowers, the sea anemones.

MAJOR MARINE PLANT AND ANIMAL GROUPS

Beyond the scientific name, biologists have erected a hierarchy of scientific classification. Hoping not to revisit the horrors of high school biology upon you, I will list the major marine plant and invertebrate animal groups with a brief description of each. For plants, this includes the major marine seaweed groups and the few marine grasses that occur in the Pacific Northwest.

Marine invertebrate animals vary incredibly in size and form. Here, they are introduced at the classification level known as the phylum (plural phyla), which unites broadly related invertebrates into a general group. The very diverse marine invertebrate phylum Mollusca, which includes such different animals as clams and octopus, is here further broken down to the more concise classification level known as the class.

The vertebrate animals in the sea include the fishes and marine mammals. Where accessible to beachcombers, most marine habitats will include few obvious fishes, so only a few are included in this guide. There are a number of field guides to marine fish available [1, 2, 3, 4, 5, 6]. One group of fish, however, cannot be ignored by this guide: the salmonids—salmon and trout of the Pacific Northwest. These fishes play an integral role in the history and economy of the Pacific Northwest, and their biology will be considered briefly in Chapter 9.

Marine mammals tend to be a wary lot and will usually only be viewed from some distance. The more common species seen in the Pacific Northwest are treated in Chapter 8. In addition, there are several good marine mammal references available [7, 8, 9].

Major Marine Invertebrate Phyla

Phylum Porifera. This phylum includes the sponges—the simplest of the multi-celled marine invertebrates. Their bodies are basically a porous filter which traps organic material down to the size of bacteria. The sponge has many small openings or pores over its entire surface that lead to chambers where filtration takes place. These chambers are lined with special cells, called collar cells, that possess long, whip-like flagella. These flagella beat to create the current that pulls water into the sponge and sends it out again through larger exit openings. Most sponges in the intertidal zone grow close to the rocky surface and spread in an encrusting

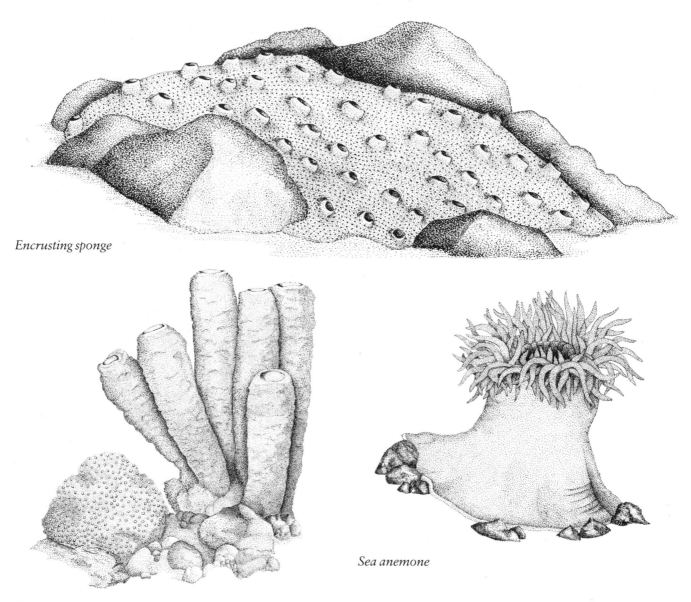

Encrusting sponge

Sea anemone

Erect sponge

sheet of sponge tissue. In deeper, quieter water, sponges grow erect and reach elaborate sizes and shapes in the more favorable habitats such as coral reefs. Sponges are often brightly colored, with red, orange, and yellow species the most common.

Phylum Cnidaria. The cnidarians include such familiar animals as sea anemones and jellyfish. All members of this phylum possess special cell organelles called nematocysts which are used to capture food and for defense. Nematocysts come in a variety of types, and some penetrate and poison their prey while others entangle it with sticky substances. The nematocyst-

bearing cells are always located on a ring of tentacles surrounding the cnidarian's mouth, and elsewhere on the body depending on the group.

There are two basic body types found in the cnidarians: the polyp and the medusa. The sea anemone is an example of the polyp body form. It consists of a column of tissue with a bottom disk for attachment and an upper disk which bears the mouth and tentacles. Polyps are attached to the substrate and often occur in colonies of many polyps, such as a coral colony. The polyps in a colony can be quite small in size, and the overall colony bush-like. These bush-like colonies are known as hydrozoan colonies or hydroids.

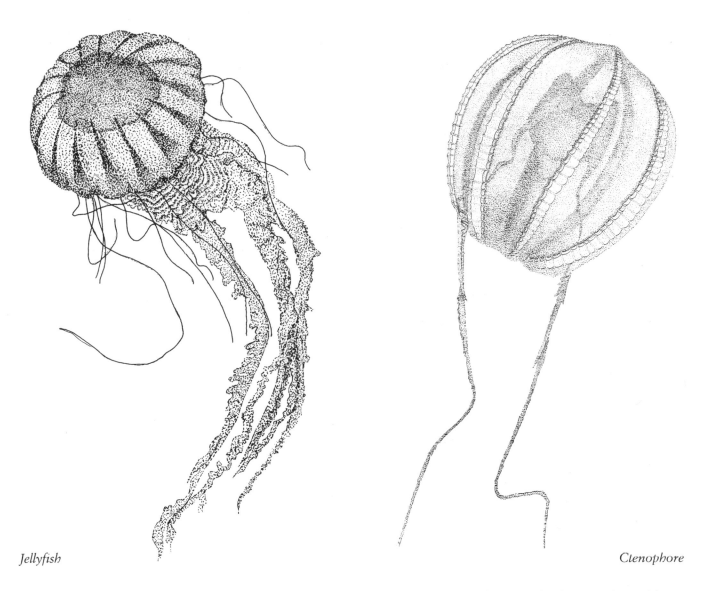

Jellyfish

Ctenophore

The jellyfish is an example of the medusa body form. It has a bell-shaped umbrella with the mouth hanging downward in the center, surrounded by a ring of tentacles around the edge of the umbrella. The medusa can swim by contraction of the bell, which forces water out and propels the animal in the opposite direction. Some cnidarians have both body forms in their life cycles, while others have only the polyp or the medusa form.

Phylum Ctenophora. Ctenophores are a small group of medusa-like animals that are commonly called comb jellies. They were once considered to be closely related to the cnidarians, as they have a circular body plan. However, ctenophores do not possess nematocysts and are now considered only distantly related to the cnidarians. Ctenophores are planktonic animals.

They swim through the water by the coordinated beating of eight bands of fused ciliary plates called ctenes. Ctenophores feed on planktonic animals which they either capture with special adhesive tentacles or swallow whole. They are sometimes quite abundant in bays and often wash up on sandy beaches.

Phylum Plathyhelminthes. The name literally means "flatworm," and includes the major parasitic groups—the flukes and tapeworms. It also includes a large group of simple, free-living worms that vary in size from microscopic to two feet in length. The marine flatworms typically encountered by the beachcomber are found under smooth rocks in the intertidal zone. These animals are usually a mottled brown or gray color, from one to two inches long, and very flat. They

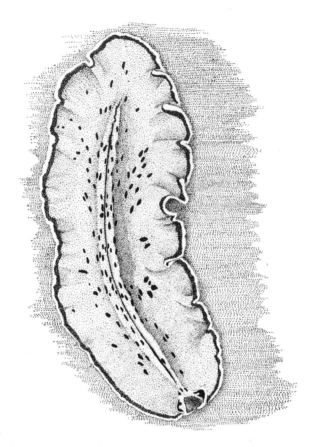

Flatworm

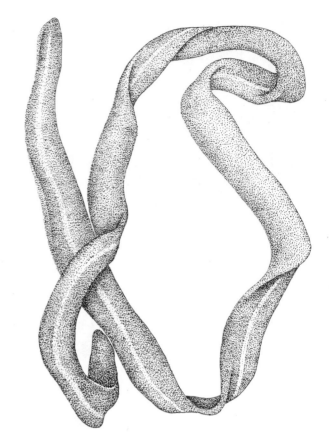

Nemertean

are usually about three times as long as they are wide and often have a series of eyespots anteriorly and along their sides. These flatworms glide along the moist rocks on cilia and can also swim by undulating their flat bodies. Intertidal flatworms have a mouth located in the center of their bottom (ventral) surface and feed on organic debris or small invertebrates.

Phylum Nemertea. The nemertean worms are known as ribbon worms or rubber band worms. They are considered to be closely related to the flatworms. However, instead of being flat, they are very elongated. The long worm body is adapted to moving through tight quarters, burrowing through the sediment or living in a tube. Ribbon worms vary in size from a few inches to several feet in length, and are capable of tremendous stretching. A worm eight inches in length when contracted can stretch to over a yard long! Ribbon worms are found in a variety of habitats including soft sediments and the rocky intertidal zone. Most make their living feeding on live invertebrate prey which they capture with a unique feeding structure

known as a proboscis. The proboscis is housed in a special cavity in the body wall and can be shot out very rapidly by the contraction of the body wall musculature. The proboscis is sticky or armed with poison barbs, and quickly entangles and subdues the prey which is then brought to the mouth and swallowed.

Phylum Annelida. The annelid worms include the familiar garden earthworm and the medicinal leech. Most marine annelids belong to the annelid class Polychaeta. Polychaete worms are widely distributed in the marine environment and have a variety of lifestyles. Several different species will be discussed in this guide. Shown is a free-living or "errant" polychaete from the genus *Nereis*. As you can see, *Nereis'* body is organized in distinct rings ("annelid" means arranged in rings) or segments, each equipped with special appendages for locomotion. These segmental appendages are strengthened by stout bristles or setae which assist the worm in gaining traction with the substrate. The head is equipped with a number of sensory appendages for testing the worm's environment as it encounters it head-

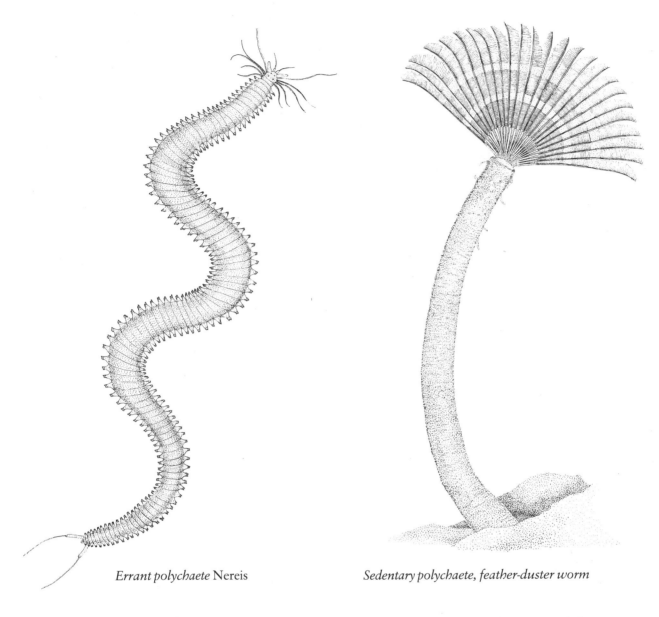

Errant polychaete Nereis   *Sedentary polychaete, feather-duster worm*

first. *Nereis* is able to evert its pharynx (the anterior region of its digestive tract) which is armed with jaws to capture prey. Errant polychaetes typically move about freely either through soft substrates or on the surface, and feed on live prey or large food particles like seaweed or carrion (dead animal tissue).

The second polychaete illustrated here is an example of a "sedentary" polychaete, and is known as a feather-duster worm. This polychaete lives in a mucous tube, and the elaborate plume of "feathers" are special ciliated head appendages which are used for filter feeding. Sedentary polychaetes typically live in a permanent or semi-permanent space like a tube or burrow. They feed on particulate organic matter or plankton which they capture by filter or deposit feeding.

Phylum Sipuncula. The sipunculid worms are commonly called peanut worms. They are considered to be close relatives of the annelids. Sipunculids are simply organized with a body consisting of a bulbous trunk region and an elongated "neck" or introvert which they can roll inward like the finger on a glove. When the introvert is rolled in all the way, the swollen trunk has the shape and size of a peanut, and thus the origin of their common name. When the introvert is unrolled (everted), the mouth opening is found at the end surrounded by a ring of tentacles which are used for filter or deposit feeding. Sipunculid species are found in soft substrates among the roots and holdfasts of surfgrass and seaweeds, respectively, and also in cracks and crevices among the rocks in the rocky inter-

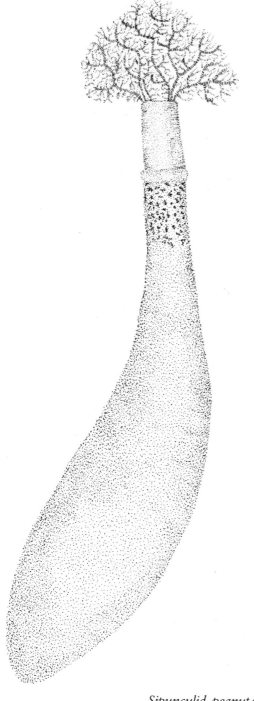

Sipunculid, peanut worm

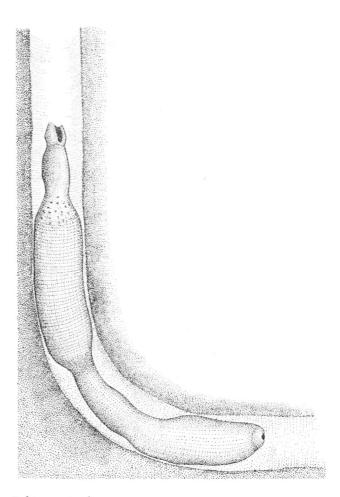

Echiuran, innkeeper worm

tidal zone. The common species found along the coast of the Pacific Northwest are small, ranging in size from one to four inches long when the introvert is fully everted.

Phylum Echiura. The echiuran worms are also considered to be closely related to the annelids. These worms are very plain-looking with a bulbous trunk and an anterior, flexible proboscis which contains the mouth. Echiurans are found in soft sediment habitats and are usually deposit feeders. The only species that may be encountered by beachcombers is the fat innkeeper worm, *Urechis caupo,* living in the sandy-mud flats of coastal embayments of southern Oregon. The innkeeper is a burrow-dwelling filter feeder.

Phylum Bryozoa. The bryozoa are small colonial animals that are often overlooked. These miniature animals live in small calcareous (made of calcium carbonate) houses that are attached together. The houses are usually rectangular in shape, and a colony consists of large numbers of these small houses that form an overall basket-weave or reticulate pattern. Bryozoans are filter feeders. They employ a tentacular device known as a lophophore for feeding which can be elevated above the calcareous house. A variety of colonial growth

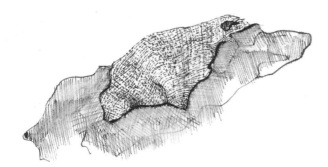

Bryozoan colony—flat, encrusting sheet

Bryozoan colony—bushy and upright

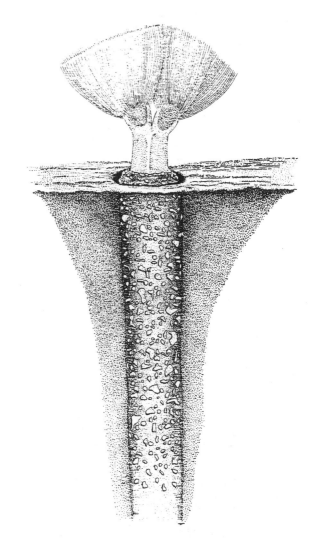

Phoronid

forms is found among bryozoan species. Some colonies grow in flat, encrusting sheets on a variety of substrates including rocks, the shells and exoskeletons of animals, and seaweeds. Other colonies grow bushy and upright and look superficially like finely branched algae.

Phylum Phoronida. The phoronids are a small group of marine worms that also have the feeding structure known as a lophophore like the bryozoans discussed above. The phoronid lophophore is a continuous double row of ciliated tentacles folded into an elaborate horseshoe shape. The phoronid has a plain, unsegmented body that remains enclosed in its chitinous (stiff, cellulose-like material) tube. The tube is oriented vertically in the substrate with the lophophore extended anteriorly above the surface for filter feeding. *Phoronopsis viridis* is a species found in southern Oregon which lives in large aggregations in the low intertidal regions of sandy mud flats in protected coastal embayments.

Phylum Mollusca. The mollusks are one of the largest and most diverse of the invertebrate phyla. Included are such various forms as clams, squid, and abalone. Mollusca means "soft body" in Latin, and at the heart of the molluscan organization is a soft, pliable body protected by a calcareous shell. The shell is secreted by a special epidermal tissue known as the mantle which completely underlies the shell. Between the shell

Snails known as limpets

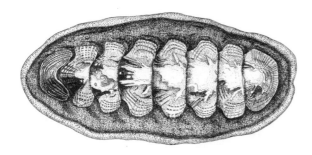

Chiton

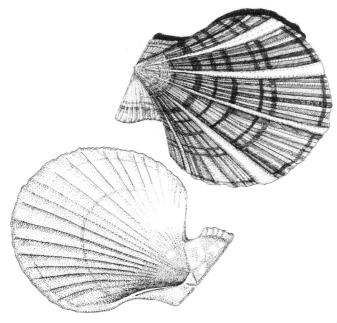

Scallops

adhere to the irregular surfaces of the intertidal rocks where it typically lives. Chitons still possess the large molluscan foot for locomotion and adhesion, and a large radula for feeding on seaweeds.

The class Bivalvia includes all the mollusks that have a shell divided into two plates or valves that completely encase the body, such as a clam or a scallop. All bivalve mollusks have a body that has been compressed laterally (from the sides) and a foot that is now spade-shaped and narrow instead of broad and flat. The shell is divided in two by a hinge made of protein along the mollusk's back which allows it to gape open at the bottom so the foot can protrude. The spade-like foot is used for burrowing into the substrate for safety. Bivalve mollusks have lost the radula and instead use their large ciliated gills to filter food. As filter feeders, the bivalves can feed anywhere they can successfully attach or burrow and have access to the water column. Thus, such diverse forms as clams, mussels, oysters, and the scallops shown here can be found.

Finally comes the class Cephalopoda which includes the familiar octopus and squid. Cephalopods are the most intelligent and motile of the mollusks. The octo-

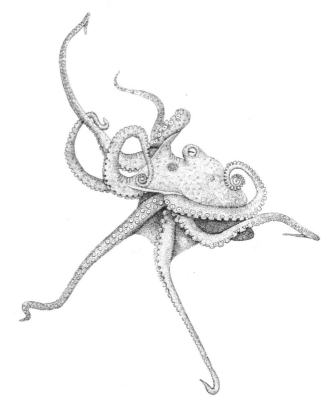

and the body is a space, lined by mantle tissue, that houses a pair of large gills used for breathing. This is called the mantle cavity. The basic mollusk hauls this shell-encased soft body around on a broad, flat muscular foot. The head is at the anterior end of the body and typically has a pair of sensory tentacles, and a special rasping feeding structure, known as the radula, within the mouth cavity. This is a description of what zoologists visualize as an ancestor to the modern mollusks, and it would look similar to a modern-day marine snail we call a limpet. Three limpet shells are illustrated here. Snails belong to the class Gastropoda which contains a wondrous number of species with and without shells, many of which will be found in this guide.

Not too far removed form the basic mollusk just described is the chiton (class Polyplacophora). The chiton has a shell divided into eight valves or plates. This gives it some flexibility and allows it to conform and

Octopus

pus moves along the bottom on eight suckered arms and swims via jet propulsion by forcing water in and out of its enlarged and muscled mantle cavity. Squids live in the water column, and their mantles are even larger and more muscular than those of the octopus, allowing them rapid movement that lets them swim and capture some fish. These animals are carnivores. They feed with stout, beak-like jaws that allow them to subdue prey and bite them into pieces.

Phylum Arthropoda. The largest of all the animal phyla is the Arthropoda. Included here are the insects, the spiders, and in the marine environment, the crustaceans (class Crustacea). The arthropods have two morphological features that are the keys to their incredible success. The first is a thickened outer covering called an exoskeleton. The second is the jointed limb ("arthropod" literally means jointed limb). The limb is actually a series of tubes joined together by flexible membranes. Each joint allows movement in only one plane. When a number of these tubes are strung together in line with muscles to flex them, with each joint flexing in a different plane, a limb with a great range of movement can be obtained. Thus we find arthropods that can walk, swim, and even fly.

The marine arthropods known as crustaceans occur in a bewildering number of shapes and sizes. Such different animals as barnacles and shrimp are both crustaceans. A review of the entire group would be too lengthy here, and the individual crustacean species will be introduced separately in the guide. However, it should be remembered that all these animals have the

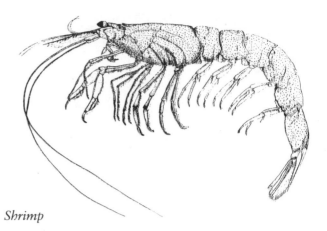

Shrimp

protective exoskeleton and the jointed limb in common. The exoskeleton is made of a tough animal material called chitin and calcium carbonate salts that give its "crusty" texture. Also, all crustaceans have the necessary limitation the exoskeleton imparts in that they must shed the exoskeleton to grow. The periodic shedding of the old exoskeleton and its replacement with a new one is known as molting. Molting is very time and energy consuming, and leaves the crustacean very vulnerable to harm. The new exoskeleton must be soft so it can be extracted from the old one, and to allow it to be stretched so the animal can increase in size. The crustacean is defenseless while it is molting and waiting for the new exoskeleton to harden. During this time, it becomes very secretive and hides from prospective predators which often include members of its own species.

Before leaving the arthropods, a little crab taxonomy is necessary. Among the crustaceans, the name "crab" is given to a variety of fairly divergent animals. Hermit "crabs," for example, are crustaceans highly modified to live in a snail shell. The appendages of their abdomen are reduced in number and size, and the last two pairs of walking legs are reduced and modified to position and hold onto the shell. Zoologists believe that hermit crabs were the ancestors of a number of other "crab" groups. This is based on a number of similarities, but the most obvious is the fact that in these groups the last (fifth) pair of walking legs is small and reminiscent of those of the hermit crabs. These crabs have only four pairs of walking legs visible (remember that the claws are modified walking legs), as the fifth pair is kept folded under the abdomen and out of sight. Porcelain crabs (family Porcellanidae) belong to one of these groups, and a second group is the lithode

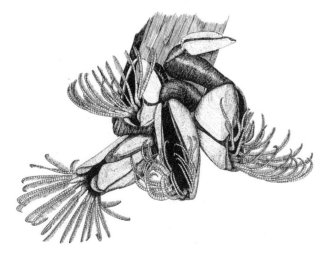

Crustacean—barnacles

crabs (family Lithodidae), members of which will be discussed in this book. These crab-like crustaceans are distinguished from "true" crabs which have five pairs of prominent walking legs visible. True crabs are further identified by having both pair of antennae located between their eyes. Hermit crabs and their allies have the second, large pair of antennae located to the outside of their eyes.

Phylum Echinodermata. The echinoderms are a group of exclusively marine animals. They are all organized in a circular or radial fashion as adults and possess a unique, internal hydraulic system known as the water vascular system. The water vascular system uses sea water as its hydraulic fluid and terminates in structures known as tube feet. Tube feet are used for locomotion, feeding, and respiration (breathing). Echinoderms include the familiar sea stars (starfish) and sea urchins. Also found in this phylum are the serpent or brittle stars and the elongated sea cucumbers.

Echinoderms have an internal skeleton like our own, composed of calcium carbonate. The individual skeletal elements may be tightly joined together like the skeleton or "test" of a sea urchin, or more loosely articulated to allow movement like that seen in the arms of sea stars or serpent stars. The tube feet are equipped with suckers in the sea stars, sea urchins, and sea cucumbers, and are used for locomotion as well as food gathering. The serpent stars use their long, thin

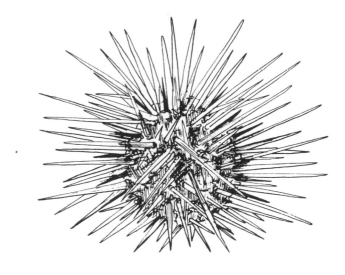

Sea urchin

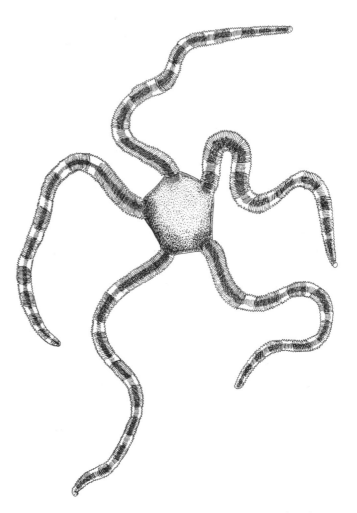

Sea star (starfish)

Serpent or brittle star

Sea cucumber

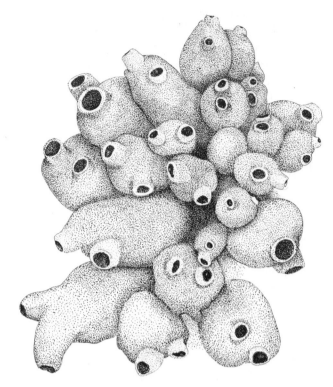

Sea squirt

arms to drag and push themselves along, and their tube feet serve mainly for food manipulation. All echinoderms use the thin-walled tube feet as sites for respiration. As a general rule, echinoderms are relatively large invertebrates, and species will be treated individually in this guide.

Phylum Chordata/Subphylum Urochordata. The chordate animals have a dorsal hollow nerve cord, a stiff rod known as a notochord, gill slits, and a post-anal tail. This phylum includes the familiar backboned animals including ourselves (subphylum Vertebrata), and the subphyla Urochordata and Cephalochordata known as the invertebrate chordates. Only the Urochordata will be treated here.

The majority of animals in the subphylum Urochordata are sessile (stationary) filter feeders known as sea squirts or tunicates. Sea squirts look very little like other chordate animals as adults, and only their larvae show the chordate characteristics mentioned above. Sea squirts vary in size from peach-sized individuals to minute animals joined together in a colony. The sea squirt is encased in a skin-like tunic which can be thick and woody or soft, transparent, and quite colorful. Within the tunic, the body of the sea squirt is dominated by a large filter-feeding basket which is the forerunner of our own throat region. Water is pumped into and through openings or slits in the basket by cilia on

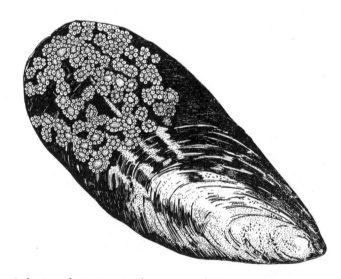

Colonies of miniaturized sea squirts living in a common tunic on a mussel shell

its inner surface. Food particles are trapped as they pass through these openings, and are carried on to the animal's stomach. Sea squirts are usually attached to a solid substrate. Large solitary species are typically attached to rocky substrates. Colonies of miniaturized individuals living in a common tunic may be found on a variety of surfaces including rocks, pier pilings, and floats, as well as the bodies of other invertebrate animals, such as the shell of a mussel as illustrated. These colonies are known as compound tunicates.

Marine Plants

The majority of large, obvious plants a beachcomber will see are seaweeds or algae. The seaweeds are considered relatively primitive plants by botanists because they lack the elaborate conductive tissues and nutrient-gathering roots of the vascular plants that dominate terrestrial environments. However, because seaweeds are bathed by nutrient-bearing water, they can survive perfectly well without these specializations, and many grow to very large sizes.

Seaweeds require light and a solid attachment site to prosper. They are attached to the substrate by a mass of root-like, adhesive processes collectively called a holdfast. Because the entire plant is capable of absorbing the nutrient fertilizers from the water, true roots are not necessary, and the holdfast tissue has no special absorptive ability. In a typical alga, stem-like structures

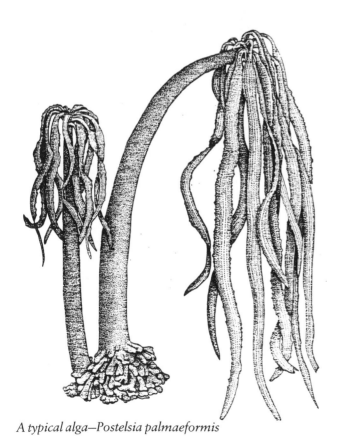

A typical alga—Postelsia palmaeformis

called stipes grow from the holdfast. The stipes in turn support flat blades. In some seaweeds, there are no recognizable stipes, and the blades grow directly from the holdfast. The relative size of the stipes and blades varies considerably from one algal species to another. The size of the holdfast is directly related to the size of the plant and the particular environment in which it grows. Algae growing in the exposed rocky intertidal zone need much larger holdfasts than those growing in a protected, quiet water environment.

Marine seaweeds belong to three main groups, the green algae (Chlorophyta), the red algae (Rhodophyta), and the brown algae (Phaeophyta). Green algae are the least diverse and tend to be found in fairly shallow, inshore environments. The plants are usually thin, sheet-like, and a bright green color. Green algae can be very abundant in a local situation and very short-lived. For example, the tissue-thin sea lettuce, *Ulva* spp. (Color Plate 1c), sometimes covers nearly every hard substrate visible, and a week or so later is almost entirely gone.

Red algae are the most diverse, and individual species occur in a range of colors and sizes (see Color Plate 2). A red alga can be red, brown, green, or violet. Species vary in size from intricately branched, lacy forms a few inches long, to broad, flat blades over two feet long. Some red algae, called coralline algae, incorporate large amounts of chalk-like calcium carbonate between their cell walls and have a coral-like texture. Red algae occur from the intertidal zone down to over 100 feet below the surface.

Brown algae are usually brown to dark brown in color. Among them are the largest of all the seaweeds, the kelps. Kelp species can reach well over 100 feet in length, and occur in large subtidal aggregations or beds. Kelp species occur from the middle rocky intertidal zone down to below 100 feet. Smaller, non-kelp brown algae called rockweeds are found in the high rocky intertidal zones.

The beachcomber might encounter several hundred common marine algae in the rocky intertidal zone. Only the largest, most obvious species will be mentioned in this guide. There are several more extensive guides available [10, 11, 12].

The so-called higher plants or vascular plants are not widely represented in the marine environments of the Pacific Northwest. Surfgrass (Color Plate 3c) is found in the middle and low rocky intertidal zones and below, and eelgrass (Color Plate 3d) occurs in quiet water habitats. There are many common salt marsh plants and plants that occur on coastal dunes. Beachcombers can find more extensive information about these plants in the following references [13, 14, 15].

REFERENCES

1. Eschmeyer, W. N., et al., *A Field Guide to Pacific Coast Fishes of North America, The Petersen Field Guide Series.* Boston: Houghton Mifflin Company, 1983, 336 pp.

2. Somerton, D. and C. Murphy, *Field Guide to the Fish of Puget Sound and the Northwest Coast.* Seattle: University of Washington Press, 1977, 71 pp.

3. Fitch, J. E. and R. J. Lavenberg, *Tidepool and Nearshore Fishes of California.* Berkeley: University of California Press, 1975, 156 pp.

4. Miller, D. J. and R. N. Lea, *Guide to the Coastal Marine Fishes of California.* Sacramento: California Department of Fish and Game, 1972, 249 pp.

5. Gotshall, D. W., *Fishwatchers' Guide to the Inshore Fishes of the Pacific Coast.* Monterey: Sea Challengers, 1977, 108 pp.

6. Feruson, A. and G. Cailliet, *Sharks and Rays of the Pacific Coast.* Monterey: Monterey Bay Aquarium Foundation, 1990, 64 pp.

7. Leatherwood, S. and R. R. Reeves, *The Sierra Club Handbook of Whales and Dolphins.* San Francisco: Sierra Club Books, 1983, 302 pp.

8. Orr, R. T., and R. C. Helm, *Marine Mammals of California.* Berkeley: University of California Press, 1989, 92 pp.

9. Flaherty, C. 1990, *Whales of the Northwest.* Seattle: Cherry Lane Press, 1990, 25 pp.

10. Abbott, I. A. and G. J. Hollenberg, *Marine Algae of California.* Stanford: Stanford University Press, 1976, 827 pp.

11. Dawson, E. Y. and M. S. Foster, *Seashore Plants of California.* Berkeley: University of California Press, 1982, 226 pp.

12. Waaland, J. R., *Common Seaweeds of the Pacific Coast.* Seattle: Pacific Search Press, 1977, 120 pp.

13. Wiedemann, A. M., *The Ecology of Pacific Northwest Coastal Sand Dunes: A Community Profile.* U.S. Fish and Wildlife Service, FWS/OBS-84/04, 1984, 130 pp.

14. Munz, P. A., *Shore Wildflowers of California, Oregon, and Washington.* Berkeley: University of California Press, 1964, 122 pp.

15. McConnaughey, B. H. and E. McConnaughey, *The Audubon Society Nature Guides: Pacific Coast.* New York: Alfred J. Knoph Inc., 1988, 603 pp.

4

THE SANDY BEACH

TYPES OF SANDY BEACHES

Sandy beaches dominate much of the open coastline of the Pacific Northwest, stretching uninterrupted for miles in many regions (Figure 4-1). These sandy beaches represent the most physically controlled of all the nearshore marine habitats, and as such one of the most difficult to live in. Some background on the formation and dynamics of sandy beaches is helpful in understanding the nature of the habitat and the animals that live there.

Sandy beaches have several things in common. All are composed of sediment particles that overlay a rocky beach platform. Beyond that, they can vary considerably. The sediments that make up these beaches are small pieces of rock, mainly the minerals quartz and feldspar. These minerals are either weathered from the continental rocks and washed down to the ocean in rivers or are the products of coastal erosion. Once these sediment particles reach the sea, they are carried along the coast until they find their way onto a sandy beach or offshore and perhaps down a submarine canyon. The transport of sediment along the coast requires water movement in the form of waves and currents.

Waves come from all directions along the open coast, and the direction is related to prevailing wind patterns. When the waves come on shore and break, they often break at an angle to the shoreline with some of their energy generating currents that run along the beach. These are called longshore currents, and as they move along the coast they carry sand particles with them. This movement of sediment along the beach is called longshore transport (Figure 4-2). In the summer, the prevailing wave direction is from the northwest, the prevailing longshore current flows towards the south, and the net longshore transport of sediment is likewise southerly. However, in the winter, the strong storm winds are from the west and southwest, and the waves likewise have a strong southerly component. Thus, net longshore current direction and transport of sediment are to the north in the winter. It should be pointed out that along the coast local conditions can vary considerably, and the deposition of sediment in the form of sand bars and sand spits can likewise vary considerably from place to place.

The larger the wave, the more energy it contains and the bigger the sand particles it can carry. As waves lose their energy, the larger, heavier particles can no longer

Figure 4-1. Long sandy beach separates the Oregon estuary, Netarts Bay, from the ocean.

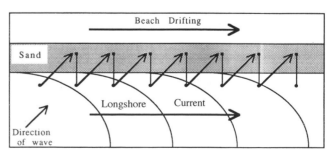

Figure 4-2. Direction of longshore transport of sediment along a beach with a prevailing northwest swell.

be carried along and fall to the bottom. The same is true for any type of water movement. The faster the movement, the larger the particles that can be transported. As the water slows down, the larger particles can no longer be held in suspension and fall to the bottom. Finally, when the water becomes still, only the smallest, lightest particles remain in suspension and available to settle to the bottom. These small, light particles, known as silts and clays, are deposited as marine muds either in protected, quiet habitats like bays and estuaries or farther offshore in deep water. This settling process is known as sedimentation, and it accounts for the formation of all soft bottom marine habitats.

Because sandy beaches are subject to relatively continuous wave action, only the larger particles, known as sands, accumulate and remain on the beach. The size of the sand particles on the beach is directly related to the size of the waves that hit the beach. On beaches that experience vigorous wave action, the finer sand grains will be resuspended and removed, leaving only large sand grains behind that feel coarse to the touch. Beaches with fine sands develop when only gentle wave action occurs, and thus only finer particles are transported to and deposited on them. Beaches will also undergo drastic changes in the type of sediment present. Strong storm waves can strip a beach of sand or leave only the largest particles behind. Likewise, small waves return fine grains to the beach, creating a gentle, sloping beach. Many beaches go through an annual cycle of sand accumulation during the spring and summer months. This is followed by a drastic loss of sand with the first strong winter storm, which leaves the beach in a winter condition [1].

Sand washed down from rivers and carried along the coast by longshore transport accumulates on rocky benches called beach platforms (Figure 4-3). These beach platforms have been carved into the rocky conti-

nent by wave action. The size of the beach platform depends on the local geological makeup of the coastline. Small, narrow wave-cut benches are found at the base of towering headlands made of erosion-resistant rocks as seen along the Olympic Mountain Range that abuts the northern coast of Washington. Long, broad beach platforms are cut from softer rocks as seen in southern Washington and Oregon where the mountains of the coastal ranges consist mainly of sedimentary rock. In some areas of the coastline, it is possible to view a series of extensive beach platforms, also called beach terraces, that rise up like stepping stones above the current sea level. These represent wave-cut terraces that were carved during periods when the sea level was higher. The extreme case of this phenomenon is seen in southern Oregon where wave-cut terraces are found that are almost 500 feet above current sea level.

In many areas of the Pacific Northwest, the sand that accumulates on the beach is blown shoreward off the beach face and forms dunes behind the beach. These dune fields can be extensive, such as those found in the Oregon Dunes National Recreation Area. Here the most spectacular dune system in the Pacific Northwest consists of a 50-square-mile area of dunes that extends down the coast nearly 40 miles between Coos Bay and Florence. Beachcombers may want to explore the unique dune habitat that includes marshes, meadows, lakes, and forests [2].

Lesser dune fields are prominent components of the coastline of central and northern Oregon and southwest Washington [2]. In fact, over forty percent of the Oregon-Washington shoreline is fronted by sand dunes which include low-lying sand spits. The community of Long Beach in southern Washington is situated on a long, sandy peninsula that fronts Willapa Bay. The city has built a long boardwalk here that traverses the dune habitat. The boardwalk is wheelchair accessible and posted with natural history information about sand dune ecology. It is worth a stop.

Sandy beaches are truly dynamic habitats. What's it like to live there? First, there is the sediment to contend with. It doesn't stay put; therefore, living on the surface or trying to excavate and live in a permanent burrow are not options. Because the sediment can shift so rapidly and unpredictably, any organism living on the beach must be able to swim and/or burrow rapidly to keep from being swept away. Then there is a problem with drainage. As the tide recedes, water drains from between the sand grains, leaving organisms burrowed

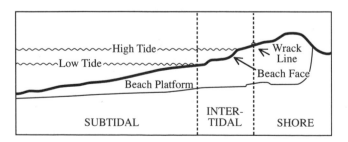

Figure 4-3. Cross-sectional view of a beach platform showing major beach zonation.

in the sand in danger of drying out. This is less of a problem on beaches made up of fine sand grains, as water is held in the small spaces between the grains by capillary action. The spaces between the grains on coarse-grained beaches are too large to hold water by capillary action. These beaches can become quite dry at high tide, especially if the sun is shining and/or the wind is blowing. Finally, there are predators. Fishes, crabs, shrimps, worms, and an occasional predatory snail forage on the beaches at high tide. Birds, small mammals, and insects take over at low tide.

If a sandy beach is such a miserable place, why live there at all? Because there is food, plain and simple. The same wave and current action that accounts for the beach's dynamic physical nature also delivers food to the sandy beach. Some of the food consists of the carcasses of large animals like fish and marine mammals, or large seaweeds that have been torn from their attachment offshore. However, the majority of the

food available to beach dwellers is in the form of small particles of animal and plant material called detritus. These particles are derived from large and small organisms produced elsewhere in the ocean that have been broken up and carried along by the moving water.

PERMANENT BEACH RESIDENTS

Crustaceans

Given the physical description of the sandy beach habitat and the nature of the food available, allow me to introduce the ultimate sandy beach animal, the mole or sand crab, *Emerita analoga* (Figure 4-4). The mole crab is found on sandy beaches from British Columbia to Baja California. The body is oval and streamlined for easy burrowing, and the hind limbs are modified for rapid digging into the sand. Mole crabs burrow backwards into the sand facing down the beach into the oncoming waves. However, they don't stay put. As the

Figure 4-4. Top and profile views of the two-inch-long mole crab, Emerita analoga; *upper: crab with antennae in feeding position.*

tide ebbs and floods, the mole crab emerges from the sand and rides the tide up or down to position itself in the swash zone. The swash zone is that area of the beach washed by both the breaking waves rushing up the beach and the water flowing back down the sloping beach. Here in the swash zone the mole crab unfurls a pair of long antennae covered with fine hairs. The antennae are held up into the water and the hairs trap detrital particles. Finally, the antennae are wiped across the mouth and the trapped particles are removed and swallowed. If a particularly strong wave should dislodge the mole crab, it is a strong swimmer and quickly finds the bottom and reburrows.

Where to find mole crabs? By digging in the swash zone, of course. The crabs will be just beneath the surface and can be easily dug up with your bare hands. However, if they are particularly abundant on the beach, some individuals invariably become stranded by the receding low tide and can be found on the exposed beach in the moist sand several inches below the surface. Mole crabs are crustaceans and must shed their outer skeletons to grow. The heavy shield-like portion of the skeleton, called the carapace, is frequently found by beachcombers on the surface of the sand.

Mole crabs are a quarter of an inch long when they settle from the plankton in the late spring and summer. Male crabs stop growing after they reach about three-quarters of an inch and live only one year. The largest female crabs grow to over two inches and can live two years. Large females may be brooding (incubating) embryos. Turn a female over and look for the bright, coral-colored mass of fertilized eggs on her underside. A female will brood her eggs for several weeks until they develop into planktonic larvae. Then the larvae break through the egg membrane and swim off into the sea. There they feed on plankton and grow until they are ready to settle and start life on the beach.

Mole crabs aren't found on every sandy beach in the Pacific Northwest. As you go north from the California-Oregon border, the presence of a mole crab population on a given beach becomes more unpredictable. On some beaches of Washington and British Columbia, the mole crabs may be missing for several years in a row and then show up again when planktonic larvae carried in by northward flowing currents settle and repopulate the beach.

The shallow holes you excavate while digging in the swash zone for mole crabs often fill with water and reveal another sandy beach crustacean known as a

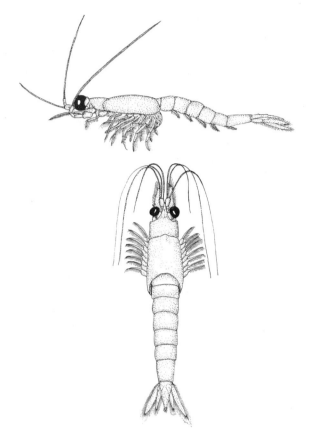

Figure 4-5. Sandy beach crustaceans known as mysid shrimp. These inch-long animals are nearly transparent in life.

mysid (Figure 4-5). You may get a glimpse of this small animal (less than one-half inch long) swimming in the water and then settling to the bottom and quickly burrowing. Agitating the sand a bit will cause it to resume swimming. Mysids are also known as opossum shrimp because they carry their eggs in a pouch located on their trunk region. They are nearly transparent, and sometimes are more easily found by looking for the shadows they cast on the bottom of the hole as they swim. Mysid species occur in a number of marine habitats including tidepools and estuaries.

Another common sandy beach crustacean is the isopod, *Excirolana* sp. (Figure 4-6), a close relative of *Cirolana harfordi* from the rocky intertidal zone. *Excirolana* is sometimes mistaken for a small mole crab because it has a similar, oval appearance. However, it has much shorter antennae and body appendages, and only reaches about one half inch in length. What it lacks in size, it makes up for in number and appetite. *Excirolana* is a scavenger, and hundreds to thousands of these animals can be found attacking any large animal carcass that

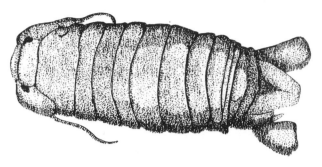

Figure 4-6. The common half-inch-long sandy beach isopod, Excirolana sp.

might wash up on the beach. It will quickly turn a dead fish into a skeleton, and some waders claim they've been nipped by the small, voracious scavengers. Several different species of isopod fill this role along the beaches of the Pacific Northwest; *Excirolana* spp. are the most common.

The sandy beach crustacean that's most familiar to many beachcombers technically doesn't live in the ocean at all. This is the small amphipod crustacean known as the beach hopper or sand flea, *Megalorchestia* spp. (Figure 4-7). Beach hoppers have moved out of the sea and can no longer withstand submergence in seawater. They live just above the reach of high tide where they pass the day in shallow burrows. Frequently, the high tide line contains large clumps of washed-up seaweed and other debris (called wrack), and the hoppers will burrow within or beneath it. During night-time low tides, the beach hoppers emerge from their burrows and scavenge in the wrack and along the beach for food. Hoppers prefer plant material, and their favorite foods are the large kelps like *Nereocystis* and *Macrocystis,* but they will eat almost anything organic if no plant material is available.

Beach hoppers can be found by visiting the wrack line on the upper beach and turning over clumps of seaweed

and other debris. If the wrack material is fresh, it will normally harbor these animals. Small beaches or very exposed beaches with very coarse sand sometimes will lack beach hoppers. Large beaches with extensive beach backshore and a steady supply of wrack usually harbor large populations. A good time to see the beach hoppers out and about is at a low tide just after sunset or just before sunrise, when literally swarms of them can be found scavenging on the beach.

There are several species of beach hoppers on Pacific Northwest beaches, and I refer you to more technical sources to distinguish them [3, 4, 5]. All species have a similar appearance and large hind appendages that they use to achieve the mighty leaps that give them their "hopper" name. Female beach hoppers brood their young and release them as juvenile animals right onto the beach. Species range from a third of an inch long as adults to over an inch and a half in length. Because they avoid submergence, beach hoppers are free from the normal marine sandy beach predators like fish that feed during high tide. However, it is not unusual to find large (one inch long) predatory rove beetles (Figure 4-8) in the wrack with the hoppers that prey on them. The small flies

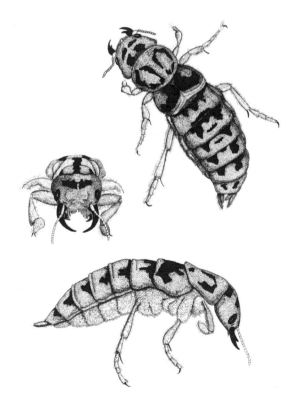

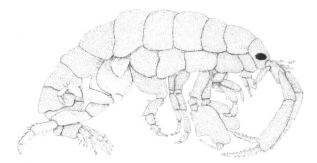

Figure 4-7. The beach hopper or sand flea, Megalorchestia sp., *a half-inch-long amphipod crustacean.*

Figure 4-8. Top, front, and profile views of the inch-long rove beetle, Thinopinus pictus, *a terrestrial predator of sandy beach crustaceans.*

that can be so plentiful in the wrack are sand flies which lay their eggs in the rotting seaweed.

Sandy Beach Polychaete Worms

There are a few obvious polychaete worms that live on the sandy beach. Usually, the most abundant on protected beaches is the blood worm, *Euzonus mucronata* (Figure 4-9). The blood worm usually is found several inches to a foot deep in a distinct band that parallels the water's edge at about the mid-tide level. As the name implies, the worm is dark red and about two inches long. Blood worms can be quite abundant, with dozens in a spadeful of sand. The worm burrows through the sand and swallows it as it goes like a terrestrial earthworm. The organic particles trapped when the sand was deposited are digested, and the remaining sand is passed out of the gut.

When digging for mole crabs in the swash zone, a shiny, gunmetal gray worm that wiggles like crazy is often discovered. This is the shimmy worm, *Nepthys*

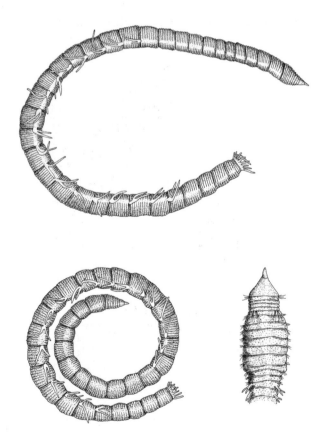

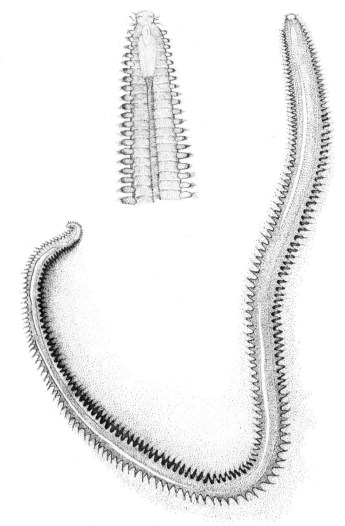

Figure 4-10. The six-inch-long shimmy worm, Nepthys californiensis, *with a close-up view of the anterior.*

californiensis (Figure 4-10), and it occurs from British Columbia to Baja California. Shimmy worms can reach six inches in length and are predators, probably eating other worms. They are armed with a wicked feeding structure called an eversible proboscis. The proboscis is an extension of their throat with jaws at the end that they can shoot out from their mouth and snag prey. Shimmy worms also use the proboscis to help them burrow. You are in no danger from the proboscis, but just be thankful this worm isn't six feet long!

A last worm to look for on the sandy beach is not a polychaete, but a nemertean (see Chapter 3). This is the robust predator *Cerebratulus californiensis* (see Figure 5-9 in Chapter 5), which is also common on protected sand flats. This worm is usually dirty-pink in color and reaches a length of three yards when extended.

Figure 4-9. The blood worm, Euzonus mucronata, *a two-inch-long polychaete worm often abundant on sandy beaches.*

Sandy Beach Mollusks

Shelled marine snails are not abundant on sandy beaches. The combination of their locomotion across the sediment surface using a wide creeping foot and the constant wash of the waves is not a good fit. However, there are a few exceptions, and these snail species burrow through the sediment instead of staying on top of it. The most common is the olive snail, *Olivella biplicata* (Figure 4-11), which occurs on sandy beaches and coastal sand flats along the entire coastline. *Olivella* has a glossy purple highlighted shell that reaches up to an inch and a half long. The shell is tapered at both ends, making it easy to maneuver through the sand. The very large foot has a special wedge-shaped front end that acts much like a ploughshare to allow the snail to push through the sand. Finally, the olive snail has a long siphon that it can project up through the sand and bring water to its gills. Olives comb the sand for deposited organic material and small prey. When the tide is out, their relatively straight burrows can often be seen on the wet beach face as narrow, upraised trails with the bulge of the burrowed snail at one end. The other species of snails found on the beach are really only occasional visitors and will be discussed later in this chapter.

Bivalve Mollusks. Clams are very successful filter feeders, and with all the suspended food available it is no surprise that several have adapted to the sandy beach environment. These animals are dependent on the high oxygen content of the wave-tossed water and cannot survive in the quiet water of sheltered bays. In the Pacific Northwest only, one species, the razor clam (*Siliqua patula*), is common.

Razor clams can be found on open sandy beaches from northern California to southern Alaska. They do not occur in the Puget Sound region. These clams (Figure 4-12) are named for their thin, elongated shells and can reach six and a half inches in length. They occur on

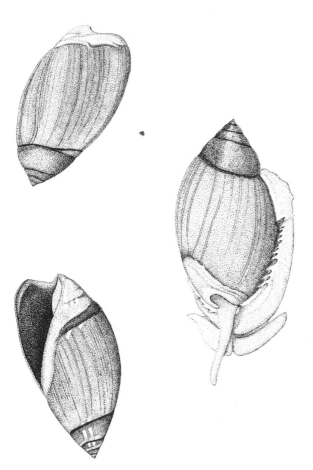

Figure 4-11. The olive snail, Olivella biplicata. *Views of the shell and extended snail showing the elongated siphon.*

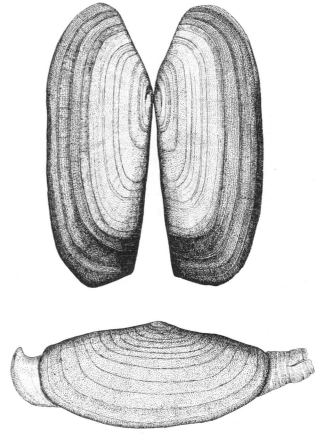

Figure 4-12. Shell and side view of the razor clam, Siliqua patula, *a rapidly burrowing species found on open sandy beaches.*

the lowest tidal region of beaches with a flat slope and small sand grains. They often reveal themselves by a small dimple in the sand made by their siphons. It takes an experienced razor clammer armed with a narrow clam shovel to unearth one of these animals. They are very sensitive to any movement and can quickly burrow out of reach. A razor clam placed on top of the wet sand can reburrow in ten seconds. A unique food chain involving razor clams has been identified along the open beaches of the Washington coast. A vigorous diatom population thrives in the surf zone providing food directly to the razor clams and other filter feeders on the sandy beach.

Remember, the season and license requirements vary for razor clamming throughout the Pacific Northwest. It is always best to check the local regulations. See the section on clamming in Chapter 3.

Besides razor clams, several other bivalve species may occasionally occur on the sandy beach. The beautiful basket cockle, *Clinocardium nuttallii,* more typical of sand flats of sheltered bays (Figure 4-13), sometimes

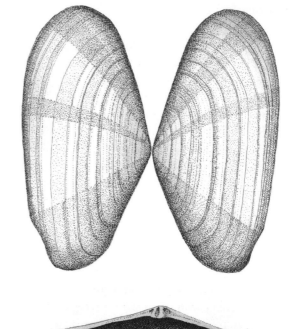

Figure 4-14. The surf clam, Tellina bodegensis, *a two-inch-long species that is common offshore of sandy beaches.*

Figure 4-13. Valves of a large (three-inch-diameter) basket cockle, Clinocardium nuttallii, *a clam sometimes found on quiet sandy beaches.*

is found on clean, fine-sand beaches. The two-inch-long surf clam or Bodega Tellin, *Tellina bodegensis* (Figure 4-14), which typically lives just offshore of the sandy beach, is also occasionally stranded on the beach by strong waves. It is also sometimes found on sand flats near the mouth of embayments.

OCCASIONAL VISITORS

In addition to the two clams mentioned above, several other animals occasionally are found on the beaches of the Pacific Northwest. I refer to these as occasional visitors because their normal habitat is either quite near or includes the intertidal beach, or they use the sandy beach to fulfill some aspect of their life cycle.

Moon Snails

A large mollusk that sometimes occurs on more protected beaches is the moon snail, *Polinices* spp. (Figure 4-15). Similar to the olive snails discussed earlier, the moon snails have a large foot with a ploughshare-like anterior modification for burrowing through sand. However, moon snail shells are very bulky (up to four inches in diameter, but usually only smaller ones are seen on the beach), and often the top third projects above the snail's burrow. This makes them susceptible to being washed out of the sand by wave action. The snails found on the beach were probably washed in from the sandy bottom just offshore.

Moon snails are more common somewhat offshore on sandy bottoms and on protected coastal sand flats all along the coast of the Pacific Northwest. These snails are interesting carnivores. They use their flexible, tongue-like radulas to bore neat, counter-sunk holes into their molluscan prey. Once the hole has been bored through the shell, the snail inserts its long snout through the opening and devours its prey. Clam and snail shells are often found on sandy beaches and coastal tidal flats with this characteristic calling card of moon snail predation (Figure 4-16).

Figure 4-15. Views of the shell and expanded foot of the moon snail, Polinices *sp. Shells can reach four inches in diameter.*

Figure 4-16. Shell of a two-inch littleneck clam, Prototheca staminea, *showing the characteristic counter-sunk hole bored by a predatory moon snail.*

Visiting Crabs and Shrimp

A crab occasionally found buried on the beach at low tide is the graceful cancer crab, *Cancer gracilis* (Figure 4-17). Found from central California northward, the graceful cancer is a much more docile crab than the other members of the genus *Cancer,* like the pugnacious red rock crab of the rocky intertidal zone, *Cancer antennarius* (see Figure 7-7 in Chapter 7). *C. gracilis* can be up to four inches wide. Many of the individuals a beachcomber will find will be females carrying a large clutch of developing eggs attached to their abdomens. The graceful cancer crab is more commonly seen on protected sand flats.

A final crustacean seen on the beach all along the Pacific Northwest are the salt and pepper shrimps, *Crangon* spp. (Figure 4-18). These two- to three-inch-long shrimps are very active carnivores found in a number of shallow water habitats. It is not uncommon for a school of these shrimps to come onshore at high tide to forage for invertebrate prey including worms and small sand crabs. If stranded by an ebbing tide, the shrimps just burrow in and wait for high tide.

Figure 4-17. Graceful cancer crab, Cancer gracilis. *Note the white-tipped claws that distinguish it from other common cancer crabs,* Cancer productus *and* Cancer antennarius.

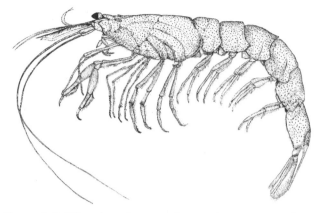

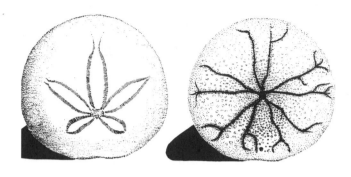

Figure 4-18. The salt and pepper shrimp, Crangon *sp., a three-inch-long predator found on sandy beaches at high tide.*

Sandy Beach Echinoderms

To the beachcomber, the Pacific sand dollar, *Dendraster excentricus,* hardly seems like an occasional visitor as it is regularly found on most open beaches of the Pacific Northwest. However, what the beachcomber typically finds here is actually the bleached white skeleton or "test" of *Dendraster* (Figure 4-19), that can measure up to three inches in diameter. Sometimes, after a storm, living sand dollars that have been washed in from just offshore of the surf zone can be discovered on the beach. These animals are distinguished from the naked skeleton by their fine covering of short, dark spines that gives them an almost velvety appearance. The Pacific sand dollar occurs in large subtidal sand dollar beds that run parallel to the shore line. Here, the sand dollars sit upright in the sand and filter food from the water moving along shore. When storms occur and large waves are generated, the sand dollars lie flat and bury themselves in the sand, but individuals are occasionally washed out and onto the beach.

WASH-UPS

The final group of organisms to consider are grouped into a category called "wash-ups." This grouping is somewhat arbitrary, as many of the "occasional visitors" described above find themselves on the beach only because they have washed up from their nearby offshore habitat. The organisms grouped here as wash-ups are animals and plants typically found well away from the sandy beach, and arrive on its surface because the relentless washes of waves have carried them in.

Figure 4-19. Above: the skeleton of a two-inch diameter Pacific sand dollar, Dendraster excentricus. *Below: typical feeding posture of live sand dollars.*

Included here are several large planktonic animals and the large kelp plants of offshore kelp beds.

Stranded Seaweeds

Let's talk about the plants first. We've already discussed the arrival of plant material on the beach and its contribution to the "wrack" used by beach hoppers. Seaweeds can only grow attached to solid substrates where they can have access to sunlight. This limits them to rocky intertidal habitats and shallow, subtidal rocky bottoms. In rocky intertidal habitats, a variety of red, green, and brown algae grows luxuriantly. Although firmly attached to the rocky substrate by root-like holdfasts, the algae can be torn loose by wave action and washed away. If a sandy beach occurs close by a rocky area, a variety of algae can be found washed up. However, if the beach is some distance from a source of algae, only the biggest, toughest algae remain intact, and the rest are shredded into detritus by wave action. Therefore, the algae most typically found on sandy beaches are the large brown algae known as kelps.

A common stranded kelp is *Macrocystis integrifolia*. This plant is closely related to the largest of all the kelps, the giant kelp *Macrocystis pyrifera,* which is the predominant kelp of southern and central California's offshore kelp forests. From central California northward, *Macrocystis pyrifera* is replaced by *Macrocystis integrifolia*. Here it grows both intertidally and subtidally along the open coast of the entire Pacific Northwest as far north as Alaska. It is found occasionally in the Strait of Juan de Fuca and around the San Juan Islands, but does not appear in Puget Sound. From a stout holdfast attached to the bottom, it grows vine-like branches called stipes that may reach over 30 feet long.

Broad, flat blades grow laterally from the stipes. Each blade is buoyed up by a bulbous, air-filled float located at its base (Figure 4-20). Depending on the degree of wave action and the time of the year, pieces of *Macrocystis* of differing sizes will wash up on the beach. During the first severe storms of early winter, whole plants will be uprooted and will wash onto the beach in tangled heaps. At other times, only a few stipes or blades will be present, and sometimes only the small inch-and-a-half-long floats will appear by themselves.

The bullwhip or bull kelp, *Nereocystis luetkeana,* grows up to 60–70 feet long and is the dominant kelp in the offshore kelp beds of the Pacific Northwest. Bull kelp (Figure 4-21) differs from *Macrocystis integrifolia* in that only a single stipe grows from a holdfast. The stipe ends in a large float from which a number of stout blades grow. Usually, the whole plant washes up, much to the delight of junior beachcombers who find no end

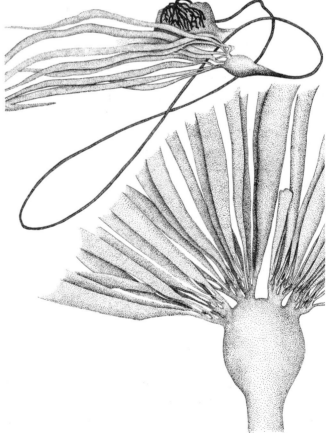

Figure 4-20. The giant kelp, Macrocystis pyrifera, *showing clockwise from below: holdfast, stipe with blades, and close-up of the inch-and-half-long float.*

Figure 4-21. The bull kelp, Nereocystis luetkeana. *Upper: illustration of entire plant; lower: view of the single large float with blades.*

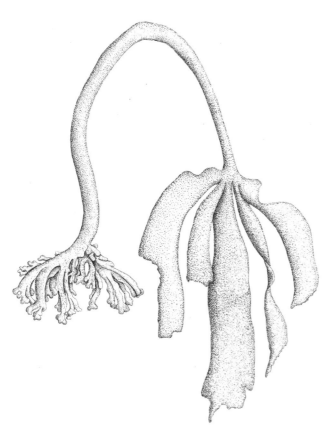

Figure 4-22. The oar weed, Laminaria *sp., a kelp plant that washes in from the low rocky intertidal zone.*

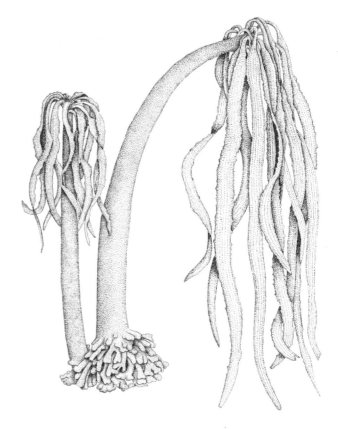

Figure 4-23. The sea palm kelp, Postelsia palmaeformis, *showing two plants attached to a common holdfast.*

of uses for it. Adults, on the other hand, are known to slice the hollow stipes and make pickles out of them.

Two smaller kelps are often contributed from the rocky intertidal habitat. The first is the oar weed, *Laminaria* spp., which grows to about five feet long in the lower intertidal zone. Oar weed (Figure 4-22) grows in the most wave-exposed area and takes a tremendous beating (see also Figure 7-35). It survives by having a very tenacious holdfast and a stipe that is very flexible and capable of bending with the back-and-forth wash of the waves. *Laminaria* has a stout blade that often splits as it grows.

The second intertidal species is the sea palm kelp, *Postelsia palmaeformis* (Figure 4-23). The sea palm grows to about three feet high in the middle intertidal zone of the most exposed rocky intertidal habitats. Like the oar weed, the sea palm weathers the onslaught of the waves by having a flexible stipe topped with short, palm-like blades. Both the oar weed and the sea palm can be found washed up on sandy beaches. The sea palm often occurs in small clumps of several stipes attached to a common holdfast.

Stranded Jellies

The broad, exposed sandy beaches collect an amazing array of gelatinous marine zooplankton. These species vary from small, marble-sized ctenophores to medusas over a yard in diameter. Usually, when these animals are found by beachcombers, they are unrecognizable mounds of jelly. However, if they are newly arrived they can be quite intact and very interesting to investigate. The "jelly" is a special type of animal material, called mesoglea, that allows the organism to float. Mesoglea is mostly water with a chemical composition slightly different from seawater that makes it a little bit lighter. Although most of these gelatinous zooplankters have some means of locomotion, they can't outswim the force of the currents. If the water mass in which they're floating comes too close to shore, they can become stranded, sometimes in very large numbers.

Scyphomedusas. The large medusas (greater than a foot in diameter) that wash up all belong to the class

Scyphozoa of the phylum Cnidaria. Cnidarians all possess special cell capsules known as nematocysts which they use to stun and entangle prey. These large medusas, known as scyphomedusas, have nematocysts all over their bodies, not just on their tentacles. Even though a medusa stranded on the beach appears motionless and apparently dead, the nematocysts are still potentially capable of discharging and imparting a nasty sting to an unsuspecting beachcomber. So to be safe, don't handle any large stranded jellyfish with your bare hands. If you wish to investigate them further, use gloves or a stick to turn them.

When the medusa is seen swimming in the water column, it is a magnificent animal to behold (Figure 4-24). The bell or umbrella contracts rhythmically, and the animal is propelled gracefully upwards with its long tentacles and oral arms extended out below it to entrap prey. However, when it becomes stranded on the beach, it is robbed of the water's supporting buoyancy and appears a round, flat, motionless blob of jelly.

The most striking of the stranded scyphomedusas is the purple-striped *Pelagia colorata* (Figure 4-24), which can reach a bell diameter of over 30 inches. It has eight long tentacles spaced evenly around the bell margin, and oral arms several yards in length extending from the mouth in the center of the bell. Nematocysts of this species sting fiercely, so be very careful with them. *Pelagia* occur all along the continental shelf of the eastern Pacific, and sometimes large numbers will be trapped in coastal embayments.

Another medusa commonly stranded along the entire open coast is the sea nettle, *Chrysaora melanaster* (Figure 4-25). The bell, which can reach a diameter of over

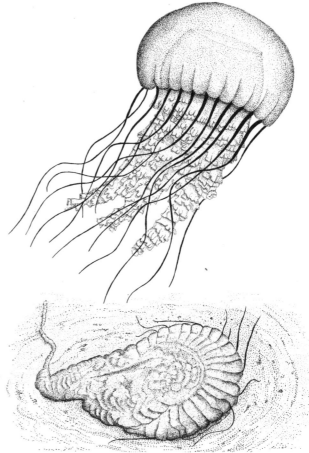

Figure 4-24. The large (30 inches in diameter) common scyphomedusa, Pelagia colorata, *swimming, and stranded on the beach.*

Figure 4-25. The 15-inch diameter sea nettle, Chrysaora melanaster, *as viewed in the water and stranded on the beach.*

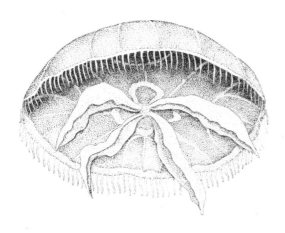

Figure 4-26. Top and bottom views of the common moon jelly, Aurelia aurita, *which can reach 15 inches in diameter.*

15 inches, has radial yellow or brown lines and 24 reddish marginal tentacles.

The frilly oral arms of the sea nettle are quite prominent. The moon jelly, *Aurelia aurita,* has a worldwide distribution. It sometimes occurs in large nearshore aggregations along the Pacific Northwest, resulting in many strandings. *Aurelia* reaches a bell diameter of 15 inches and has numerous short tentacles around the margin of its scalloped, saucer-shaped bell (Figure 4-26). The bell is translucent gray or blue with four large horseshoe-shaped gonads clearly visible through the top. The male gonads are purple, and those of the females are yellow to white. The moon jelly is unique among the large medusa species in that it does not capture its prey with its tentacles. Instead, it traps zooplankton in mucus coating the outer surface of the bell and the oral arms. The sessile polyp stage of *Aurelia* is well known, and can occur in large numbers attached to floats in quiet harbors.

Figure 4-27. Large scyphomedusa, Cyanea capillata, *known as the lion's mane jelly.*

A final large medusa to look for is the lion's mane medusa, *Cyanea capillata* (Figure 4-27). This medusa is named for the "mane" of brownish-gold tentacles that hang down from its scalloped bell in eight distinct bundles of about 70 tentacles each. These tentacles can extend over six feet into the water to entangle prey. *Cyanea* can grow quite large, up to 20 inches in diameter, and is known to pack a nasty sting, so be careful if you encounter one stranded on the beach.

Hydromedusas. Many smaller medusas also become stranded along open sandy beaches. These animals belong to the cnidarian class Hydrozoa, and are called hydromedusas. They usually have a sessile polyp form in their life cycles as well. Only two of the largest, most common species are included here. Further information on hydromedusas can be found in more detailed references [4, 5, 6].

The first species is the graceful *Polyorchis pencillatus* (Figure 4-28). *Polyorchis* can be very common in coastal embayments in the spring, and often large numbers can be found stranded along the adjoining beaches. *Polyorchis* is about the size of a hen's egg, with one end opened outward to form the bell margin. The rather tall umbrella is ringed with up to 90 tentacles each with a bright red eyespot at its base where it joins the bell margin. *Polyorchis* has four prominent radial canals each with numerous long, slender gonads suspended from them hanging down into the bell. *Poly-*

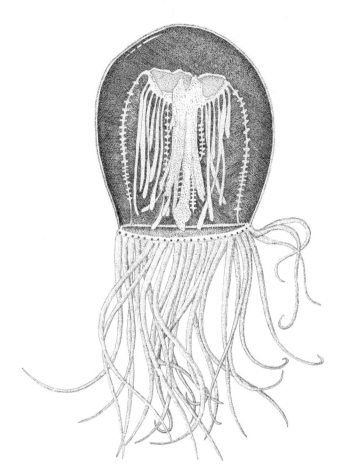

Figure 4-28. The egg-sized hydromedusa, Polyorchis pencillatus. *Note the eyespots at the bases of the tentacles.*

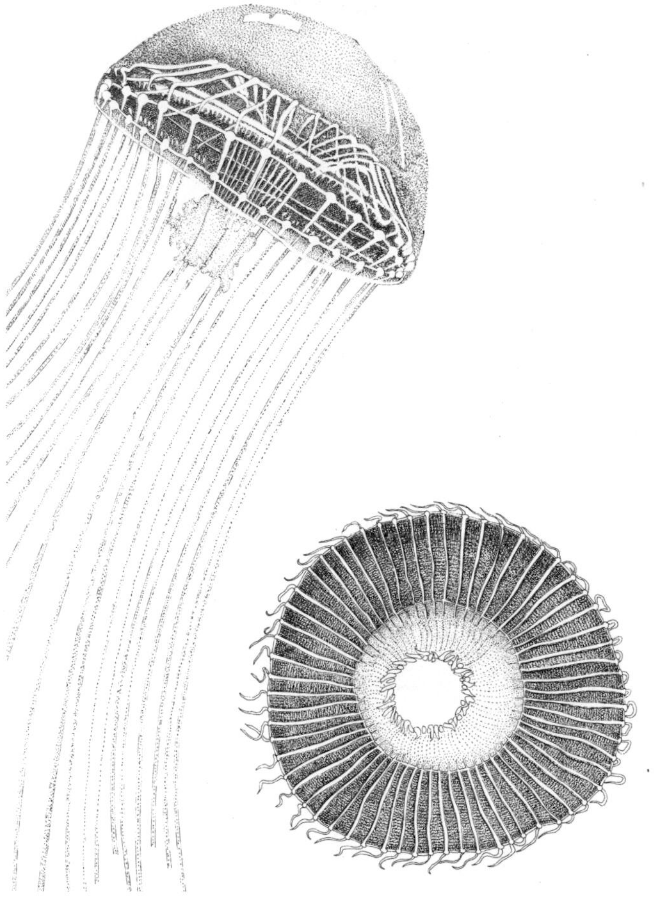

Figure 4-29. The three-inch diameter, many-ribbed hydromedusa, Aequorea aequorea, *viewed from the side and from below.*

orchis has relatively harmless nematocysts and is small enough so that a freshly stranded specimen can be suspended in a plastic bag of seawater. Try it!

While *Polyorchis* has a tall, graceful bell, the many-ribbed hydromedusa, *Aequorea aequorea* (Figure 4-29), is saucer-shaped. *Aequorea*'s bell reaches over three inches in diameter and is about an inch in height. The bell is thick and glossily transparent with 60 narrow radial canals and up to 80 long marginal tentacles. The mouth is surrounded by ruffled lips. *Aequorea* is very bioluminescent. At night, live stranded specimens can give off a bright flash of light when disturbed.

Both these larger species of hydromedusa and a number of others can often be seen swimming gracefully near the docks and floats in coastal embayments and estuaries. Likewise, the larger scyphomedusas also show up occasionally. Look for them when you are waiting to pull up your crab traps.

By-the-Wind Sailors. Another cnidarian "jellyfish" that can sometimes be very abundant on the beaches of the Pacific Northwest is not a medusa at all, but instead is a large (up to three inches long) floating polyp. This is the by-the-wind sailor, *Velella velella* (Figure 4-30). *Velella* has a stiff exoskeleton made of chitin which includes a gas-filled float and a transparent sail. The sail is mounted diagonally to the left or right of the long axis of the body, so that the animal tacks at a 45-degree angle to the left or right of the true wind direction. *Velella* generally remain offshore; however, shifts in wind direction or currents can drive these animals onshore. When the wind pattern shifts to a northwesterly direction in early spring, depending on its strength and persistence and the abundance of *Velella* offshore, windrows (narrow rows of deposited material that accumulate along the upper edge of the previous high tide) of beached by-the-wind sailors several inches deep

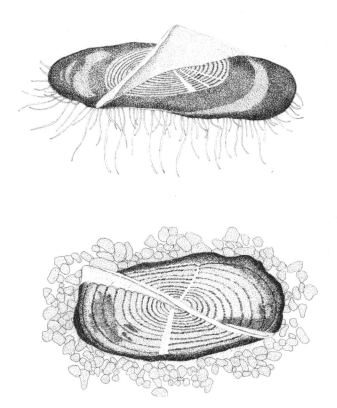

Figure 4-30. *The floating hydroid known as the by-the-wind sailor,* Velella velella, *which can reach three inches in length.*

can pile up on exposed sandy beaches. These animals create quite a stink for a short time, but quickly decompose, leaving behind only the thin, blue, cellulose-like chitinous exoskeletons which can persist on the beach for months.

Comb Jellies. Sometimes, the beach can be littered with round, marble-sized jellies. Often these are also not medusas, but closely related animals known as ctenophores or comb jellies. The most common animal is the sea gooseberry or cat's eye ctenophore, *Pleurobrachia bachei* (Figure 4-31). Ctenophores lack the stinging nematocysts typical of cnidarians, and instead use tentacles with special adhesive cells to snare their zooplankton prey. Ctenophores can be quite marvelous to behold when suspended in a plastic bag of seawater. Their eight rows of ciliary plates (ctenes) beat rhythmically and catch the light in a flashing spectrum of color.

Oregon beachcombers have the unique opportunity to view many of the jellies discussed above at the jellyfish exhibits at the Oregon Coastal Aquarium in Newport, Oregon. The jellyfish are maintained in specially

Figure 4-31. *The cat's eye ctenophore,* Pleurobrachia bachei, *swimming in the water. Stranded animals are the size of a marble.*

designed aquaria that allow them to swim freely for the public to view.

Squid Egg Cases. Sometimes in summer or early fall, open beaches may be strewn with a few or many jelly sausages. These are six to eight inches long and a quarter to a half inch in diameter. Closer inspection reveals that the sausages themselves are packed with round, quarter-inch in diameter spheres. These are the egg

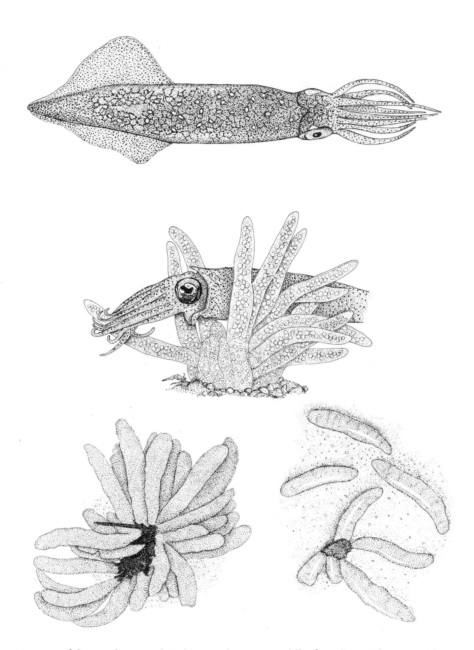

Figure 4-32. Upper: top view of the market squid, Loligo opalescens; *middle: female squid amongst her egg cases; below: egg cases stranded on the beach.*

cases of the market squid, *Loligo opalescens* (Figure 4-32). The squids mate in large aggregations some distance offshore over sandy bottoms. The females receive special sperm packets from the males, fertilize their eggs, and then extrude the eggs into these special egg cases that they anchor into the sandy bottom. Often, either by wave action or some other disturbance, the cases are uprooted and wash ashore. Unfortunately, the embryos in these uprooted egg cases are lost to the population. Depending on the degree of development the embryos have achieved, tiny squid may be seen through the egg membranes with the use of a hand lens.

Attached Pelagic Animals

Pelagic Barnacles. Often, after a particularly severe storm, the more exposed beaches will be littered with pieces of debris that have been floating at sea for some time. These can include such mundane junk as bottles

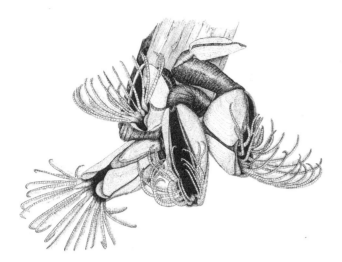

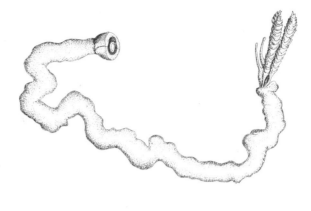

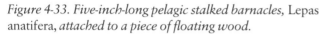

Figure 4-33. *Five-inch-long pelagic stalked barnacles,* Lepas anatifera, *attached to a piece of floating wood.*

and plastic bags or such exotica as glass or plastic fishing floats used by the Japanese on nets in their mid-Pacific fisheries. These floating substrates are the homes of a sea-going group of crustaceans known as pelagic stalked barnacles. Barnacles make their living by filtering food out of the water using the hairs on their body appendages. The closer together the hairs, the smaller the particle they can filter. On exposed beaches of the Pacific Northwest, large pieces of driftwood are sometimes covered with the barnacle *Lepas anatifera* (Figure 4-33). This species is distinguishable from other pelagic stalked barnacles because of its large size (up to six inches long) and the smooth white plates that make up its shell. It is also found on glass floats, bottles, and Styrofoam.

A smaller (one inch long) stalked barnacle, *Lepas fascicularis,* is also commonly stranded by seasonal onshore winds. This barnacle secretes a material at the base of its stalk that contributes to a common float that may be shared by several to many barnacles. It has thin shells that show the blue color of the underlying tissues.

Shipworms. Driftwood that has been at sea for some time is often riddled with wood-boring invertebrates. If the wood is soft enough, breaking off a piece may reveal the white, four-fifths-inch diameter, calcium-carbonate-lined burrows of shipworms. Shipworms are not worms at all, but are bivalve mollusks with shells specially modified for boring into wood. The shipworms use the excavated sawdust they produce from boring as food. They have a special pouch in their

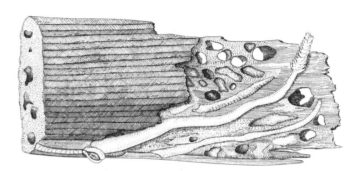

Figure 4-34. *Above: a clam removed from its burrow; below: driftwood riddled with the burrows of* Bankia setacea, *wood-boring bivalves known as shipworms.*

stomach for storing sawdust and harbor symbiotic bacteria that digest the cellulose in the sawdust. Many shipworms also filter feed.

The most common species of shipworm encountered in the Pacific Northwest is *Bankia setacea.* The fleshy bodies of this species can reach over a yard in length and are tipped by long, delicate siphons that reach to the burrow opening (Figure 4-34). The siphons are tipped with calcareous, feathery-looking structures known as pallets that plug the burrow opening when the siphons are retracted.

The Dungeness Crab. A final animal often found on open beaches in the late winter really isn't there at all! No, it is not a ghost, but the molted outer skeleton (exoskeleton) of the large male market or Dungeness crab, *Cancer magister* (Figure 4-35). In the late winter, male Dungeness crabs molt offshore in close temporal synchrony in preparation for the spring and summer breeding season. They can be so abundant in some years that large windrows of cast male exoskeletons pile

Figure 4-35. Male Dungeness crab, Cancer magister. *This crab is light brown to buff-colored in life.*

up on sandy beaches (Color Plate 13b). Because the crab molts its entire outer covering intact, a fresh molt can easily be mistaken for a live animal. However, as the molt washes about, it pulls apart and soon is in pieces. The solid, shield-like carapace that covers the head and body of the crab remains intact for some time and is often found by itself on the beach. Dungeness crab exoskeletons can be found throughout the year on the beach; they are just more common in the late winter.

A FINAL NOTE ON SANDY BEACHES

As stressed here, sandy beaches are dynamic, rigorous habitats that serve a specially adapted fauna. However, given the variety of combinations of sand availability, exposure to waves, local geology, and larval settlement patterns, no two sandy beaches are going to be identical. In the Pacific Northwest, especially in Puget Sound and the San Juan Archipelago, there are many small, protected beaches that receive little to no wave action. Beachcombers should not expect to find mole crabs and razor clams on these beaches, as these animals are dependent on wave action to transport their suspended food to them. Other sandy-beach animals may be found here, such as beach hoppers and shimmy worms. On some of these quiet sandy beaches, large numbers of lug worms, discussed in the next chapter (see Figure 5-4), can occur. Their presence can be discovered by the telltale spiral mounds of fecal castings deposited on the beach surface.

Finally, it should be noted that this chapter introduces only the very common organisms that typically show up on sandy beaches. Because of the immense reaches of shoreline the beaches traverse, virtually anything in the sea may be found on the beach at some time or another. A 60-foot-long blue whale washed up 15 miles from my home one summer. Many of the organisms presented elsewhere in this guide may wash up on the beach, so flip through the other chapters if you are stumped. Sometimes, knowing what the adjacent shoreline looks like can be helpful. If there is a rocky intertidal habitat nearby, many of the shells and algae probably came from there. If the beach is near the outlet of an estuary or enclosed embayment, the organisms may have been carried out with the tide and washed ashore on the beach. Keep your eyes open, and good hunting!

REFERENCES

1. Bascom, W., *Waves and Beaches,* revised. Garden City: Anchor Press, 1980, 366 pp.
2. Wiedemann, A. M., *The Ecology of Pacific Northwest Coastal Sand Dunes: A Community Profile.* U.S. Fish and Wildlife Service, FWS/OBS-84/04, 1984, 130 pp.
3. Ricketts, E., et al., *Between Pacific Tides,* 5th Ed. Stanford: Stanford University Press, 1985, 652 pp.
4. Smith, R. I. and J. Carlton, *Light's Manual: Intertidal Invertebrates of the Central California Coast,* 3rd Ed. Berkeley: University of California Press, 1975, 716 pp.
5. Kozloff, E. N., *Seashore Life of the Northern Pacific Coast.* Seattle: University of Washington Press, 1983, 370 pp.
6. Kozloff, E. N., *Keys to the Marine Invertebrates of Puget Sound, the San Juan Archipelago, and Adjacent Regions.* Seattle: University of Washington Press, 1974, 226 pp.

5

QUIET-WATER HABITATS: BAYS, ESTUARIES, AND LAGOONS

HOW QUIET-WATER HABITATS ARE FORMED

The coastline of the Pacific Northwest is constantly changing. Sandy beaches can be transformed in a matter of hours during winter storms. Coastal bluffs are continuously weathered by wind and wave. Sea level changes and plate tectonic activity over geologic time have alternately inundated and uncovered vast areas of coastal land. Against this backdrop of change, a number of habitats are created that have one thing in common: These are coastal areas that become shielded from the onslaught of the waves and develop into quiet-water habitats.

For example, estuaries are typically formed when a large river is flooded by rising sea level. The sediment carried from the land accumulates as a delta in the drowned river mouth. Sand flats, mud flats, and finally, salt marshes develop as the delta grows and stabilizes. Typically, a long, finger-like sand spit forms along the interface between the estuary and the ocean as is seen all along the coast of central Oregon and southern Washington. Another example is a strong longshore current (see Figure 4-2) transporting sediment along the coastline and depositing it behind a headland. The deposited sediment builds up a sand bar, and finally, a sand spit gradually cuts off a cove behind the headland, forming a protected coastal embayment. As tidal action moves water in and out of the embayment, the fine sediments are deposited, and sand and mud flats are formed. A final example is a coastal lagoon. Sea level drops, and rivers carve large channels into the exposed, wave-cut terrace. Sea level again rises, and the channels become flooded with salt water. Subsequently, the connection to the sea closes, and a trapped body of sea water, i.e., a lagoon, is created.

Quiet-Water Marine Environments

These quiet-water, soft-bottom habitats provide an environment very different from the sandy beach. Here, organisms can create burrows in the soft substrate that will be somewhat permanent. An organism can move across the substrate at high tide and not be washed away by wave action. Tidal action continues to bring suspended food into these habitats that combines with local plankton production to provide ample resources for a host of filter feeders. In estuarine areas, organic detritus is brought downstream by freshwater flows. Finally, as the water becomes quiet in the most sheltered regions of these habitats, the fine organic material carried in suspension is deposited. This provides food for animals called deposit feeders that feed on organic matter that accumulates on and within the soft sediment.

As the types of substrates and opportunities for feeding are similar in these quiet-water habitats, they tend to host similar types of animals. However, there are some differences. Coastal embayments typically contain normal, undiluted seawater. In comparison, estuaries have a gradient of salinities running from fresh water at the head of the estuary, where the river or other freshwater source enters, to pure seawater at the mouth of the estuary where it enters the sea. Saltwater lagoons vary in salinity depending on the source(s) of water that supplies them.

Estuaries are an aquatic interface between the riverine (fresh water) and marine environments They serve a vital role for many organisms whose life cycles involve both these environments. Most obvious of these are the salmonid fishes that spawn in upstream freshwater habitats and migrate to the sea to feed and mature. These fishes typically pass through an estuary to reach the sea. The graded range of salinites found in the estuary allow the young salmonids to acclimate gradually from fresh to salt water.

Estuaries also play important roles as nurseries for early stages in the life cycles of many marine organisms. An example of this is the Pacific herring, *Clupea harengus*. Schools of adults enter the estuary to lay their sticky eggs on algae and eelgrass. The eggs hatch, and larvae and young fish use the estuary as a refuge to feed and grow before they finally enter the ocean. There is a substantial fishery for both the adult herring when they enter the estuary and for the eggs attached to marine plant material. The latter is mainly sold to the Japanese who consider it a delicacy.

Another very important commercial species that uses the estuary as juveniles is the Dungeness crab, *Cancer magister* (see Chapter 9). Advanced larvae enter the estuary from offshore and soon metamorphose and settle to the bottom as young crabs. The crabs may spend up to three years feeding and growing in the estuary before they move towards the mouth and out to sea. In large estuaries like Coos Bay and Grays Harbor, adult populations of Dungeness crabs can be found year-round in the more saline waters of the estuary mouth. Likewise, the "inland seas" of Puget Sound and the Strait of Georgia harbor year-round adult populations of Dungeness crabs [1]. Although these bodies of water are technically estuaries because they receive freshwater input that drains from the land, they are predominately marine in character.

Besides these examples of commercial species, many other marine animals enter the estuary to seek food and/or avoid predators. Thus, estuaries provide a vital habitat not only for the strictly estuarine organisms, but also for residents of the adjacent marine and, in the case of the salmon that move offshore to feed, oceanic habitats.

Estuarine Organisms. The internal body fluids of marine animals contain essentially the same types of chemical elements (e.g., sodium, chloride, calcium, etc.) as pure seawater, and in the same concentrations. When the salinity of the water varies, these animals become stressed. Thus, a lagoon, a coastal embayment, and the more saline water at the mouth of an estuary can all potentially support a very similar marine fauna. But the upper, less saline reaches of the estuary will harbor a unique fauna adapted to the lower salinities that occur there.

A final word on estuarine organisms. Very few marine animal groups have successfully evolved the ability to withstand the low salinities found in estuaries. On the other hand, those groups that have adapted to estuarine conditions tend to be very hardy. They are easily transported by human conveyances such as in the ballast water tanks of ships or among estuarine food species, like oysters, transported for human consumption. The estuarine fauna along the coast of the Pacific Northwest is very poorly developed, and the native fauna found in a given estuary contains very few species. Because the estuaries of the Pacific Northwest have such limited faunas, and because estuaries, such as Coos Bay, Willapa Bay, and especially Puget Sound, tend to be such intense sites of international human commerce, large numbers of estuarine animals from around the world have been introduced there.

Shorebirds. Obviously, the most conspicuous animals seen in these quiet water habitats are the shorebirds that forage there during low tide and other waterfowl that take refuge on the calm water during high tide. Salt marshes are great places to view herons and snow-white egrets. Mud flats team with foraging shorebirds with a variety of bill shapes and sizes and a range of leg lengths. Different combinations of bill shape and leg length allow the birds to spread over the mud flat and share the food resources found there. Sanderlings move about like wind-up toys on their short legs using their short, pointed bills to probe the surface of the exposed substrate. In contrast, the long-legged curlews are able to wade and probe deeply into the substrate with their long, curved bills. Unfortunately, there is not room to cover birds in this guide. There are several excellent guidebooks to western birds [2, 3] and marine birds [4, 5], and I refer you to them.

In this chapter, I will discuss specific quiet-water habitats such as sand flats and mud flats and introduce the marine organisms that are commonly found in these habitats wherever they occur. I will also point out those organisms that are unique to these habitats in estuaries.

MUD FLATS

The Mud Flat Environment

In the quietest reaches of protected habitats, the water becomes very still, and the finest particles carried in suspension by the water are able to settle out. These fine sediments are mainly clay and silt particles, and collectively they form muds. A word of caution to beach-combers about mud flats: They can be so soft that they will not support a person's weight, and you can quickly sink up to your boot tops and become mired. Always proceed with caution onto any soft-sediment substrate. Use a shovel or some other probe to determine how soft the sediment is ahead of you. Depending on the composition of the substrate, you may be able to continue with only a slight bit of sinking or you may decide to move somewhere else and try again.

It should be pointed out here that although mud flats and sand flats are treated as separate habitats, they are part of a continuum of sediment types that grade from the finest clay muds to cobblestone beaches on up. In the quiet water habitats discussed here, the soft substrate is often a mixture of several sediment sizes reflecting the different types of water movement that occur over a particular area. For example, a region in an embayment that is generally only influenced by gentle tidal currents may occasionally experience locally generated waves when the wind comes from a different direction than normal. This could result in some larger sand grains being transported in and mixing in with the finer sediments. Marine biologists might describe one such sediment as a sandy mud and another, with slightly more sand, as a muddy sand—arbitrary terms that suggest the general composition of the substrate. Therefore, although this section is entitled "mud flats," many of the organisms discussed will be found over a range of soft sediment habitats.

Because of the gradual way mud flats are formed, they tend to be quite flat with little physical relief. However, the surface signs of the burrowing and feeding activities of the resident organisms can sometimes be quite extensive (Color Plate 12e). Mud flats might seem to be the last place you would find seaweeds, but sometimes extensive growths of the green algae *Ulva* spp. and *Enteromorpha* spp. (Color Plates 1b and 1c) can be found. Also, occasional red algae will grow attached to an exposed shell or other debris. There are even some species of red algae that specialize in growing in sandy mud substrates. During the spring and summer months, the surface of mud flats is often coated with a brownish-green layer of single-celled plants, called diatoms, that add substantially to the food available to mud flat dwellers. (These diatoms are related to those found in the plankton, but they grow on the sediment surface, typically in long filamentous chains.) Finally, mud flats often will be fringed by salt marsh vegetation or eelgrass beds, and these habitats also provide an additional, locally derived detrital food source. Salt marsh and eelgrass habitats will be discussed later in this chapter.

Mud Flat Cnidarians. Soft sediment habitats may seem like strange places to find cnidarians because their nematocyst-bearing tentacles give them a typically delicate appearance. However, cnidarians are very simple animals that breathe across their body surface and have no elaborate gills to clog with sediment. As long as they have access to oxygenated water, they can survive quite well in soft substrate habitats.

A large cnidarian sometimes seen at the low tide edge of sandy mud flats is the fleshy sea pen, *Ptilosarcus gurneyi* (Figure 5-1). This pale white to orange, colonial animal is a close relative of corals and sea anemones. Along the bulbous, 20-inch-long central axis are numerous small polyps mounted on lateral leaflike branches. The sea pen can contract and force water from the colony and achieve a considerable reduction in size. In Puget Sound, fleshy sea pens occur subtidally in large beds on soft bottoms up to depths of 150 feet. They form the nucleus of a community (Figure 5-2) that includes several sea stars and nudibranchs that prey directly on the sea pens or each other.

Two nudibranch predators of fleshy sea pens are *Armina californica* (Figure 5-3) and *Tritonia festiva* (Color Plate 11f). *Armina* is a striking animal, formally dressed with white and dark brown stripes running along its back. *Armina* can reach just under three inches in length. It sometimes wanders into the shallow water of quiet bays and occurs just beneath the substrate. *Tritonia* is also a stunning animal. It varies in color from pale white to orange to light brown. A frontal veil of finger-like processes project from its head, and a series of gill plumes is spaced regularly along either side of its back. A series of fine white lines forms a diamond pattern between the rows of gill plumes. In addition to sea pen beds, *Tritonia* can sometimes be found in low intertidal tidepools along the open coast.

The orange-red *Mediaster aequalis* (Figure 5-2) is a sea star predator of the sea pen. This somewhat stiff sea star reaches a diameter of six inches and is rarely seen in the intertidal zone. A second sea star that feeds on the sea pen is the rose star, *Crossaster papposus* (Figure 5-2). Rose red in color, sometimes with a circle of a lighter cream color, this star reaches 10 inches in diameter and has from 8 to 14 arms. It is also known to feed on nudi-

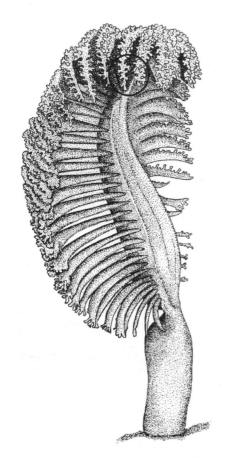

Figure 5-1. The fleshy sea pen, Ptilosarcus gurneyi. *Circle shows detail of polyps.*

branchs, bryozoans, and bivalve mollusks. The leather star, *Dermasterias imbricata* (see Figure 6-21), is another sea star that feeds on the sea pen. This star also occurs in the rocky intertidal zone where it feeds on sea anemones and is illustrated in the next chapter. A final star that is

shown is the multi-rayed sea star, *Solaster dawsoni* (Figure 5-2), which feeds almost exclusively on other sea stars, especially the closely related *Solaster stimpsoni* (see Figure 7-15), but also *Crossaster, Mediaster,* and *Dermasterias. Solaster dawsoni* can reach up to 20 inches in diameter and has 12 to 13 arms. It is usually gray, cream, yellow, or brown in color, with an occasional orange or red individual seen.

A second cnidarian of Pacific Northwest mud flats is a tube-dwelling, anemone-like animal known as *Pachycerianthus fimbriatus.* This animal can reach 14 inches long when fully extended and lives in a black, slippery tube that projects above the mud bottom. *Pachycerianthus* emerges from the tube at high tide and spreads a double whorl (circle) of tentacles to collect zooplankton prey. If disturbed, the cnidarian can quickly retreat into the safety of its tube. *Pachycerianthus* is also found subtidally on muddy sand bottoms.

Several other small cnidarians occur on mud flats. Small anemones, typically with bulbous, mushroom-like anchors, emerge on the sediment surface at high tide and spread their tentacles for feeding [6, 7].

Polychaete Worms. The mud flat is a haven for a bewildering variety of worms. The polychaete worms are particularly well represented here. It is impossible to cover all the species a beachcomber might find by digging into the substrate; therefore, only the largest, most abundant worms are included in this guide.

The lug worms (Figure 5-4) of the genera *Arenicola* and *Abarenicola* give their presence away by the formation of spiral mounds of fecal material on the sediment surface. A lug worm species can be up to 12 inches long, and lives in an L-shaped burrow with its head facing into the base of the "L." It uses its blunt proboscis to engulf the sandy mud sediment, which continues to fall into the burrow from the surface, forming a recognizable dimple. The worm passes the ingested sediment through its digestive tract to remove any organic matter contained, and the remainder is defecated onto the surface in the characteristic spiral fecal mounds.

Another large polychaete worm that announces its presence on the sandy mud flat is *Pista pacifica* (Figure 5-5). *Pista* lives in a tube formed of stiff mucus mixed with sand. The tube projects an inch or so from the surface as a fringed hood, as seen in the illustration. During high tide, the worm moves to the top of its tube and spreads out a wreath of long tentacles along the sediment surface. The tentacles are quite sensitive and

Figure 5-2. *Members of the fleshy sea pen bed community: Clockwise from top:* Ptilosarcus gurneyi, Crossaster papposus, Mediaster aequalis, Armina californica, Tritonia festiva, *and* Solaster dawsoni.

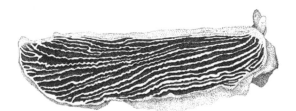

Figure 5-3. *The nudibranch* Armina californica, *a predator of fleshy sea pens.*

Figure 5-4. *A lug worm,* Arenicola *sp., a burrow-dwelling polychaete. Note the blunt anterior and tapered posterior of this four-inch-long specimen.*

pick up deposited organic matter and transport it back to the worm's mouth located in the center of the tentacles. The beachcomber may find quite a few of these funnel-shaped hoods in an eelgrass bed or on a mud or sand flat, but never see the worm. The tube of a large worm (they are up to 15 inches long) may reach three feet into the sediment. Before you can reach the worm at the bottom of its tube, the sides of your excavation cave in around you.

Sometimes, a shovel full of sandy mud will reveal a large (up to 28 inches long) red polychaete with a pointed snout. This is a blood worm, *Glycera* sp. (Figure 5-6). Several species occur in the Pacific Northwest,

the more common being *Glycera robusta* illustrated here, and *Glycera americana*. These worms are voracious carnivores. They excavate a series of interconnected burrows called a gallery and wait for prey to pass over and disturb the water in the gallery burrows. When an unsuspecting worm or small crustacean wan-

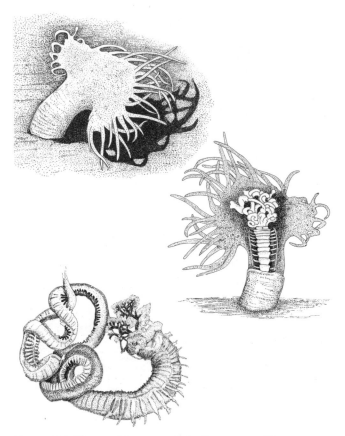

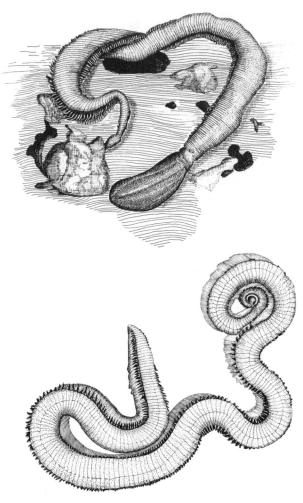

Figure 5-5. Views of the tentacle-feeding worm, Pista pacifica. *The upper left drawing shows the characteristic funnel-shaped tube opening.*

ders over the gallery, *Glycera* quickly emerges and everts a proboscis that can stretch over a third the worm's length. The proboscis ends in four black, hooked jaws, each equipped with its own poison gland. Prey items are quickly subdued and swallowed whole. Interestingly, these worms also use the proboscis to assist them in burrowing. If you should dig up a blood worm, don't pick it up. The larger specimens can deliver a nasty bite.

Another large errant polychaete found in sandy mud is the clam worm, *Neanthes brandti* (Figure 5-7). The clam worm can reach up to a yard in length and over an inch in circumference. It is a nereid polychaete as described in Chapter 3, and occurs in a variety of habitats including sandy mud flats and the rocky intertidal zone. Clam worms are omnivorous, taking whatever comes along including smaller worms and bits of algae. A number of other, smaller nereid species may be found in the soft sediment habitats. They are all recognizable by the familiar set of nereid head appendages as seen here in the clam worm.

Figure 5-6. The carnivorous polychaete, Glycera robusta. *The upper illustration shows the worm with its proboscis everted (extended).*

Figure 5-7. Anterior of a clam worm, Neanthes brandti, *a large polychaete found in several Pacific Northwest habitats.*

An excavation in a sandy mud flat may often turn up a tangle of thin red worms. They can be identified as polychaetes because close inspection reveals that their stretched bodies are segmented. A variety of polychaete species burrow through the sediment, ingesting it as they go like earthworms. The species *Lumbrinereis zonata* (Color Plate 7a) can reach up to three feet long when fully extended. These worms can be very abundant and are found on mud flats from Alaska to Baja California.

A final polychaete to look for is *Hesperone adventor* (Figure 5-8). *Hesperone* has a series of flattened plates or scales that cover its back, which give it its common name, scale worm. This worm reaches two inches in length and lives in the same burrow as the large innkeeper worm, *Urechis caupo*, and feeds on its discards. A number of other similar-appearing scale worms occur in the burrows and tubes of large invertebrates [7].

Other Mud Flat Worms. *Urechis caupo* (Figure 5-8) is an echiuroid worm that is common in central and northern California estuaries, and occasionally seen in southern Oregon. The smooth, pinkish skin and sausage-like shape have contributed to its common name, the weenie worm. Large *Urechis* can reach a length of 20 inches. The worm lives in U-shaped burrows on sandy mud flats at mid tide level or below. The two openings often are marked by low, volcano-shaped mounds of sediment and are usually 16–30 inches

apart. *Urechis* is a filter feeder. It spins a fine-meshed mucous net which it attaches to one end of its burrow. It then pumps water through its burrow and net using peristaltic contractions of its body. Periodically, the innkeeper ceases contractions and ingests the net. Particles that are discarded are fought over by the scale worm, *Hesperone adventor* (Figure 5-8), and a small (less than one-half inch wide) pea crab, *Scleroplax granulata* (Figure 5-8), that also lives in the burrow. A third resident of the inn, a small (one inch long) fish known as the arrow goby, *Clevelandia ios,* only uses the burrow for protection during low tide. The arrow goby is also found in other large invertebrates' burrows, like those of mud and ghost shrimps, as well.

When digging in sandy mud flats, you may come across long, narrow, flat worms that lack segmentation. These are probably nemertean worms of the Phylum Nemertea. Nemerteans are known as rubber band or ribbon worms, and their ability to elongate their bodies makes them successful burrowers. Nemerteans possess an eversible feeding structure and are very adept carnivores on other worms and small crustaceans. Illustrated here is *Cerebratulus californiensis* (Figure 5-9), a

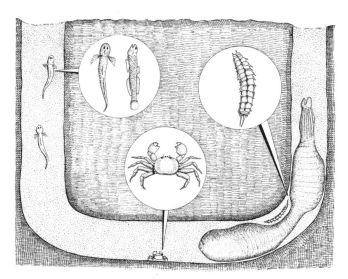

Figure 5-8. The fat innkeeper worm, Urechis caupo, *in its burrow. Guests are the scale worm,* Hesperone adventor; *the pea crab,* Scleroplax granulata; *and the arrow goby,* Clevelandia ios.

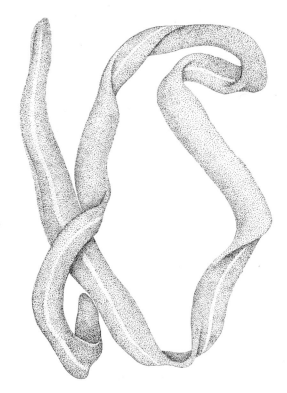

Figure 5-9. Cerebratulus californiensis, *a common large (up to three yards!) nemertean worm of coastal flats and sandy beaches.*

relatively common worm in sandy mud. This species is also found on sandy beaches. *Cerebratulus* is usually dirty-pink in color and reaches a length of three yards when extended!

Another nemertean seen on the surface of mud flats, especially those with a covering of green algae, is *Paranemertes peregrina* (Color Plate 6e). This species is dark brownish purple above and pale yellow below. It can stretch to a length of over six inches. This ribbon worm is also common in rocky intertidal habitats and prefers a diet of polychaete worms.

It is probably a good idea not to pick up any nemerteans you find, as they fragment into many pieces when handled. As with all the worms discussed here, gently bury them in a shallow excavation, and they'll take care of the rest.

Mud Flat Clams. Clams are very much at home in protected, soft substrate habitats. The relatively undisturbed nature of the substrate allows them to sit vertically in semi-permanent burrows. Their posterior elongated siphons allow them to reach the water for suspension feeding while keeping their body safely beneath the sediment surface. The siphons are especially effective for clams that live in very muddy substrates where there is little water circulation below a very shallow surface sediment layer. Beneath this layer, oxygen is depleted by decomposing bacteria, and the substrate takes on a dark brown to black color and has the odor of rotten eggs. Obviously, this isn't a hospitable place for an aerobic (oxygen-consuming) organism, but it's perfect for clams that can burrow safely into this anaerobic mud and reach the surface with their siphons. Often the shells of clams taken from such a substrate will be stained black.

Sometimes when walking about on a mud flat, the beachcomber may be startled by a sudden spout of water squirting out of the substrate. Stomping your foot will sometimes produce several such spouts in the immediate vicinity. This is most likely the work of the large gaper or horseneck clam, *Tresus capax* (Figure 5-10). The siphons of the gaper clam are so large that they cannot be fully retracted into the shell, so the posterior end of the shell gapes open to allow the clam to close its shell around the rest of its body. Gaper clams can reach a length of over eight inches, and the clam can weigh upwards of four pounds. A clam this size could be burrowed over three feet into the sediment. With any disturbance, including the tread of hip

Figure 5-10. The large northern gaper or horseneck clam, Tresus capax.

waders, the clam quickly retracts its siphons into its burrow, and the water contained within them is forced out to produce the water spouts mentioned above.

Tresus capax is the common gaper found in the Pacific Northwest. The shells can reach a length of eight inches and are a chalky white with a brown, flaky outer layer, called the periostracum. The large, muscular siphons are joined together, and the tips that reach the surface are protected by leathery patches. In *Tresus capax,* these siphon patches are comparatively thin and are not strengthened by hard, horny plates as they are in its southern relative, *Tresus nuttallii,* discussed later in this section. In both species, the siphon tips will sometimes project above the substrate surface when the tide recedes, revealing their presence. *Tresus capax* also differs from *T. nuttallii* by having a thin skirt of mantle tissue that projects beyond the edge of the shell.

Tresus capax's skirt of mantle tissue is very frequently the home of a mated pair of the small commensal pea crabs, *Pinnixa faba* (Figure 5-11), or *Pinnixa littoralis.* The female crab is the larger of the pair, reaching an inch in width. The more slender, elongated male seldom reaches half an inch. The female remains stationary by the clam's gills while the male moves around the clam's body, often climbing up into the long siphons. There are several species of these small pea crabs that form commensal relationships with larger invertebrates. They either live in their host's tube or burrow or within the body of the host itself as they do with the horseneck clam, *Tresus capax.*

In a symbiotic relationship known as a commensalism, the commensal species (in this case, the pea crab) shares space and/or food with its host, and does not harm it. However, some studies suggest that the pea

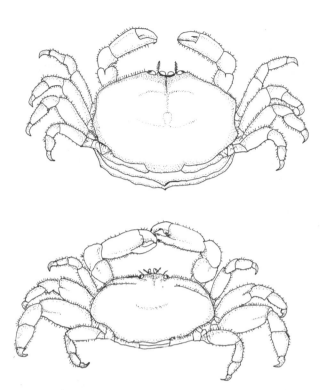

Figure 5-11. Female (above) and male pea crabs, Pinnixa faba, *found with northern gaper clam.*

Figure 5-12. The southern gaper clam, Tresus nuttallii. *The siphons can not be fully retracted into the shells.*

differs from *Tresus capax* in that the shell is more elongate and the outer periostracum layer is thicker. *T. nuttallii* does not serve as a host to pea crabs.

While the gapers are real master burrowers, they are not the champions of the mud flat. This honor goes to the geoduck, *Panope generosa.* The common name, geoduck, is derived from the Native American name for this immense (up to a yard long, including the siphons) clam that can weigh upwards of 12 pounds. The siphons of *Panope* (Figure 5-13) are so large that the eight-inch-long shells gape widely to accommodate them. Geoducks can be buried up to five feet in the substrate, and only the most determined, well-equipped beachcomber will unearth one. Geoducks are found in mud flats from British Columbia to central California, but are not abundant intertidally. In the Pacific Northwest, they are taken commercially from subtidal clam beds by divers using hydraulic digging gear.

When excavating for the deeply buried gaper and geoduck clams, another relatively large (up to four

Figure 5-13. The geoduck clam, Panope generosa. *The shells gape widely around the large siphon.*

Figure 5-14. The Washington or butter clam, Saxidomus giganteus.

crab's presence inside the gill cavity of a bivalve might negatively affect the bivalve's growth. If this is the case, the pea crabs would be considered parasites of their clam hosts.

The second species of gaper clam, *Tresus nuttallii* (Figure 5-12), reaches the northern end of its distribution in the estuaries of southern Oregon. Although both species can be found in Coos Bay, *T. nuttallii* is not common north of Tomales Bay in California. Besides the differences mentioned above, the southern gaper further inches) mud flat calm sometimes is turned up. This is the Washington or butter clam, *Saxidomus giganteus* (Figure 5-14). Washington clams are also deep burrowers and may have black-stained shells. The shells are thick and heavy and ornamented with a continuous series of concentric rings. *Saxidomus giganteus* occurs throughout the Pacific Northwest and reaches as far south as central California, although uncommon south of Humboldt Bay.

Saxidomus nuttalli (Figure 5-15), a similar-looking, close relative of *S. giganteus,* occurs from Humboldt Bay, California, to Baja California. *S. nuttalli* grows to a larger size, five inches, and the shell is more elongate and the concentric rings are heavier than those of its northern cousin. Both species are known by the common names Washington or butter clam, which demonstrates how unreliable common names can be.

One of the more interesting mud flat clams is the bentnosed clam, *Macoma nasuta* (Figure 5-16). The bentnosed clam lies burrowed on its left side with the bent posterior end of the shell facing upwards. The yellow siphons of this clam are long, thin, and separated from one another. The incurrent siphon, which brings water into the clam, probes about the substrate surface for deposited organic matter. The siphon vacuums the food into the mantle cavity, where it is trapped on the surface of the gills in the same manner as a filter-feed-

Figure 5-16. The bentnosed clam, Macoma nasuta, *two inches long. Note the upward bend in the shell of the upper specimen.*

ing clam. The bentnosed clam quickly vacuums up any available food on the surface and must move to a new spot. This is accomplished by a large, thin digging foot that allows the bentnosed clam to burrow sideways in the sediment. Bentnosed clams are usually two inches in length (four-inch specimens are occasionally seen), and are found in bay and estuarine mud flats throughout the Pacific Northwest. Their range extends from Alaska to Baja California.

Another common mud flat species is the softshell clam, *Mya arenaria* (Figure 5-17). This six-inch-long species was probably introduced into West Coast estuaries along with the Virginia or blue point oyster, *Cras-*

Figure 5-15. The southern butter clam, Saxidomus nuttalli. *Note the strong concentric rings on the shell in the foreground.*

Figure 5-17. Three-inch-long shells of the softshell clam, Mya arenaria. *Note the conspicuous spoon-shaped projection on the rear shell.*

Figure 5-18. Four-inch-long shells of the Virginia or blue point oyster, Crassostrea virginica.

Figure 5-19. The false mya, Cryptomya californica, a half-inch clam with short siphons found in the burrows of other large invertebrates.

sostrea virginica (Figure 5-18). The oysters were initially brought around the horn of South America in clipper ships during the California gold rush to satisfy the palates of newly rich 49ers. When the transcontinental railroad was completed, oysters were brought in by the train-car load along with a plethora of uninvited hitchhikers. The softshell was seen as a welcome addition by many, as the clam is able to live in low-salinity estuarine waters, grows rapidly, and is delicious. The Virginia oyster was quickly planted in estuaries in Oregon and Washington, and the softshell clam tagged along. *Mya* is now one of the most common bay clams from Alaska to Elkhorn Slough in central California. The thin, brittle shells of the softshell clam are chalky white with a brown, flaky layer, called the periostracum, along the hinge region. When the shells disarticulate (come apart) as seen in the illustration, the right-hand valve has a spoon-shaped shelf projecting outwards that strengthens the hinge region in life. It is the only common clam in mud flats that has such a structure.

Often, when innkeeper worm, ghost shrimp, or large clam burrows are excavated, a small (one-half inch long), dull-white clam appears, sometimes in abundance. This is most likely the false mya, *Cryptomya californica* (Figure 5-19). *Cryptomya* is initially an enigma because it has very short siphons yet occurs very deep in the substrate. However, this clam taps into the burrows of other large invertebrates, and uses the water they circulate through their burrows for its own filter feeding. *Cryptomya* is common throughout the Pacific Northwest wherever its many hosts occur.

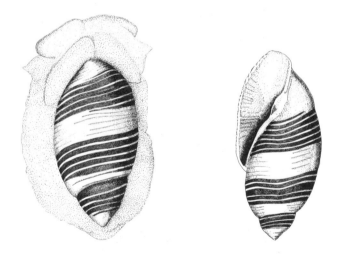

Figure 5-20. The barrel-shell snail, Rictaxis puntocaelatus, less than an inch in height.

Mud Flat Snails. There are a number of obvious snails to be found on mud flats. The barrel-shell snail, *Rictaxis puntocaelatus* (Figure 5-20), occurs on the mud flats of bays, occasionally in large numbers. This deposit-feeding snail is less than an inch long, but is clearly marked with narrow black bands that wind around the shell. The range of *Rictaxis* is Alaska to Baja California, but it is not often found in abundance north of the California-Oregon border.

Batillaria attramentaria (Figure 5-21) is another deposit-feeding snail common in some muddy bays of the Pacific Northwest. This snail was introduced from Japan along with the Pacific oyster, *Crassostrea gigas*. It reaches a length of one-and-a-half inches. Its tapering, slate gray to brown shell is unmistakable. Smaller specimens may have pigment bars crossing the fine spiral ridges at right angles. In addition to mud flats, this snail can also be found in salt marshes.

In Willapa Bay, Washington, another introduced mud snail, known as *Nassarius obsoletus* (*Illyanassa obsoleta* in some texts) (Figure 5-22) occurs. The deposit-feeding mud snail was probably introduced along with the Virginia oyster (Figure 5-18), and has taken up residence with a vengeance. Mud flats and salt marsh channels throughout the estuary are peppered with these one-inch-long snails with the dull black to brown shells. The female mud snail packages her fertilized eggs into eighth-inch high, vase-shaped egg cases, which she attaches to any hard surface. It was probably such egg cases, attached to oyster shells, that led to the mud snail's introduction.

A close relative of the mud snail is the native snail species known as the channeled basket shell, *Nassarius fossatus* (Figure 5-23). This beautiful snail, which reaches two inches in shell length, is found in sand and sandy mud habitats all along the West Coast. In the Pacific

Figure 5-21. The tall-spired snail, Batillaria attramentaria, *introduced into the Pacific Northwest from Japan with Pacific oysters.*

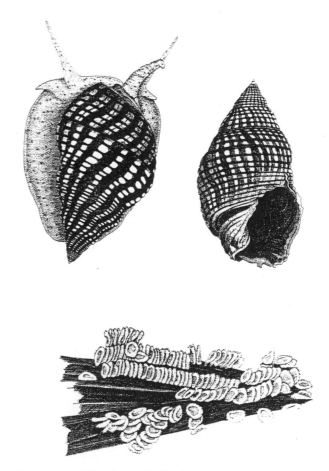

Figure 5-22. The mud snail, Nassarius obsoletus, *an import from the east coast. Note the elongated siphon.*

Figure 5-23. The channeled basket snail, Nassarius fossatus. *Lower: the snail's egg cases that are three-eighths of an inch in height.*

Northwest, it is occasionally found on intertidal flats, at mid tide or lower. In the spring, look for the three-eighths-inch-long egg cases laid by female snails attached to any handy solid substrate like a bottle, empty shell, or sand dollar skeleton. *Nassarius fossatus* is a carnivore/scavenger and a very lively, fast-moving snail. If you have a plastic bag, emerge this snail in seawater and watch as it quickly comes out of its shell and begins to explore its surroundings. Look for the long, agile siphon that the snail uses for breathing and testing the water ahead for the presence of prey.

A delightful snail to look for in these sandy mud habitats is the long-horned nudibranch, *Hermissenda crassicornis* (Color Plate 10d). *Hermissenda* is one of the most common of the shell-less sea slugs. It is found in the rocky intertidal zone and on pier pilings and dock floats. *Hermissenda* occasionally shows up on sand and mud flats, usually in tandem with large amounts of drifting green algae that wash up and become stranded on the intertidal flats. This nudibranch eats a wide variety of prey including carrion (dead animal tissue), and can reach up to three inches in length. It is readily distinguished by an orange area flanked by vivid light blue lines running down the center of its back.

Mud Flat Crustaceans. *Hemigrapsus oregonensis* (Figure 5-24). is the most abundant and widely distributed mud flat crab in the Pacific Northwest. *Hemigrapsus* males reach up to two inches across the carapace, and

Figure 5-24. The mud crab, Hemigrapsus oregonensis, *common on soft substrates of bays and estuaries.*

their claws are proportionately much larger than those of the smaller females. The mud crab is colored drab grayish-green with small blotches of red and yellow. A portion of the population will usually have some white on the carapace, sometimes extending onto the hairy legs. This crab can be found under any debris on the mud flat or in shallow burrows during low tide, and roaming the mud flat during high tide. *Hemigrapsus* is primarily a detritus feeder, but will also take small invertebrates and carrion when they are encountered.

In Willapa Bay and San Francisco and Humbolt Bays to the south, a new crab has made a recent appearance. This is the green crab, *Carcinus maenas* (Figure 5-25). The green crab was discovered in Willapa Bay in the

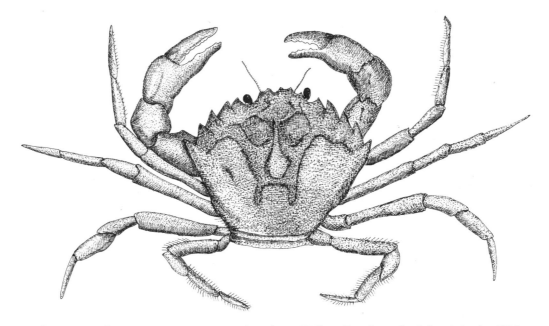

Figure 5-25. The green crab, Carcinus maenas, *introduced into Willapa Bay from the Atlantic in the 1930s.*

Figure 5-26. The red ghost shrimp, Callianassa californiensis. *This three-inch-long specimen is a female.*

Figure 5-27. The blue mud shrimp, Upogebia pugettensis, *a burrow-dwelling filter feeder.*

1930s, in San Francisco Bay in 1991, and in Humbolt Bay in 1994. The green crab is native to Europe and was introduced to the East Coast long ago. How it arrived on the West Coast and where it came from is currently a mystery. The green crab reaches about three inches across the carapace and is a voracious predator of clams and other soft substrate invertebrates. It is of particular concern in the Pacific Northwest estuaries because it may compete with juvenile Dungeness crabs for food and perhaps even prey on the smaller juveniles.

A third mud flat crustacean occurs beneath the sediment in burrows. This is the red ghost shrimp, *Callianassa californiensis* (Figure 5-26). Ghost shrimp are very active burrowers and their excavations can reach two or more feet beneath the mud flat surface. As the shrimp burrows through the sediment, it shifts out and eats organic particles that were buried within the sediment when the mud flat was formed. Ghost shrimp ventilate their burrows by pumping water through them via the rhythmic sculling of their flat abdominal appendages. The male shrimp is larger (up to three inches long) than the female and has one claw much larger than the other (Color Plate 12d). The shrimp uses his claw like a bulldozer blade to push sediment out of the burrow onto the surface. In the process, he buries organic material that has been deposited on the substrate. The shrimps' continuous excavations can result in the upper layer of a local mud flat area being turned over several times a year (Color Plate 12e), sometimes burying valuable oyster cultures.

The blue mud shrimp, *Upogebia pugettensis* (Figure 5-27), is closely related to *Callianassa,* but usually

occurs lower in the intertidal zone. The blue mud shrimp is actually bluish white, reaches about six inches long, and lacks the large claw seen in male *Callianassa.* It is also a burrower, but does not need to burrow in order to feed. Instead, *Upogebia* excavates a burrow and pumps water through it with its flat abdominal appendages in the same fashion as the ghost shrimp, *Callianassa,* discussed above. As the water flows over the shrimp's body, it strains suspended material with its legs and collects and swallows the food with its head appendages. Like *Callianassa* and many other large invertebrate burrow dwellers, blue mud shrimp may have "guests" or commensals living with them including pea crabs, scale worms, and the small arrow goby, *Clevelandia ios* (Figure 5-8).

In addition to these large, obvious crabs and shrimp, many smaller crustaceans also occur on the mud flats. These include legions of small, tube-dwelling amphipods and burrowing isopods. These animals, along with numerous small worms, are the main food source for the foraging shorebirds at low tide and the small fishes and shrimp that come in at high tide [8].

SAND FLATS

The Sand Flat Environment

As mentioned above, sand flats are part of a continuum of soft substrate habitats. Many mud flat animals overlap into sand flats, especially the burrowers. Sand flats occur in protected environments where there is an appreciable flow of water and a source of sediment. For example, in an estuary, sand flats typically form near the estuarine mouth adjacent to the main channel where relatively constant tidal currents keep the finer sediment particles in suspension and only the larger sand grains settle out. Sand flats are also common in coastal embayments for similar reasons. The combination of tidal currents and locally generated waves transport sand into the embayment, where it is dropped when the water movement slows. The most attractive feature of sand flats to beachcombers is that they are firm and easily traversed. With a little patience, a good shovel, and a decent low tide, sand flats are very rewarding places to explore.

Sand Flat Cnidarians. The moonglow anemone, *Anthopleura artemisia* (Color Plate 5d), can be found on sand flats from Alaska to southern California. However, this animal will always be anchored to a rock or some other solid substrate below the sand's surface. The moonglow anemone can reach a size of three inches across the tentacles and stretch upwards through the sand for over ten inches. Its color varies considerably, but the tentacles are usually transparent and brightly marked with either black, red, orange, white, or blue. The moonglow anemone also occurs in the middle and low rocky intertidal zones, usually under rocks where some sediment has accumulated.

Sand Flat Polychaetes. As mentioned above in the mud flat section, many polychaete species overlap both sandy mud and sand flats. Lug worms, blood worms, scale worms, and most others can show up on sand flats.

The ice cream cone worm, *Pectinaria californiensis* (Figure 5-28), is a sand bottom specialist. *Pectinaria* uses the sand to construct a beautiful tube of individually selected sand grains. The cone-shaped sand tube fits snugly around *Pectinaria*'s tapered body. Sealing off the end of the tube are elegant, gold-colored bristles that the worm uses for digging. *Pectinaria* feeds using anteriorly positioned feeding tentacles that bring sand and organic detritus to the mouth. The tube may reach three inches in length and harbor a two-and-a-half-inch-long worm. Ice cream cone worms occur in the lower intertidal zone of sand flats from Puget Sound to Baja California.

A final sand flat polychaete sometimes seen is related to the shimmy worm of the sandy beach, *Nepthys californiensis* (see Figure 4-10). This is *Nepthys caecoides,* and it is a somewhat more robust version of its

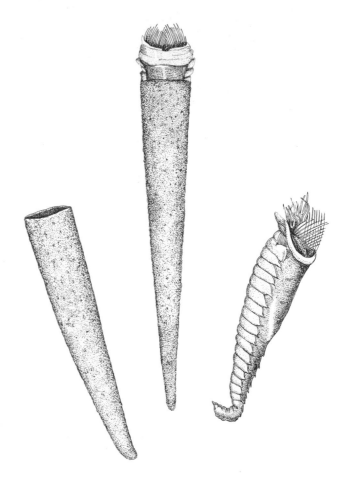

Figure 5-28. The ice cream cone worm, Pectinaria californiensis. *Note the tapered body of the exposed two-and-a-half-inch-long worm.*

beach-dwelling cousin. This three- to four-inch-long worm is a carnivore/scavenger and freely burrows through the sediment looking for food. It occurs from British Columbia to southern California.

Other Sand Flat Worms. Ribbon worms (Figure 5-9) and (in southern Oregon) an occasional fat innkeeper worm (Figure 5-8) may also occur on sand flats.

On some sand flats in the Pacific Northwest, the flexible, chitinous tubes of the phoronid worm *Phoronopsis harmeri* (Figure 5-29) can be found. When the tide covers these slender, three- to five-inch-long worms, a white, double-spiraled filter-feeding structure called a lophophore protrudes from the opening of the vertically oriented tubes. In some places in Puget Sound, this worm is found in substrates that are a mixture of mud, coarse sand, and gravel. Here, coastal embayments, stronger wave action. For the clams that live here, this means that a burrow may occasionally be disrupted or buried. Most sand flat clams live shallower in the substrate than those on mud flats and have correspondingly shorter siphons. To compensate for the occasional disruption that can sometimes wash them out of the sand, these clams have a very large digging foot and are excellent burrowers.

The basket cockle, *Clinocardium nuttallii* (Figure 5-30), is an excellent example of a sand flat clam and can be found throughout the Pacific Northwest. This bivalve mollusk has a robust, heavily ribbed shell that can reach

Figure 5-29. The phoronid worm, Phoronopsis harmeri, *in its sand-grain encrusted tube. The worm is three inches long.*

the tubes grow crooked and have large sand grains attached to them. On sand flats of central and northern California, and occasionally in southern Oregon, a similar-sized, green phoronid, *Phoronopsis viridis,* is found. This worm also lives in vertically oriented tubes, but while *P. harmeri* is never found in high abundance, *P. viridis* is typically found in large beds with individual tubes packed closely together.

Sand Flat Clams. The sand flat is a more physically active habitat than the mud flat. It is subjected to stronger water currents and sometimes, especially in

Figure 5-30. The heavily ribbed shell of the basket cockle, Clinocardium nuttallii, *is unmistakable. This small specimen is one-and-a-half inches across.*

Figure 5-31. A small (one inch) littleneck clam, Protothaca staminea. *Note the short siphons that give it its common name, "littleneck."*

four inches in diameter. *Clinocardium*'s siphons are very short, barely protruding beyond the posterior end of the gaped valves. The foot is immense, stretching out over twice the length of the shell when fully extended. The cockle lives at such a shallow depth that it is easily excavated by the predatory sea star, *Pisaster brevispinus* (Color Plate 16c). However, *Clinocardium* has a remarkable escape response up its sleeve (shell?). It protrudes its large foot and folds it under its shell, than rapidly stretches the foot its full length. The clam is pole-vaulted free of the substrate surface and out of the grasp of the sea star. A few more of these jumps and the clam has successfully avoided the slow-moving predator.

Sometimes co-occurring with the basket cockle is the common littleneck clam, *Protothaca staminea* (Figure 5-31). The white to tan, three-inch shell of this clam is also ribbed, but the ribbing is not as strong as *Clinocardium*'s, and is combined with a series of weak concentric rings. The common name "littleneck" is in reference to the clam's short siphons, and it is seldom buried deeper than three inches. *Protothaca* is not as good a digger as the basket cockle, so it is not found in habitats with shifting sands. Besides being found on protected sand flats, *Protothaca* also occurs in packed mud and in gravel mixed with sand and mud. *Protothaca* will also settle into pockets of sand and gravel that collect in the rocky intertidal zone (Figure 5-32), sometimes becoming trapped in the rocks as it grows. *Protothaca*'s occurrence in the rocky intertidal zone has led to its other common name, the rock cockle.

Figure 5-33. *The Japanese littleneck clam,* Tapes japonica. *This introduced clam is found in bays and estuaries all along the West Coast.*

Figure 5-34. *Shells of the white sand clam,* Macoma secta. *This clam is two-and-a-half inches long.*

Figure 5-32. *A large (two-and-a-half inches) littleneck clam,* Protothaca staminea, *found in a sand pocket in the middle rocky intertidal zone.*

A clam very similar to *Protothaca,* but from the other side of the Pacific, is the Japanese littleneck, *Tapes japonica* (Figure 5-33). *Tapes* was first found in Puget Sound in the 1930s and is now one of the most abundant clams in the Sound, where it is harvested commercially. *Tapes* grows to about three inches in diameter and prefers a sandy mud to sandy sediment with some shell or rock mixed in. It is found in bays, sloughs, and estuaries from British Columbia to southern California.

The smooth, clean shell of the white sand clam, *Macoma secta* (Figure 5-34) is unmistakable. This clam is found in clean sand, from Vancouver Island to Baja

California. It is especially abundant near the mouth of bays. Like its bentnosed cousin, *Macoma nasuta* (Figure 5-16), the white sand clam is a deposit feeder, and it has long, separated siphons and an agile digging foot. With this morphology, the sand clam can burrow down to 18 inches or more, putting it out of reach of most surface-feeding predators. The sand clam reaches up to four inches in length.

Often occurring with the sand clam is the closely related Bodega Tellin, *Tellina bodegensis* (see Figure 4-14), introduced in the sandy beach chapter. This clam is also a deposit feeder and an excellent burrower.

Sand Flat Gastropods. The two most common snails on most sand flats are the olive snail, *Olivella biplicata* (see Figure 4-11), and the moon snail, *Polinices* spp. (see Figure 4-15). Both these snails were introduced in the sandy beach chapter. The olive can sometimes be found in large aggregations, either attracted to a common food source or in search of mates. Olives are most active at night, when they can be found actively burrowing just beneath the sand, often with the top of their shell exposed.

Moon snails are solitary, usually showing up as a burrowed bulge in the sand or with just the top of their shell showing on the surface. When one of these large predatory snails is unearthed at low tide, it often has its huge foot extended. Gentle prodding of the foot will cause the snail to retract into its shell, but hold it well away from you as you may get wet. Unlike most mollusks which extend the foot internally by inflating special blood sinuses, the moon snail actively pumps water into special chambers in its foot to help it expand. When the snail retracts into its shell, this water is forced out. The last thing visible as the snail retreats into the safety of its heavy shell is the horny operculum that closes off the entrance to the shell and protects the snail's soft body.

In the spring and summer, beachcombers may find a sand-colored structure as big around as a saucer or small dinner plate that looks like a discarded plunger or plumber's friend. This is the egg collar of a moon snail (Figure 5-35). It is formed by the female who places her fertilized eggs within a matrix of mucus combined with sand grains. As the embryos develop within the collar, it gradually deteriorates so that it falls apart at the time the embryos are ready to swim away as planktonic larvae. As many as half a million embryos are contained in a single large egg collar.

Figure 5-35. Six-inch diameter egg collar deposited by female moon snail, Polinices lewisii.

Sand Flat Crustaceans. First, some familiar animals that were introduced in the sandy beach chapter. The graceful cancer crab, *Cancer gracilis* (Figure 4-17), found from central California north, is at home foraging on sand flats. It would be buried in the sand at low tide. Also from central California north, juvenile Dungeness crabs (less than three inches in carapace width), *Cancer magister* (Color Plate 13d), are often found on estuarine sand flats. As an adult, this large, commercially important crab typically shows up on sandy beaches in the form of molted exoskeletons (Color Plate 13b). Juveniles, however, will venture far up into estuaries, as they are tolerant of much lower salinities than the adults. The estuaries of the Pacific Northwest serve as important nurseries for the juvenile Dungeness crabs, allowing them to feed and grow free of many of their open ocean predators.

Two other cancer crabs, *Cancer antennarius* and *Cancer productus* (Figures 7-7 and 7-8, respectively), are occasionally found on sand flats, especially if there are some rocks or jetties nearby. However, these two large, brick-red crabs with black-tipped claws are much more common in the rocky intertidal habitat and are treated in Chapter 7.

The combination of sand flats and nearby rocky areas will also yield the mud crab, *Hemigrapsus oregonensis* (Figure 5-24), and, in southern Oregon, the larger (up to two-and-a-half inches in carapace width), green-lined shore crab, *Pachygrapsus crassipes* (Figure 5-41). You may find both of these crabs under the same rock lying on the sand flat surface. *Pachygrapsus* is a scavenger and also very common in the rocky intertidal zone and on pier pilings from southern Oregon south. These crabs can also be found together in the tidal creeks that drain salt marshes. *Hemigrapsus* excavates burrows in the creek banks, and *Pachygrapsus* usurps and enlarges them.

The salt and pepper shrimp, *Crangon* spp. (Figure 4-18), introduced in the sandy beach chapter, are also common on sand flats. They come in at high tide and forage for prey. If stranded, they burrow in and wait for the next high tide. The familiar mole crab of sandy beaches, *Emerita analoga* (Figure 4-4), is sometimes found on sand flats if any wave action occurs.

A large hermit crab (over an inch and a half in carapace length) is found on the sand flats and subtidal sandy bottoms from Alaska south to San Diego, California. This is the black-eyed hermit, *Pagurus armatus* (Color Plate 13f), and it typically lives in moon snail (*Polinices*) shells. As the common name implies, this hermit has large black eyes, and the legs and claws have some orange banding. Like most hermit crabs, it is a scavenger and forages on the sandy bottoms for bits of organic detritus that it picks up with its claws. The black-eyed hermit is one of the largest and most commonly observed sandy bottom hermits on the Pacific coast [9]. It is also common in sea pen beds in Puget Sound. Another hermit similar in size, habitat, and appearance to the black-eyed hermit is *Pagurus ochotensis* (not shown). This hermit likewise is typically found in a moon snail shell, but can be distinguished from the black-eyed hermit by the yellow-green color of its eyes. The two species seldom co-occur, with one or the other dominating in a given habitat.

Sand Flat Echinoderms. As their name suggests, you would expect to find sand dollars on sand flats. The common Pacific sand dollar, *Dendraster excentricus* (Figure 4-19), is occasionally found exposed on sand flats in Puget Sound, usually near a tidal channel or some other source of moving water. Elsewhere in the Pacific Northwest, sand dollars are much more common offshore of sandy beaches as was discussed in the previous chapter. When exposed on the sand flat, the sand dollars usually lie flat and are completely or partially burrowed.

A much more obvious echinoderm on sand flats is the sea star known as the pink or short-spined pisaster, *Pisaster brevispinus* (Color Plate 16c). This sea star is found in many habitats from sand flats and the rocky

Figure 5-36. Pale white worm-like cucumber, Leptosynapta clarki.

intertidal zone to pier pilings, and well offshore on subtidal sand and mud bottoms. It is known to occur from Alaska to San Diego. On sand flats, *P. brevispinus* feeds primarily on bivalve mollusks. It has the ability to find and extract a burrowed clam from the substrate either by digging after it or using special tube feet located around its mouth. These tube feet can penetrate the substrate to a depth equal approximately to the length of the sea star's arm. The tube feet are equipped with suckers that attach to the clam's shell and allow it to be pulled up to the sea star's mouth. The pink sea star can reach a diameter of over two feet in subtidal habitats, but the sand flat individuals are usually less than a foot across.

There are other echinoderms sometimes seen on or in the sand flat. Worm-like sea cucumbers work through the sediment a few inches from the surface, swallowing it as they go much like earthworms. One common species found in the Pacific Northwest is the worm-like, pale white cucumber, *Leptosynapta clarki* (Figure 5-36). *Leptosynapta* lacks tube feet on its body typical of most echinoderms and looks like a nondescript worm. However, when observed in a quiet setting, the cucumber elongates up to four inches and feeding tentacles emerge from the mouth and begin to probe the bottom. These feeding tentacles are modified tube feet.

ROCKY SHORES OF PROTECTED COASTAL HABITATS

This chapter is intended to introduce habitats with soft substrates. However, in many of these environments, some amount of rocky substrate occurs, either natural or introduced by humans. The organisms found here are usually a subset of the open coast rocky intertidal zone, and Chapters 6 and 7 should be con-

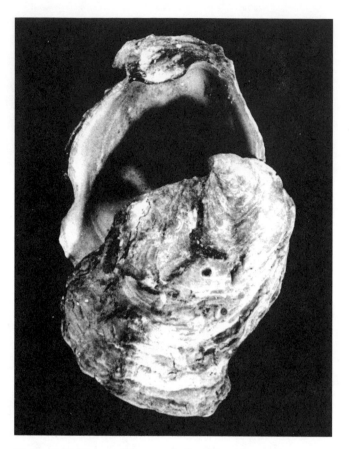

Figure 5-37. Top and bottom shells of the Olympia oyster, Ostrea lurida. *Top shell is one-and-a-half inches long.*

sulted. Indeed most of the rocky substrate inside the greater Puget Sound region would fall into this category, but the rocky intertidal of the Sound is treated inclusively in the next two chapters on the rocky intertidal. There are a few unique animals that occur on the protected rocky shores of estuaries, and these will be mentioned here briefly.

In many estuaries, a small native oyster is found. This is the lurid or Olympia oyster, *Ostrea lurida* (Figure 5-37). This bivalve reaches about two inches in diameter and can be found on the undersides of rocks and on concrete pilings, as well as attached to the shells of other mollusk species (Color Plate 8f). Oyster larvae prefer a shell substrate for settlement and sometimes this oyster will be found in small aggregations, but nothing like the huge shell reefs formed by some oyster species along the East Coast.

From 1850 to 1880, the Olympia oyster was collected in enormous quantities in the great estuaries of Washington's southern open coast, Willapa Bay and Grays Harbor, by local Indians. The oysters were shipped by oyster schooners to San Francisco to slake the appetites of hungry '49ers fresh from California's gold fields. In the late 1800s and early 1900s, the Olympia oyster was raised commercially in Puget Sound and in Oregon's Yaquina Bay. However, despite its delectable flavor, it grew too slowly and to too small a size to keep up with the demand of the growing human population. It also did not fare well with the pollution that logging and lumber mill operations dumped into the estuaries. Scientists at Oregon State University's Hatfield Marine Science Center and Oregon's Department of Fish and Wildlife are working to reintroduce *Ostrea lurida* back into Oregon's estuaries.

At the turn of the century, the Virginia oyster, *Crassostrea virginica* (Figure 5-18), was introduced into the Pacific Northwest; later in the 1900s, the Pacific oyster, *Crassostrea gigas* (Color Plate 8f), was imported from Japan. Both species of oyster grew successfully in the Pacific Northwest, but only the Pacific oyster reproduced successfully. *Crassostrea gigas* now forms large aggregations on rocky substrate or attached to shells in Puget Sound. It is especially abundant along Hood Canal.

One reason for *Crassostrea gigas*'s success in competition with the native oyster, *Ostrea lurida*, is its superior ability as a filter feeder. The native oyster filters detritus and large phytoplankton from the water as its main food. It is unable to capture the smaller phytoplankton, called nannoplankton. In contrast, Pacific oysters can filter nannoplankton in addition to the detritus and large phytoplankton taken by the native oyster, and thus have access to more food. *Crassostrea gigas* grows much faster than *Ostrea lurida* and to a much larger size. However, oyster lovers will tell you that the native oyster has a much better flavor and the flesh has a firmer consistency than that of the Pacific oyster.

The shell of the Pacific oyster can reach a foot in length, although it is generally smaller. The left valve is cemented to the substrate and is cupped (Color Plate 8f), while the right valve is usually flat and fluted. The shell shape varies from long and thin when grown close together on a soft substrate, to round and deep when grown uncrowded attached to a hard substrate. The shell exterior is chalky tan or white, often with purple streaks, and the interior is shiny white. Great heaps of these shells are a familiar sight along the road in many Pacific Northwest estuaries.

Often, a snail with a pretty, ornamented, inch-and-a-half-long shell is found close by oysters. This is the Atlantic oyster drill, *Urosalpinx cinerea* (Figure 5-38), which was introduced unintentionally with the Virginia oyster. This snail is now found in estuaries form British Columbia to Newport Bay, California. It feeds chiefly

on barnacles and bivalves, and occasionally on other snails. As the common name implies, this snail uses its radula to drill a hole in its prey in the same manner as the moon snail.

A common mollusk on these protected rocky shores is the mussel *Mytilus trossulus* (Figure 5-39). (This mussel was previously identified as *Mytilus edulis,* the edible or blue mussel, but now has been reclassified.) This mussel is usually about two inches long, although four-inch individuals are found. It occasionally occurs on the open coast, usually with the much more robust California mussel, *Mytilus californianus* (see Figure 6-50). Mussels attach to the substrate using special hairs made of protein, called byssal threads. These are attached by the foot directly to the rock or, in mussel clumps, to one another, and anchor the mussel solidly. When large clumps of mussels accumulate, they become safe havens for scores of small crustaceans, worms, and other small invertebrates.

A final animal must be mentioned, simply because it is such a curiosity. This is the fish known as the plainfin midshipman, *Porichthys notatus* (Figure 5-40). This 15-inch-long fish has a double row of white, light-produc-

Figure 5-38. The East Coast snail known as the oyster drill, Urosalpinx cinerea. *The shells are one inch in height.*

Figure 5-39. The mussel Mytilus trossulus, *two-and-a-half inches long. Note the "beard" of attachment fibers, called byssal threads.*

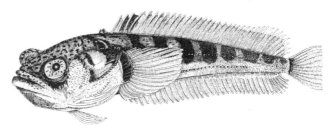

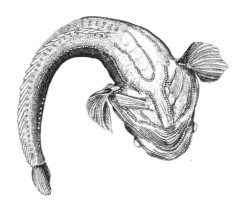

Figure 5-40. Side and bottom views of the singing toadfish or midshipman, Porichthys notatus, *that can reach 15 inches in length.*

ing organs (photophores) along its underside that look like the buttons on the front of a junior marine officer's trousers, and thus the common name "midshipman." *Porichthys* is also known as the singing toadfish because of the loud croaking sounds it produces during mating season. The croaking is the reason for the midshipman's notoriety. The fish comes into estuaries to mate in the late spring. The males set up territories near rock piles and, when night falls, proceed to croak their presence to the females. A female comes in and lays her pea-sized eggs in a tight cluster under a rock that the male will then guard until they hatch. These rocky nursery areas are sometimes in the low intertidal zone, and an investigating beachcomber may discover a guarding male and his brood of eggs under a rock. After a quick look, carefully replace the rock and let daddy do his duty.

Now for the interesting part. The singing toadfish produces its croaking song by rapidly contracting the muscles attached to its swim bladder, an internal gas chamber that fish use to adjust their buoyancy. The muscle contractions set up a rhythmic vibration in the swim bladder, which acts as a resonating chamber to produce a deep, almost mechanical hum. In the mid-1980s, when a group of love-starved toadfish set up camp and started singing beneath the houseboats in Sausalito, California, on San Francisco Bay, they created quite a stir. The combined humming of the toadfish was heard at night through the keels of the houseboats. Experts on underwater sound were called in. Speculation on the source of the alien sound ranged from miniature Russian submarines on clandestine, nocturnal forays to illegal pumping of pollutants into the bay. The mystery sound made the local newspapers and, as it was the slow-news days of summer, it was picked up by the wire services and made national news. The reaction when I identified the culprit fish gave me my 15 minutes of fame, and made the toadfish a local hero. For a few years thereafter, there was a toadfish festival, complete with parade, in Sausalito.

OTHER HARD SUBSTRATES

In addition to the unique marine and estuarine organisms discussed here, quiet-water habitats attract human animals as well. Estuaries and coastal embayments are the preferred location for harbors, marinas, fish-processing plants, etc. Consequently, the beachcomber will find a number of hard substrates provided by humans in quiet-water habitats. Pier pilings and floating boat docks are among the most common, and I will briefly discuss them here.

Pier Pilings. Pier pilings represent a hard substrate that receives normal tidal exposure. As a result, it harbors a variety of organisms that prefer and/or tolerate these conditions. The upper part of a piling is usually the domain of hardy barnacles and a smattering of limpets typical of the upper intertidal zone of the rocky coast (see Chapter 6). Lower on the piling, another barnacle that stands out because of its large size is the horse barnacle, *Balanus nubilus* (Color Plate 14d). This attached crustacean can reach a diameter of up to four inches and is distinguished by the pointed, arching plates that protrude from the shell as the animal feeds via sweeps of its thoracic appendages. Horse barnacles are also common on floating piers and occur in the low rocky intertidal zone of the open coast.

Also found on pier pilings in southern Oregon is the green-lined shore crab, *Pachygrapsus crassipes* (Figure 5-41). Below the barnacles, at approximately mid tide level, the mussel, *Mytilus trossulus* (Figure 5-39) will be common, often in sizable clumps. Mixed in with this mussel may be the open coast mussel, *Mytilus californianus* (Figure 6-50). The mussels provide attachment sites for a variety of organisms including barnacles, limpets, sea anemones, and encrusting forms like sponges and bryozoans. If the clump is especially well developed, it will harbor sea star predators like *Pisaster ochraceus* (Color Plate 16b), *Pisaster brevispinus* (Color Plate 16c), and *Evasterias troschelii* (Color Plate 16e), and a myriad of small invertebrates. See the treatment of the mussel clump habitat in Chapter 6.

Floating Docks. The sides and bottoms of floating boat docks are the other common hard substrates the beachcomber may find in quiet-water habitats. These are typically made of panels of high-density plastic foams that have high flotation properties and are impervious to seawater. However, they are not impervious to marine life. Unlike the pier piling discussed above, these substrates are never exposed to tidal action. Consequently, they harbor a suite of fragile, space-grabbing invertebrates, many of which grow in flat, encrusting colonies. Look for the browns, grays, and bright reds and yellows of marine sponges (Color Plates 4a and 6f). Also plentiful are the purple and orange colonies of compound tunicates, and the deli-

Figure 5-41. *A large green-lined shore crab,* Pachygrapsus crassipes, *clings tenaciously to a barnacle-encrusted pier piling.*

Figure 5-42. *A cluster of the tunicate known as the sea vase,* Ciona intestinalis, *found commonly on hard substrates in quiet-water habitats.*

Figure 5-43. *Several specimens of the delicate white anemone,* Metridium senile. *The largest anemone is an inch-and-a-half tall.*

cate, basket-weave patterns of encrusting bryozoan colonies (see Chapter 3; also Figure 7-5). Erect or branching bryozoan colonies are also common, along with a variety of colonial hydroid cnidarians. Barnacles and mussels will also grow on these structures, and they provide yet more substrate for the encrusting species.

Several species of relatively large solitary tunicates do very well on these floating substrates. The transparent tunicate known as the sea vase, *Ciona intestinalis* (Figure 5-42), occurs worldwide in ports and bays. Individuals three to five inches long can be very abundant in local situations. This animal can pump over five gallons of water a day through its body for filter feeding and respiration. Also look for the leathery tunics of the Monterey tunicate, *Styela montereyensis* (see Figure 7-39).

Small sea anemones can also be very common, especially the delicate, translucent-white *Metridium senile* (Figure 5-43). Occasionally, a large relative, *Metridium giganteum* (Color Plate 5e), occurs, projecting well away from the float into the water. These large metridiums are often seen by divers on rocky surfaces in subtidal areas, especially in the San Juan Islands and the Straits of Georgia and Juan de Fuca. They are also a favorite exhibit of marine aquariums.

Look for the bright-colored fans of feeding tentacles belonging to feather-duster worms (Color Plates 7b and 7c) protruding from their protective tubes. Clumps of the maroon-tentacled *Eudistylia vancouveri* (Color Plate 7c) and the slightly smaller *Schizobranchia insig-*

The level of the marsh is raised, and the margin of the marsh increases outward until it reaches a dynamic equilibrium with the local pattern of water movement that controls sedimentation. As the marsh becomes more extensive, drainage channels, called tidal creeks, develop that direct the flow of water out of the marsh as the tide recedes. These tidal creeks can become deeply eroded, and their bottoms and banks create a habitat for invertebrates.

The west coast of North America does not contain the vast acreage of salt marshes as is seen along the southeastern seaboard or the Gulf of Mexico. However, there are some very substantial salt marshes in the Pacific Northwest, especially in southern Washington and along the Fraser River estuary that enters the Strait of Georgia.

Unfortunately, much of the salt marsh habitat in the Pacific Northwest has been diked and drained and turned into pasture or commercial real estate, or dredged and turned into docking facilities. The value of salt marshes and other wetlands has only recently become apparent to decision makers, and there is some move to preserve and even restore wetlands, including salt marshes. The salt marsh habitat we do have is now generally protected.

The average beachcomber is not going to venture too far into a salt marsh. The vegetation is thick and the underfooting often unsure. Likewise, the bottom of tidal creeks can be very muddy and hard to traverse. Some salt marshes in the Pacific Northwest provide viewing trails built along the marsh uplands. The walk along the salt marsh and eelgrass beds of Padilla Bay near Fidalgo Island in Puget Sound is an excellent example.

The portion of the marsh that is affected by the tides is dominated by two plants. Along the lower intertidal a fringe of the tall (up to three feet) cord grass, *Spartina* spp. (Figure 5-45) can be found. This fringe may be fairly extensive, but eventually gives way to species of the shorter pickleweed or glass wart, *Salicornia* spp. (Figure 5-46), that grow at higher tidal elevations and typically dominate the salt marsh. The marsh is laced with meandering tidal creeks that usually drain out across a low intertidal flat. Above the pickleweed is a community of upland marsh plants, and I refer you to a more detailed account for reference [10].

Unfortunately, like much of the estuarine environment, the salt marsh has not been spared from invaders. The East Coast cord grass, *Spartina alterniflora* (Color Plate 3e) has been introduced into a number of bays in the Pacific Northwest, most notably Willapa Bay in Wash-

Figure 5-44. The branched feeding tentacles of the fan worm, Schizobranchia insignis, *extend beyond its parchment-like tube.*

nis (Figure 5-44) are especially abundant in estuaries along the open coast. The tentacles of *Schizobranchia* fork dichotomously several times along their length, and are colored red, orange, brown, gray, or green. These tube worms with the elaborate tentacles are also commonly called fan worms.

SALT MARSHES

Protected coastal environments are typically created by the flow of sediment into a bay, river mouth, or other shallow area, forming a delta. As the delta builds up, it can be colonized by special plants adapted to seawater-inundated soils, and a salt marsh is born. Once the salt marsh plants take hold, their spreading root and underground stem systems trap more sediment.

ington. This cord grass species grows much more vigorously than the native and also grows successfully over a greater tidal range. There is a danger that this plant will encroach onto the mud flats that border the salt marshes along the low tide margin and remove habitat important to birds and oyster culture.

The marsh itself is home to a mixture of terrestrial and marine organisms. The terrestrial component includes many insects, small mammals, and of course the birds. Among the plants are many small marine invertebrates including crustaceans and mollusks [6, 7, 8]. The tidal creeks are invaded by many of the same animals that were discussed above as occurring on mud and sandy mud flats.

EELGRASS MEADOWS

A final protected, soft substrate habitat that may be seen by the beachcomber is the eelgrass meadow. Eelgrass, *Zostera marina* (Color Plate 3d), grows along the intertidal edge of sand and mud flats up to plus 6.0 feet MLLW and in shallow, subtidal protected habitats to a depth of about 20 feet. A second, smaller species, *Zostera japonica*, introduced from Japan along with the Pacific oyster, co-occurs with *Z. marina* from Coos Bay northward. *Zostera japonica* has a strictly intertidal distribution from plus 4.0 to 8.0 feet MLLW. The two species overlap between plus 3.3 and 5.0 feet MLLW [11].

Eelgrass meadows require a salinity of at least 20 parts per thousand salt (normal seawater is about 33–35 parts per thousand salt) and currents that do not exceed 3–5 miles per hour. If the water is clear, the subtidal eelgrass meadows can be quite extensive. The three largest eelgrass meadows in the Pacific Northwest occur in Padilla Bay near Fidalgo Island, in Grays Harbor and Willapa Bay estuaries, and in Humboldt Bay in northern California. The largest eelgrass meadow in Oregon is found in Netarts Bay, and there are good-sized meadows in Coos Bay and Yaquina Bay. Eelgrass meadows are estimated to cover nine percent of the bottom of Puget Sound. There is a nearly continuous ring of eelgrass around Hood Canal [11].

Eelgrass meadows create important habitats for fishes, shrimps, juvenile crabs, and waterfowl. The plants spread along underground stems called rhizomes, and the combined roots and rhizomes form a mat that stabilizes the otherwise unconsolidated sandy mud substrate. The leaves float up into the water and slow the flow of water through them. This results in a great deal of sedi-

Figure 5-45. A small stand of cord grass, Spartina foliosa, *abuts a mud flat. This tall grass is found along the outer edges of salt marshes.*

Figure 5-46. The low-growing pickleweed or glass wart, Salicornia sp., *the most common plant in salt marshes of the Pacific Northwest.*

ment being trapped in the meadow and sediment level rising. The eelgrass leaves provide sites for the attachment and growth of epiphytic plants and animals, and the root-rhizome mass harbors many animals like polychaetes, brittle stars, and ribbon worms. The meadow itself provides protection and food to a large number of juvenile fishes like English sole and starry flounder. Juvenile chum salmon are particularly dependent on eelgrass meadows which provide the substrate for the copepod prey on which they feed before going to sea [11]. Pacific herring spawn on eelgrass leaves, and this provides the basis for a very lucrative fishery in British Columbia. Juvenile (Color Plate 13d) and adult Dungeness crab, *Cancer magister,* can be abundant in eelgrass meadows, as can the kelp crab, *Pugettia gracilis* (Color Plate 14a), coon stripe shrimp, *Pandalus danae* (Color Plate 12f), and sand shrimp, *Crangon* spp. (Figure 4-18).

Eelgrass is eaten by a number of waterfowl. Black brant geese are especially fond of it. It is also eaten by Canada geese and a number of species of ducks. Many shorebirds graze on the epiphytic organisms growing on the leaves. The majority of the plants' growth is not eaten directly by herbivores, but instead enters the estuarine food chain as suspended organic detritus and finds its way into the diets of filter and deposit feeders.

The intertidal eelgrass meadows accessible to the beachcomber will yield a number of familiar animals already described in this chapter for mud and sand flats, including many of the clam and worm species. The matted root-rhizome mass of the grass is a particularly good place to observe polychaetes.

Because of the root-rhizome mat, footing is pretty stable and an intertidal eelgrass meadow can be explored without too much worry about sinking into the mud. A memorable beachcombing outing can be had by visiting a meadow that has a foot or so of standing water over it. This will allow the leaves to be buoyed up so that you can see the organisms on the leaves as well as the mobile animals on the bottom between the plants. Also look for the tips of clam siphons and the hood of the large polychaete, *Pista pacifica* (Figure 5-5). You will occasionally see a large foraging sea star like *Pycnopodia helianthoides* (Color Plate 16a) or *Pisaster brevispinus* (Color Plate 16c) searching for clams. Take your time and remember the size rule introduced in Chapter 2. Adjust your search to things that fit along the edge of a blade of eelgrass and prepare to be amazed at what you find.

A number of other unique invertebrates occur in the eelgrass meadows. One of the most interesting is the nudibranch *Melibe leonia* (Color Plate 12a). This three- to four-inch-long, shell-less sea slug is colored yellowish brown to olive green. It holds onto a blade of eelgrass with its narrow foot while stretching its broad oral hood into the water to sweep up zooplankton prey. When a prey item like a copepod or an amphipod contacts the hood, the two sides are rapidly swept together, and the fringing tentacles interlock forcing the animal into the nudibranch's mouth. *Melibe* is also found in kelp beds and occasionally in the lower rocky intertidal zone. Once you've seen *Melibe,* you'll never forget it.

Eelgrass meadows are fascinating habitats, and beachcombers looking for something out of the ordinary should plan a visit.

REFERENCES

1. Simenstad, C. A., *The Ecology of Estuarine Channels of the Pacific Northwest Coast: A Community Profile.* U.S. Fish and Wildlife Service, FWS/OBS-83/05, 1983, 181 pp.
2. Peterson, R. T., *A Field Guide to Western Birds,* 3rd Ed. Boston: Houghton Mifflin Company, 1990.
3. Udvardy, M. F., *The Audubon Society Field Guide to North American Birds: Western Edition.* New York: Alfred J. Knoph Inc., 1977.
4. Harrison, P., *Seabirds: An Identification Guide.* Boston: Houghton Mifflin Company, 1983.
5. Hayman, P., et al., *Shorebirds: An Identification Guide.* Boston: Houghton Mifflin Company, 1986.
6. Ricketts, et al., *Between Pacific Tides,* 5th Ed. Stanford: Stanford University Press, 1985, 652 pp.
7. Smith, R. I. and J. Carlton, *Light's Manual: Intertidal Invertebrates of the Central California Coast,* 3rd Ed. Berkeley: University of California Press, 1975, 716 pp.
8. Rudy, P. and L. H. Rudy, *Oregon Estuarine Invertebrates: An Illustrated Guide to the Common and Important Invertebrate Animals.* U.S. Fish and Wildlife Service, FWS/OBS-83/16, 1983, 225 pp.
9. Jensen, G. C., *Pacific Coast Crabs and Shrimps.* Monterey: Sea Challengers, 1995, 87 pp.
10. Joselyn, M. N., *The Ecology of San Francisco Bay Tidal Marshes: A Community Profile.* U.S. Fish and Wildlife Service, FWS/OBS-83/23, 1983, 102 pp.
11. Phillips, R. C., *The Ecology of Eelgrass Meadows in the Pacific Northwest: A Community Profile.* U.S. Fish and Wildlife Service, FWS/OBS-84/24, 1984, 85 pp.

6

THE ROCKY INTERTIDAL
ENVIRONMENT: UPPER ZONES

A beachcomber's first trip to the rocky intertidal zone of the Pacific Northwest (Figure 6-1) is bound to be a memorable one. This is especially true if your beachcombing has been along the coast of the Gulf of Mexico, with its miles and miles of sandy beaches, or the southeastern seaboard, with its extensive marshlands and estuaries. These soft-bottom habitats, though certainly impressive, do not prepare beachcombers for their first encounter with an extensive rocky intertidal habitat. The diversity of the plant and animal life can initially be overwhelming; however, it is well worth the effort.

PHYSICAL FACTORS

Attempting to cover the Pacific Northwest rocky intertidal habitat in a general guidebook has been a daunting task. As we'll see, the rocky intertidal habitat

Figure 6-1. Extensive rocky intertidal zone found at Cape Alava, Washington.

is really several habitats stacked vertically on one another along a gradient of tidal exposure. As reviewed in the first chapter, tidal exposure is one of the three main physical factors affecting the distribution of marine intertidal organisms. The other two are degree of exposure to wave action and the type of substrate.

Wave exposure is related to several factors. The geographical location of a rocky habitat will determine if it is directly in line to receive the full force of the Pacific's storm waves. Most of the Pacific Northwest's big storms come out of the west or southwest. The presence of large offshore islands that come between the rocky intertidal habitat and the storm waves absorb the brunt of their force. Thus, they can be important influences on the degree of local wave exposure. Examples are the Queen Charlotte Islands and Vancouver Island that shield large portions of the continental coast of British Columbia which receive very minor wave exposure as a result. The Strait of Juan de Fuca connects to the open coast, and a declining gradient of wave exposure is encountered as you travel eastward along the Strait towards the San Juan Island Archipelago. Only the west and south sides of the San Juan Islands that are exposed directly to the Strait experience any appreciable wave action. Finally, the impact of wave exposure is related to the type of rocks making up the rocky substrate.

Rocky intertidal substrates vary in their composition. Remember that the basic materials making up the rocky coastline you see today probably had their origin in a previous geological epoch. The rocks were most likely formed under vastly different circumstances compared to their present situation. Some habitats are hewn from sturdy igneous rocks that originated from fiery volcanic activities. Other rocky habitats consist of sedimentary rocks, formed by pressure on the compacted layers of sands, silts, and clays that once formed the bottoms of coastal embayments or estuaries, or the conglomerate rocks composed of compressed glacial till. Sedimentary rocks like limestone, sandstone, siltstone, and mudstone are softer, and provide less secure attachment sites for animals like barnacles and mussels. These substrates are eroded by wave action in different patterns than are the igneous rocks. Sedimentary rocks are also more easily penetrated by boring organisms, which in turn weaken the rocky substrates and influence the way they will erode.

Very hard, dense, igneous rocks like basalts will resist erosion and tend to weather evenly. Sedimentary rocks are more easily broken up by wave action, and often intertidal boulder fields will be found, consisting of broken pieces of the reef surface. Likewise, the weathering of coastal cliffs can contribute loose rocky material to the intertidal zone at their base. In places where different types of rocks intergrade, an uneven pattern of erosion can result. Wave-cut surge channels, tunnels and caves, shallow and deep tidal pools, upraised outcroppings, fringing tidal reefs, and even towering headlands and seastacks so familiar to Pacific Northwest seascapes all can be formed from differential erosion patterns.

The extent of the rocky intertidal zone depends on the slope of the wave-cut bench. This slope is again related to the type of rock and the immediate geography of the area. Rocky intertidal areas are often found at the base of steep, rocky cliffs. These areas tend to be likewise steep with very narrow, vertical intertidal habitats. Other rocky intertidal areas occur on broad, wave-cut terraces. These tend to have extensive rocky intertidal areas with a very gradual slope.

The result of the interaction of wave and substrate is a rocky intertidal habitat that can vary considerably from place to place. The reef may be simple bedrock with little diversity of habitat. In contrast, it may consist of a mix of flat areas strewn with algae and boulder fields, upraised substrate, tidepools, and surge channels, and contain a myriad of niches for organisms to inhabit. The extensive rocky intertidal of Washington's Cape Alava (Figure 6-1) is a striking example of such habitat diversity.

ORGANIZATION OF ROCKY INTERTIDAL TREATMENT

Tidal Zonation Scheme

As previously mentioned, the presentation of the rocky intertidal habitat as a single entity would be an overwhelming task. In this guide, I will describe the rocky intertidal habitat by zones as suggested by the pioneer marine biologist Ed Ricketts in his book *Between Pacific Tides* [1]. Ricketts describes the intertidal habitats found along the West Coast and provides a general scheme of intertidal zonation for rocky shorelines in which each zone is described separately. The tidal elevations relative to MLLW (mean lower low water—the zero point of the tide tables; refer to Chapter 2) that these zones typically encompass differ from place to place in the Pacific Northwest. For example, because of the shape of the Puget Sound tidal basin, tides reach greater extremes than they do on the open coast of Oregon. I will give the range of tidal elevations covered by the different zones in the Puget Sound region and along the open Oregon coast. The tidal elevations of the four intertidal zones for the Washington and western Vancouver Island open coasts fall in between those for Puget Sound and the open Oregon coast. Beachcombers can determine the tidal range for the particular area they wish to investigate by procuring a tide table from a local bait shop or sporting goods store. These tide tables will nearly always have tide levels corrected for local conditions.

The intertidal zones and their elevations are:

1. Zone 1, the high intertidal zone, which includes the uppermost area wetted by the highest high tide and sea spray. This zone is sometimes called the splash zone or supralittoral fringe zone. In Puget Sound, the highest tides are 13 feet above MLLW, and the lower boundary of Zone 1 is set at 9 feet above MLLW. In contrast, the highest tides on the open Oregon coast are 7–8 feet above MLLW, and the lower boundary for Zone 1 is set at 5 feet above MLLW.
2. Zone 2, the upper intertidal zone, which in Puget Sound includes the tidal elevations from 9 feet to 3–4 feet above MLLW, and on the open Oregon coast from 5 feet to 2.5 feet above MLLW.

3. Zone 3, the middle intertidal zone, which extends from 3–4 feet above MLLW down to 0.0 feet MLLW in Puget Sound, and from 2.5 feet down to 0.0 fcet MLLW along the Oregon coast.

4. Zone 4, the low intertidal zone, which for all locations extends from 0.0 feet MLLW down to the lowest level the tides reach. In some treatments, this zone is called the infralittoral fringe.

In this chapter, I will describe the upper and high intertidal zones and the tidepool, exposed-rock surface and mussel clump habitats of the upper and middle intertidal zones. In Chapter 7, I will describe the remaining habitats of the middle and low intertidal zones, including those of the open reef flat, under-rock, burrowing, low tidepool, and surge channel.

As mentioned, exposure to wave action, tidal level, presence or absence of standing water, slope, rocky substrate type and erosion pattern, and many other factors contribute to the makeup of these zones. Therefore, although these descriptions are presented separately, you will observe that they are seldom discrete units, but instead integrate and overlap one another. Similarly, many organisms will be present in several different zones, while others will be unique to only one.

Finally, there will be a group of organisms that are common to the rocky intertidal zone throughout the Pacific Northwest and others that are restricted to some portion of it. I will present the most common organisms a beachcomber is likely to find throughout the Pacific Northwest. If any of the plants or animals I include has a restricted distribution, such as those organisms found only on the exposed open coast and missing from the quieter rocky intertidal zone of Puget Sound, I will mention where they are known to occur.

HIGH INTERTIDAL ZONE/ UPPERMOST HORIZON

The highest rocky intertidal habitat recognized is called the uppermost horizon or Zone 1 by Ricketts [1]. This is the region covered only by the highest tides and the narrow strip above the high water mark that is still influenced by the sea, primarily by the splash from waves and wind-borne sea spray. This is a zone of transition between the land and the sea, and many of the organisms dwelling here take advantage of aspects of both environments (Figure 6-2).

Figure 6-2. A vertical cliff face in the rocky intertidal zone. Note how the barren upper and high intertidal zones grade into the abundance of mussels and algae of the middle intertidal zone.

Lichens. Lichens often are at the top of the uppermost tidal horizon. These very interesting organisms are symbiotic associations between a microscopic alga and a fungus. Though most lichens are not technically marine, several species thrive here at the border between the land and the sea. Illustrated here is *Caloplaca* sp. (Color Plate 1a), one of the most obvious because of its bright orange color. *Verrucaria* (not shown) is also very common, sometimes forming a black band in the highest intertidal. Lichens are a predictable feature of the high intertidal zone in more protected rocky habitats and less so on the exposed coast.

Seaweeds. Prominent here also are algae that depend on the sea spray and fresh water seeping out of cliffs that often back rocky intertidal zones. Bright green patches of the green alga *Enteromorpha* sp. (Color Plate 1b) can be found in shady, moist areas. Another bright green alga seen here is the sea lettuce, *Ulva* spp. (Color Plate 1c), although it is much more common in the lower zones. *Ulva* spp. come and go quickly, often completing their life cycles in a few weeks. However, they can occur in great profusion throughout the intertidal zone, often growing on other algae as well as the rocky substrate.

A few hearty rockweeds (see below) hang on in the lower part of this zone. Algae of the high intertidal zone are more prominent in the winter when warm sunny days are few, and when sea spray, wave splash, and rain are plentiful, keeping this zone moist. In the spring and summer, the high intertidal zone dries out, and the algae die back. Other algae grow in this zone; however, they are small blue-green algae and diatoms that grow close to the rock surface and are not readily visible to us. These microscopic plants are most important to the few animals that live here, primarily marine snails that feed on this thin algal film growing on the rocks.

High Intertidal Snails. The highest dweller in this zone is the gray periwinkle, *Littorina keenae* (Figure 6-3), which can be found in shady cracks in the rock. This snail can withstand exposure to air for up to three months as well as live totally submerged. Its shell can reach three-quarters of an inch in height and is gray-brown in color. It has a white band on the interior of the aperture (opening), and the shell is often much eroded. *L. keenae* feeds on the fine film of small algae and diatoms that grow on high intertidal rocks. When exposed to air, it can secrete a mucous holdfast around the aperture of its shell. This glues the animal to the rock surface and seals it off from excess drying. The gray periwinkle is found in southern Oregon, and ceases to be common north of Coos Bay.

North of the Oregon-Washington border, the Sitka periwinkle, *Littorina sitkana* (Figure 6-4), is commonly found in the high intertidal zone along the open coast as well as in Puget Sound. Unlike the gray periwinkle, the Sitka periwinkle is not restricted to the high intertidal and occurs well down into the upper intertidal zone. The shell reaches a little over a half-inch in size and typically has some strong spiral sculpturing compared to the smooth shell of the gray periwinkle. Shell color in the Sitka periwinkle varies from monotonous brown or gray to lighter areas on the shells of some animals, sometimes colored yellow or orange.

Limpets also occur in this zone. Limpets are snails with broad conical shells that nestle flat against the rock to prevent water loss. There are three types of limpets found in the rocky intertidal zone. Keyhole limpets have an opening at the apex (top) of their shells and occur in the middle and lower intertidal zones. Slipper limpets are specialized filter feeders that have a distinct shelf on the underside of their shells. They are usually attached to another snail or concealed in a hole or crevice in the middle or low intertidal zones. Regular limpets lack a shell opening or shelf and are found from the high intertidal zone on down. The taxonomy of the regular limpets has undergone several revisions over the years. As a result, the scientific names of many species have been changed, usually at the generic (genus) level. In

Figure 6-3. Five half-inch-long specimens of the eroded periwinkle, Littorina keenae, *share the shade of a high intertidal crevice.*

Figure 6-4. Three Sitka periwinkles, Littorina sitkana.

this book, I have used the most up-to-date scientific name available for the limpet species. Although it may be potentially confusing, I have also included the former generic (genus) name of the species in parentheses in case a beachcomber wishes to read more about a given species in the less recent literature.

On shady, vertical surfaces, the digit or ribbed limpet, *Lottia* (formerly *Collisella*) *digitalis* (Figure 6-5), can be found in small aggregations. This limpet is common on vertical rock faces in high and middle intertidal zones. It also occurs on mussels and stalked barnacles in mussel clumps in the middle intertidal zone. The shell reaches a length of one-and-a-quarter inches, and the apex of the shell is well forward, sometimes overhanging the shell margin (edge). *Lottia digitalis* receives the common name digit limpet because it looks like the flexed digit of a finger when viewed from the side.

Another limpet seen in this zone in southern Oregon is the rough limpet, *Collisella scabra* (Figure 6-6). This limpet is common in high and upper intertidal zones

Figure 6-5. A high intertidal limpet, Lottia digitalis, *one half inch long. Note how far forward the apex (top) of the shell protrudes.*

Figure 6-6. The high intertidal limpet, Collisella scabra, *shown next to its excavated home scar. The limpet is three-quarters of an inch long.*

Figure 6-7. Robust high intertidal limpet, Tectura persona.

A third limpet sometimes encountered in this highest intertidal zone is the robust *Tectura* (formerly *Notoacmea*) *persona* (Figure 6-7). This animal is not out in the open like the other two limpets mentioned; instead, it remains in a crevice, on the roof of an overhang, or under the lower edge of a boulder by day. At night it emerges to forage on the same low-growing algal crop grazed by the other limpets. *Tectura persona* reaches two inches in length, and the shell has an inflated or blown-up look to it. It is typically checkered with white dots against an olive green background, although the upper part of the shell may be eroded to a dull gray ground color. Because this limpet shows such sensitivity to daylight, some researchers believe it is able to judge light and dark by the amount of light passing through the large, nearly translucent white regions at the anterior of its shell.

High Intertidal Crustaceans. A semi-terrestrial isopod, *Ligia pallasi,* known as the rock louse, treads the fine line between air and water in this zone. *Ligia pallasi* (Figure 6-8) occurs from San Francisco, California, to Alaska. Males of this species have greatly expanded side plates, and have always reminded me of mini-trilobites, those ancient relatives of the crustaceans. *L. pallasi* lives in crevices in cliffs above the high tide mark and is especially abundant in sea caves. It spends most of the day hiding in crevices or under stones above the high tide mark. It emerges in the late afternoon to work the night shift. Like the limpets and periwinkles, this inch-and-a-quarter-long crustacean also feeds on the microscopic film of algae growing on the rocks. The rock louse will

on horizontal and sloping rock faces. The shell is up to an inch-and-a-quarter long, and the apex is forward of center; it is heavily ribbed with a scalloped margin. The rough limpet exhibits "homing behavior." Using its shell and its rasping tongue (radula), the rough limpet excavates a depression in the rock, called a home scar, that exactly matches its scalloped shell. Like the digit limpets, these animals move about at high tide to feed on the microscopic film of algae on the rocks, but the rough limpets always return to their "home scar" to wait out the low tide period. Predators include shorebirds, the green-lined shore crab, *Pachygrapsus crassipes* discussed later, and sea stars.

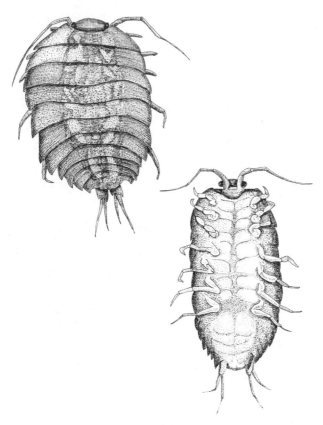

Figure 6-9. A small green-lined shore crab, Pachygrapsus crassipes, *nestled in an upper intertidal crevice.*

Figure 6-8. Top and bottom views of the rock louse, Ligia pallasi, *one-and-a-half inches in length.*

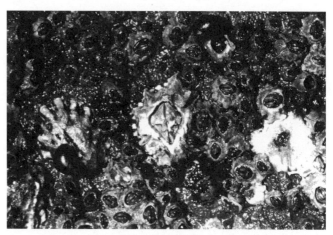

Figure 6-10. The common acorn barnacle, Balanus glandula *(center), surrounded by the smaller barnacle* Chthamalus sp., *a rough limpet, and periwinkles.*

also scavenge on decaying algae. Although it cannot withstand continuous submersion, it needs to keep its breathing apparatus moist. The rock louse can be seen moving down to tidepools and dipping its rear end, which contains its gills, into the water.

A more obvious crustacean, the green-lined shore crab, *Pachygrapsus crassipes* (Figure 6-9), is sometimes found here. This crab is found throughout the high and upper intertidal zones of the southern coast of the Pacific Northwest as far north as Ecola State Park, Oregon. It occurs in crevices in the high intertidal zone, under rocks and in crevices in the upper intertidal, and among the mussel clumps of the middle intertidal zone. Male *Pachygrapsus* reach a carapace width of two inches. The crab is dark in color and marked with shades of red, purple, or green. *Pachygrapsus* is an excellent scavenger, feeding on a variety of plant and animal material and occasional live prey such as limpets or *Littorina*. Its main food is the low-growing, microscopic algae that it scoops up with spoon-like claws. *Pachygrapsus* is a nimble-footed, aggressive

species that challenges predators and humans alike with a pugnacious, claws-raised-and-outstretched stance. However, when given the chance, it quickly scuttles to the safety of a crevice or under a rock.

Small patches of acorn barnacles occur in the lower portion of the high intertidal zone. The small, volcano-shaped species *Balanus glandula* (Figure 6-10) occurs throughout the intertidal on upraised substrates, and is at its physiological limit to drying out here in the high intertidal zone. This species is the most common intertidal barnacle in the Pacific Northwest, and like all acorn barnacles, is a filter feeder. It occurs in large patches, and it is probable that its larvae are attracted to already-settled individuals, accounting for the dense settlements of these quarter-of-an-inch animals sometimes seen. Another acorn barnacle found here is the gray or brown *Chthamalus dalli* (Figure 6-10), which is about half the size of *Balanus glandula.* Acorn barnacles are eaten by a number of sea stars and carnivorous snails.

UPPER INTERTIDAL ZONE

The upper intertidal zone (Figure 6-11) extends from 5 feet to 2.5 feet above MLLW along the Oregon coast and from 9 feet to 3–4 feet above MLLW in the Puget Sound region. The prevailing physical factors operating here are exposure to air and sunlight during low tide. Thus, the organisms that exist successfully in this zone are well adapted to withstand drying out (desiccation).

Upper Intertidal Seaweeds. Several hardy seaweeds are found here. The dark-red brillo-pad weed, *Endocladia muricata* (Color Plate 2e), grows in saucer-sized tufts and larger patches. *Endocladia* is a red alga and will dry to almost crispness at low tide; it quickly rehydrates when the tide returns. Another common red alga is the Turkish towel, *Gigartina* sp. (Figure 6-12), so named for the nubby texture of its blades. In late spring and summer, small salt-sac alga, *Hallosaccion glandiforme* (Figure 6-13), can be found here, sometimes in large patches. A little lower down, and especially on the sides of slightly raised surfaces, the brown algae known as rockweeds, *Fucus* sp. and *Pelvetiopsis* sp. (Figure 6-14) occur. These algae survive the exposure of the upper intertidal by secreting a slick muscilage coating that inhibits water loss.

Often occurring with the rockweeds is the green alga known as sponge weed or dead man's fingers, *Codium fragile* (Color Plate 1e). Sponge weed is the most mas-

Figure 6-12. One of several species of the genus Gigartina, *red algae of the high and middle intertidal zones.*

Figure 6-11. The relatively barren rocks of the upper intertidal zone flank a high tidepool.

Figure 6-13. A red alga known as the "salt sac," Hallosaccion glandiforme; *the largest "sac" is three inches long.*

Figure 6-14. Fucus *sp., one of several upper intertidal brown algae known collectively as "rockweeds."*

Figure 6-15. *Three small (three-eighths of an inch high) checkered periwinkles,* Littorina scutulata.

sive of the green algae, reaching over a foot in length with clumps weighing several pounds. The plant has dark green to black finger-like fronds. A smaller green alga, *Cladophora* sp. (Color Plate 1d), grows here also in dense, pincushion-sized tufts of bright green which hold water like a sponge. Look for them on flat surfaces often mixed among other algae.

Upper Intertidal Snails. Several marine snails occur in the upper intertidal zone all along the Pacific Northwest coast. The small, black, checkered periwinkle, *Littorina scutulata* (Figure 6-15), occurs high in the upper zone, especially in depressions and cracks, and is common in both the upper and middle intertidal zones. It is very abundant in high tidepools and among mussel clumps. The shell is smooth, conical, and taller in proportion to diameter than either *L. keenae* or *L. sitkana,* both of which may co-occur with the checkered periwinkle. The shell of the checkered periwinkle

reaches a half inch in height although it is usually much smaller, and is brown to black, often with white markings in a checkerboard pattern. *L. scutulata* feeds on microscopic algae as well as the larger algae that co-occur with it, including *Cladophora* and *Ulva.* It is preyed upon by the sea star *Leptasterias hexactis* (see Figure 6-26).

A little lower in the upper tidal zone, the black turban snail, *Tegula funebralis* (Figure 6-16), makes its first appearance along the open coast of the Pacific Northwest. The black turban is a herbivore, and is the most abundant and broadly distributed large snail in the protected rocky intertidal habitat along the open coast of Oregon and Washington. This snail is found as far north as Vancouver Island, but is not found away from the open coast and is missing from the rocky intertidal zone of Puget Sound.

Smaller black turbans are found in the upper intertidal zone, with larger animals occurring lower in the

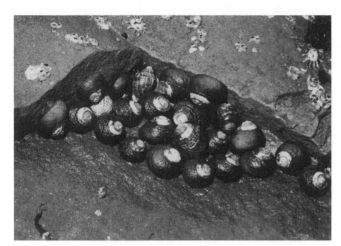

Figure 6-16. A small aggregation of the black turban snail, Tegula funebralis, in a moisture-holding crevice.

Figure 6-17. The small limpet, Lottia asmi, that lives on Tegula spp. and other gastropods.

intertidal. The black turban snail reaches a shell diameter of one-and-a-quarter inches. The shell is dark purple to black with silver white on the bottom. The spire (top) of the shell is often eroded, revealing the pearly shell layers beneath. The foot is black on the sides and pale beneath. *Tegula funebralis* eats several different types of algae including microscopic films growing on the rock surface, attached large algae, and drift plant material. *Tegula* is preyed upon by rock crabs and sea stars, especially *Pisaster ochraceus* (Color Plate 16b).

Tegula often has smaller snails living on the outside of its shell. The first of these is the small black limpet *Lottia* (formerly *Collisella*) *asmi* (Figure 6-17). This limpet feeds on the tiny plants that grow on Tegula's shell. It changes *Tegula* shells when the turban snails aggregate during low tide. Studies have shown that each *L. asmi* changes *Tegula* hosts at least once a day. *L. asmi* can grow to one-half inch long, but is usually smaller. It is not unusual for a large *Tegula funebralis* to have more than one black limpet on board as well as one or more of a second snail, the hooked slipper limpet, *Crepidula adunca* (Figure 6-18), on its shell. *Crepidula* is also found occasionally on *Tegula brunnea* (see Figure 6-24), *Searlesia dira* (see Figure 6-25), and *Calliostoma* spp. (Color Plate 9e). The hooked slipper snail gets its name from the high, beak-like apex that overhangs the posterior margin of its shell. This snail may reach a length of one inch, although it is usually smaller. Unlike the herbivorous *Lottia asmi*, *Crepidula adunca* is a filter feeder.

The three limpet species of the high intertidal zone are also found here in the upper intertidal zone. The

Figure 6-18. Two slipper limpets, Crepidula adunca, on a Tegula funebralis. Note the characteristic hooked shell apex.

digit limpet, *Lottia digitalis,* is found on shady vertical surfaces throughout the Pacific Northwest. The nocturnal forager, *Tectura persona,* is also common here, again in crevices or under boulders until the sun goes down. Finally, the rough limpet, *Collisella scabra,* is seen on horizontal surfaces from Coos Bay south.

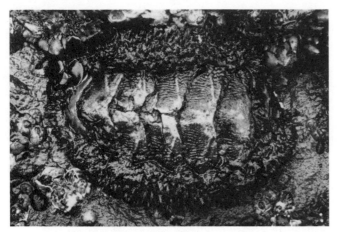

Figure 6-19. The mossy chiton, Mopalia muscosa. *Note how the shells are eroded.*

Figure 6-20. Two identical clone mates of the aggregating anemone, Anthopleura elegantissima. *Each anemone is one inch across.*

Another mollusk common in the upper intertidal zone is the mossy chiton, *Mopalia muscosa* (Figure 6-19). Remember, chitons are herbivores with their shells divided into eight plates. This species is usually found nestled up against a tuft of alga or some other organism that will harbor a reservoir of moisture during low tides. The mossy chiton reaches three-and-a-half inches in length, and the shells are dull brown, although frequently eroded or covered with encrusting animals and plants. The tough, fleshy girdle that surrounds the shell plates is tan and is densely covered with stiff, round, reddish-brown bristles. The bristles give this chiton its "mossy" appearance. The mossy chiton is active only at night during high tides when it feeds on algae such as *Endocladia, Gigartina,* and *Cladophora.* Many mossy chitons show homing behavior and move within a radius of about 20 inches from home base to which they return. Small mossy chitons in tidepools fall prey to sea stars, especially *Pisaster ochraceus.*

Upper Intertidal Cnidarians. A widely distributed, intertidal cnidarian that makes its first appearance in the upper intertidal zone is the colonial, aggregating anemone, *Anthopleura elegantissima* (Figure 6-20). In most situations, this anemone stops growing after it reaches an inch in diameter and increases its number by dividing itself in half, a process known as longitudinal fission. Because of this mode of reproduction, an aggregation of this anemone is a genetic clone, the result of repeated asexual divisions stemming back to the original pioneering anemone that grew from a planktonic larva. As a result, all the anemones in an aggregation have the same color pattern (Figure 6-20) and are the same sex.

High in the upper intertidal zone, *A. elegantissima* often occurs in a single-file line following the trace of a moisture-holding crevice. A little lower in the zone, this anemone can be found in solid sheets on the shady sides of crevices and small upraised portions of rock, called outcroppings. When exposed at low tide, these colonial aggregations of anemones appear to be layers of shell particles and other debris (Color Plate 4d). These materials are held by the retracted anemones to shield them from the sun and prevent water loss. When the tide returns, the anemones open up to form meadows of deadly, pink-tipped, flower-like polyps waiting for unwary prey.

Once the beachcomber has identified clones of the aggregating anemone, look for places where a clear strip of rock separates two clones (Color Plate 4d). This space is a "no man's land" that represents the area where two clones have come into contact, fought, and finally retreated. The anemones from the different clones actually attack one another, and fire their deadly stinging nematocysts in the battle. Eventually, both clones will pull back and the clear strip remains as a buffer. I call it "clone wars."

Large, solitary individuals of *A. elegantissima* (Color Plate 4e), up to eight inches across the oral crown of tentacles, occur in the lower intertidal zones and in tidepools. These large animals are distinguished from other anemones by the conspicuous radiating lines on their oral disc. Anemones feed on zooplankton and

Figure 6-21. A predator of sea anemones, this leather star, Dermasterias imbricata, *is five inches in diameter.*

small intertidal animals that are captured by their tentacles. They are preyed upon by shell-less snails known as nudibranchs and the leather sea star, *Dermasterias imbricata* (Figure 6-21).

The upper intertidal zone will often include large numbers of acorn barnacles, *Balanus glandula* and *Chthamalus dalli* (Figure 6-10), especially on slightly vertical surfaces.

UPPER TIDEPOOLS

Tidepools are considered by many beachcombers to be the most interesting of all the intertidal habitats. Tidepools are formed by depressions in the rocky substrate that trap water at low tide (Figure 6-11). Thus, they provide a habitat that frees organisms from one of the most stressful factors of intertidal life—drying out. Tidepools may contain a more diverse and often different association of organisms than found on adjacent, exposed substrate.

Physical Factors

Tidepools are not without physical stresses, however, especially during low tide periods. A small volume of seawater trapped in a tidepool can experience a critical elevation in temperature on a warm, sunny day. Similarly, evaporation caused by wind and sun can raise the salinity to a sometimes dangerous level. Conversely, a very cold day can cause a decrease in water temperature during low tide, and a rainy low tide period may cause a reduction in salinity. The change in physical factors experienced within a tide pool habitat is related to

the tidal level of the pool, its shape, and the volume of water it contains. A small, shallow pool located in the high intertidal zone would experience the greatest fluctuations, while a large, deep pool in the low intertidal zone would experience the least change.

Therefore, instead of visualizing tidepools as a single habitat, it becomes obvious that they constitute a continuum of habitats depending on the particular situation of the individual pool. With this in mind, two tidepool habitats are described here. The first, called the upper tidepool, will encompass the tidepools of the upper, high, and middle tidal zones, from approximately 9 to 0.0 feet above MLLW. I will treat tidepools of the middle intertidal zone before I describe the organisms living on the other, exposed middle intertidal substrates, as there is considerable overlap in the species found. A second tidepool habitat more characteristic of the lower intertidal zone will be discussed in the next chapter.

All the organisms described for the upper tidepool will not necessarily be found in every pool. The volume and tidal elevation, as well as the nature of the pool's bottom (i.e., algae, gravel, cobble, sand, bare rock) will be important. However, the more common organisms will be well represented. First of all, organisms overlapping from the upper intertidal zone will occur: *Tegula funebralis, Anthopleura elegantissima, Littorina scutulata,* and various limpets will be seen often.

Tidepool Plants. In all but the highest pools, some form of coralline algae (Color Plates 2a and b) will appear. These red algae are called "corallines" because they incorporate calcium carbonate into their cell walls, which gives the plant a rigid, coral-like texture. Some coralline species occur as pale, pastel encrusting patches or sheets on the sides and bottoms of tidepools and on the rocks in tidepools. Other species grow upright from holdfasts and have joint-like regions of articulation along their length; these are called erect or articulated coralline algae. Because of their crusty texture, coralline algae are tough fodder for most intertidal herbivores and are not readily eaten. Therefore, they are more likely to be seen in tidepools compared to the softer, more palatable species of fleshy brown and red algae that can be more easily consumed by the tidepool-dwelling herbivores.

Another plant that may be seen here is known as surfgrass, *Phyllospadix* spp. (Color Plate 3c). Surfgrass is not an alga; it is a flowering plant like the terrestrial grasses to which it is related. As such, it requires soil into which it can sink its roots to acquire the nutrients needed for growth. You will find surfgrass only in pools with sediment on the bottom. Large patches of surfgrass may occur in the middle and low intertidal zones as well.

How to Observe a Tidepool. The best way to investigate a tidepool is to approach it slowly and avoid stirring the water. Observe the pool quietly for a few minutes, and soon you will begin to detect movement. The swiftest animals in the pool will probably be the small (two to three inches long) fish known as tidepool sculpins (*Clinocottus* spp. and other genera, Color Plate 16f). These fish will remain almost motionless on the bottom, and their mottled color pattern makes them difficult to detect. Suddenly they will dart out, and then they can be followed.

Other rapidly moving, but less-often seen animals, are small shrimp like the red-banded shrimp, *Heptacarpus* spp. (Figure 6-22). These small shrimp (one inch long or smaller) can be quite numerous in lower pools. However, they vary in color, and often have red bands that break up their outline making them very difficult to see when still. The shrimp are quiet during mid-day, but start moving actively at dawn and dusk. They are omnivorous, and will feed on whatever they can scavenge or catch. Several species of these colorful shrimp occur in the intertidal zone of the Pacific Northwest.

To see these tidepool shrimp, carefully search any algae or surfgrass present in the pool; separate the blades slowly and watch for movement. Another method is to sweep a small aquarium net over and

Figure 6-23. A hermit crab, Pagurus *sp., emerges from its shell. These crabs are usually quite abundant in tidepools.*

among any algae growing in the pool and frequently inspect your catch. Once discovered, the speed and number of these agile crustaceans will amaze you.

Hermit Crabs. The industrious hermit crabs (*Pagurus* spp., Figure 6-23) can be seen moving around the pool during the day and night. Hermits carry their protection with them in the form of an empty snail shell into which they will retreat quickly if bothered. Otherwise, they scavenge about the pools in search of animal and plant debris that serves as their food—they are very effective scavengers. Hermit crabs have been described as the garbage men of the intertidal zone. Hermits will carefully inspect prospective shells, and only after careful scrutiny will they try one on for size. Large hermit crabs (half an inch or more in carapace length) are not above evicting smaller hermits from a shell they fancy.

In the spring and early summer, many very small hermit crabs can be found in these pools living in the small shells of the periwinkles, *Littorina* spp. On the open coast, most of the larger hermit crabs will be housed in the empty shells of the black turban snail, *Tegula funebralis,* which may be found alive in the tidepools as well. Other open coast hermits live in the shell of the two-and-a-half-inch-tall brown turban snail, *Tegula brunnea* (Figure 6-24). This top snail occupies tidepools as well as other mid- and lower-intertidal habitats along the exposed Pacific Northwest coast. In the quieter waters of Puget Sound, the larger hermit crabs in these tidepools are commonly found in the shells of *Calliostoma* spp. (Color Plate 9e) and *Nucella* spp. (see Figures 6-42, 43, and 6-44).

Figure 6-22. The red-banded shrimp, Heptacarpus *sp., one of several common small tidepool shrimps.*

Figure 6-24. Two-inch-tall brown turban snail, Tegula brunnea. *Note the light-colored (orange) margin at the base of the foot.*

Another gastropod mollusk (snail) found in the tidepools is the dire whelk, *Searlesia dira* (Figure 6-25). Its tall, gray to brownish, spire-shaped shell is up to an inch and a half in height. The shell is handsomely sculptured with spiral grooves and is often encrusted with a pink or whitish coralline alga. *Searlesia* is a carnivore and feeds on limpets and other snails, chitons, and barnacles. It is also an accomplished feeder on carrion, able to detect dead organisms from considerable distances. Another neat feeding trick observed in this snail is its ability to help itself to the meal of Pacific sea stars, *Pisaster ochraceus,* by slipping its elongated proboscis into prey items held in the grasp of a feeding star. Besides tidepools, dire whelks occur under rocks from

Figure 6-25. Shell of a dire whelk, Searlesia dira, *one-and-a-half inches long. Note the small patch of light-colored encrusting alga near the anterior.*

the middle intertidal zone on down. *Searlesia* is commonly found throughout the Pacific Northwest and ranges from Alaska to Monterey, California.

Tidepool Cnidarians. Many other carnivores occur in tidepools. The stationary hunters—the anemones—include the aggregating anemone, *Anthopleura elegantissima,* previously mentioned, and its much larger relative, the giant green sea anemone *Anthopleura xanthogrammica* (Color Plate 4c). The green anemone will also be found in lower tidepools, and reaches its largest size in the low intertidal surge channels.

Two other large sea anemones occur in Pacific Northwest tidepools. Like the giant green sea anemone mentioned above, these animals also are common in low intertidal niches as well as tidepools. These are the anemones, *Urticina* (formerly *Tealia*) *crassicornis* and *U. coriacea.* Although these anemones are similar in size and shape, reaching four inches in column diameter and up to six inches across the oral disk, with a little patience they can be distinguished from one another. The painted urticina, *U. crassicornis* (Color Plate 5b), is the easiest to detect because its column often contains large, irregular streaks of red against an olive green background (such as seen in the animal in the photograph). In Puget Sound, the column tends to be uniformly red or pale tan. The tentacles are greenish gray or olive gray and have some light bands. Besides occurring occasionally in tidepools, *U. crassicornis* is found on the sides and undersides of rocks and the undersides of ledges in the low intertidal zone. It is also found on pier pilings and floats.

The stubby rose anemone, *Urticina coriacea* (Color Plate 5c), lacks the red streaks on the column as seen in *U. crassicornis.* Instead, the upper part of the column is bright red and often has shell or rock particles sticking to it. The tentacles around the oral disk are stubbier than those of *U. crassicornis,* and the prevailing colors are a mixture of red and gray with some light banding. *U. coriacea* is seen less frequently than *U. crassicornis* and tends to occur in tidepools or the low intertidal zone where some sand, gravel, or bits of shell are available to cover the column.

For comparison purposes, a third species, the white-spotted rose anemone, *Urticina lofotensis,* should also be mentioned here. *U. lofotensis* does not regularly occur in tidepools with its two congeneric species, but is found in the low intertidal zone, especially on the vertical rock faces of surge channels. It differs from the others in having a column of scarlet red set with regularly spaced white tubercles. The tentacles are longer and more slender than the other two *Urticina* species and colored from scarlet to crimson. It is truly a spectacular animal when fully inflated and waiting for its next meal to stumble by.

The proliferating anemone, *Epiactis prolifera* (Color Plate 6a), a smaller anemone (one inch in diameter) delicately patterned with white lines, may also be found in tidepools. *Epiactis* ranges in color from cherry red to orange, to bright green. Compared to the other anemones that attach only to the solid bedrock, *Epiactis* frequently may be found attached to small stones, shells, or even a blade of alga. The red animal in the photograph has a smaller anemone attached to its column. *Epiactis* reproduce sexually, and the young are brooded by the female in her stomach cavity. When they grow larger, they crawl out through the mouth and attach to mom's column. Here they stay, feeding and growing until finally they crawl off and take up an independent existence.

Tidepool Sea Stars. Motile predators include the sea stars. Some sea star species have a truly intertidal distribution, while others appear to forage into the intertidal zone from below during high tide and retreat to tidepools when the tide recedes. The small (up to four-and-a-half inches across), six-rayed sea star, *Leptasterias hexactis* (Figure 6-26), appears to remain in the intertidal zone and often shows up in tidepools where it searches for small molluscan prey and barnacles. The

Figure 6-26. Two six-rayed sea stars, Leptasterias hexactis, *against a backdrop of encrusting coralline algae. Stars are one-and-a-half inches across.*

six-rayed star ranges from the San Juan Islands and the Strait of Juan de Fuca south to the Channel Islands of southern California.

The large (up to eight inches across) leather star, *Dermasterias imbricata* (Figure 6-21), may also be found in tidepools. The leather star is smooth, slippery, and blue-gray in color with red or orange mottling. Leather stars prey on sea anemones including *Epiactis prolifera* and the two *Anthopleura* species. In the absence of anemones, it will eat sea urchins, chitons, and sponges. *Dermasterias* has a pungent odor described variously as smelling of garlic or discharged gunpowder. The leather star is found from Prince William Sound, Alaska, to as far south as San Diego, California.

The Pacific sea star, *Pisaster ochraceus* (Color Plate 16b), is a generalized predator that will feed on a wide variety of invertebrate prey. Although capable of withstanding complete exposure during low tide from the middle intertidal zone downward, *Pisaster ochraceus* will also show up in tidepools, and therefore deserves mention here. The Pacific sea star is the most common large sea star in the middle and lower intertidal zones from Alaska to Santa Barbara, California. It is also abundant in mussel clumps. This sea star reaches a diameter of over 18 inches, although usually smaller, and varies in color from yellow or pale orange to dark brown or deep purple. It has many small white spines on its aboral surface (side opposite the mouth) which form a pentagonal pattern on the central disk. *Pisaster ochraceus'* role in the mussel clump is described later in this chapter. Besides mussels, it also feeds on a variety of other prey including *Tegula* spp., chitons, barnacles, and limpets.

Evasterias troschelii (Color Plate 16e), a sea star somewhat similar to *Pisaster ochraceus,* may also occur in tidepools. It may reach a diameter of 22 inches, but most specimens are a foot or less across. *Evasterias* also has many white spines on its surface, but these never form the characteristic pentagon described for *Pisaster.* The arms of this sea star are more slender, and the disk is smaller in proportion to the arms than those of *Pisaster ochraceus,* giving it a more graceful appearance. Most specimens are orange, but color varies considerably from gray to green to brown to reddish. Like *Pisaster, Evasterias* takes a wide variety of invertebrate prey including mussels, limpets, and barnacles. These two sea stars are also found together on pier pilings and floating docks, where they are the chief predators in res-

Plate 1a. Caloplaca *sp., a splash zone lichen.*

Plate 1b. Enteromorpha *sp. growing on a cliff face.*

Plate 1c. The sea lettuce, Ulva *sp.*

Plate 1d. Pin cushion alga, Cladophora.

Plate 1e. Dead man's fingers alga, Codium fragile.

Plate 1

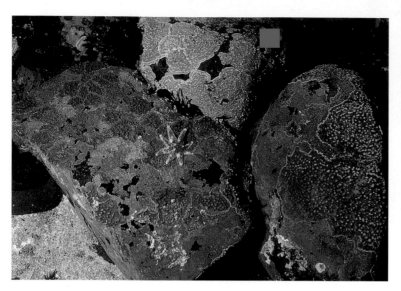

Plate 2a. Rocks covered with encrusting coralline algae.

Plate 2d. Red algae of the middle to low intertidal zones, Iridaea *spp*.

Plate 2b. Erect or articulated coralline algae.

Plate 2e. Two red algae, Endocladia muricata *(wiry alga) and* Gigartina *sp.*

Plate 2c. Porphyra *sp., a red alga commonly known as laver or nori.*

Plate 2f. The sea cabbage, Hedophyllum sessile.

Plate 2

Plate 3a. Surge channel lined with brown algae.

Plate 3b. Wing kelp, Alaria marginata.

Plate 3c. Surfgrass, Phyllospadix sp., with red algal epiphyte, Smithora naiadum.

Plate 3d. Eelgrass, Zostera marina, growing on an estuarine sand flat.

Plate 3e. Invasive Atlantic cord grass, Spartina alterniflora, stands tall among native species, Spartina foliosa.

Plate 3

Plate 4a. Red sponge with two Leptasterias hexactis *sea stars, and two red sponge nudibranchs,* Rostanga pulchra.

Plate 4b. A red sponge nudibranch, Rostanga pulchra, *and its egg spiral.*

Plate 4c. Giant green sea anemone, Anthopleura xanthogrammica.

Plate 4d. Three clones of the anemone Anthopleura elegantissima; *open rock spaces separate the clones.*

Plate 4e. Large solitary Anthopleura elegantissima.

Plate 4

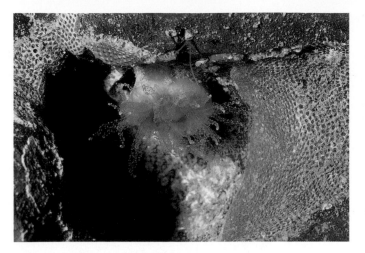

Plate 5a. Solitary orange cup coral, Balanophyllia elegans.

Plate 5b. Painted urticina, Urticina crassicornis.

Plate 5c. Stubby rose anemone, Urticina coriacea.

Plate 5d. Moonglow anemone, Anthopleura artemisia.

Plate 5e. White-plumed anemone, Metridium giganteum.

Plate 5f. Two clones of the strawberry anemone, Corynactis californica.

Plate 5

Plate 6a. *The proliferating anemone,* Epiactis prolifera. *Note young on column.*

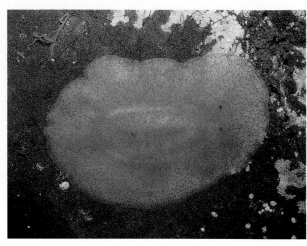

Plate 6b. *Large flatworm,* Kaburakia excelsa.

Plate 6c. *The nemertean worm,* Tubulanus polymorphus, *near a purple sea urchin.*

Plate 6e. *The common intertidal nemertean* Paranemertes perengrina.

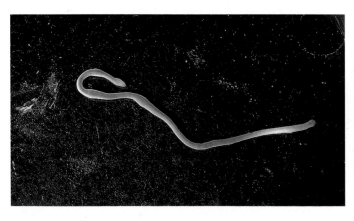

Plate 6d. *White nemertean,* Amphiporus imparispinous.

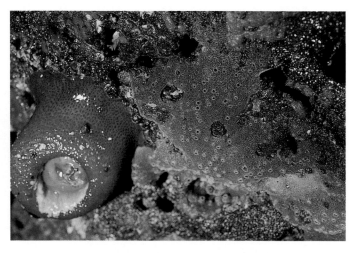

Plate 6f. *Gray sponge next to a retracted sea anemone.*

Plate 6

Plate 7a. Sand flat polychaete worms, Lumbrinereis zonata, *exposed in a shovel full of sand.*

Plate 7b. Calcium carbonate tube and filter-feeding tentacles of the fan worm, Serpula vermicularis.

Plate 7c. A cluster of Eudistylia vancouveri *on a pier float.*

Plate 7d. The mossy chiton, Mopalia lignosa.

Plate 7e. Arctonoe vittata, *a polychaete commensal with* Diodora aspera *and* Cryptochiton stelleri.

Plate 7

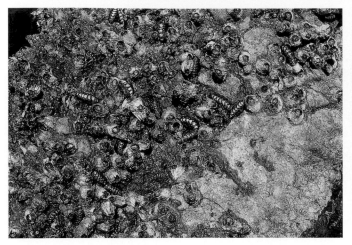

Plate 8a. An aggregation of the Katy chiton, Katharina tunicata.

Plate 8d. The veiled chiton, Placiphorella velata.

Plate 8b. The lined chiton, Tonicella lineata.

Plate 8e. Cooper's chiton, Lepidozona cooperi.

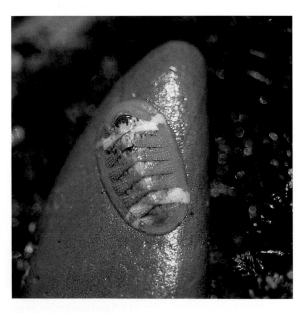

Plate 8c. Mertens' chiton, Lepidozona mertensii.

Plate 8f. Small Olympia oyster, Ostrea lurida, *growing on the shell of a Pacific oyster,* Crassostrea gigas.

Plate 8

Plate 9a. The common scallop, Chlamys hastata.

Plate 9b. The rough piddock or boring clam, Zirfaea pilsbryi.

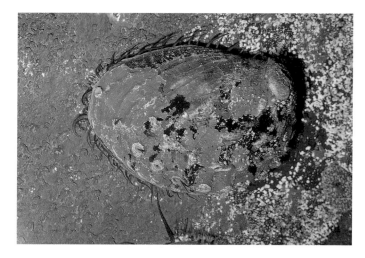

Plate 9c. Pinto abalone, Haliotis kamchatkana.

Plate 9d. The dunce cap limpet, Acmaea mitra.

Plate 9e. Three top snails, Calliostoma annulatum *(right),* C. ligatum, *and* C. canaliculatum.

Plate 9

Plate 10a. *The active snail,* Amphissa columbiana.

Plate 10b. *The wentletrap snail,* Epitonium tinctum.

Plate 10c. *Mating aggregation of* Nucella lamellosa.

Plate 10d. *The common long-horned nudibranch,* Hermissenda crassicornis.

Plate 10e. *The shag rug nudibranch,* Aeolidia papillosa, *a sea anemone predator.*

Plate 10

Plate 11a. *The yellow-edged cadlina,* Cadlina luteomarginata.

Plate 11b. The ring-spotted dorid, Diaulula sandiegensis.

Plate 11c. The sea lemon nudibranch, Anisodoris nobilis.

Plate 11d. Triopha catalinae *(upper) and* Triopha maculata.

Plate 11e. Laila cockerelli.

Plate 11f. Tritonia festiva.

Plate 11

Plate 12a. Melibe leonia, *showing large oral hood.*

Plate 12b. Janolus fuscus.

Plate 12c. Small red octopus, Octopus rubescens.

Plate 12d. Male (upper) and female red ghost shrimps,
Callianassa californiensis.

Plate 12e. Surface of mud flat showing burrowing activity
of Callianassa californiensis.

Plate 12f. Coon-stripe shrimp, Pandalus danae.

Plate 12

Plate 13a. The umbrella crab, Crytolithodes sitchensis.

Plate 13b. Molted exoskeletons of the market or Dungeness crab, Cancer magister.

Plate 13c. Cancer productus *pair in mating embrace.*

Plate 13d. Young Dungeness crab, Cancer magister.

Plate 13e. The pygmy cancer, Cancer oregonensis.

Plate 13f. The large hermit crab, Pagurus armatus.

Plate 13

Plate 14b. *Large isopods*, Idotea wosnesenskii.

Plate 14a. Pugettia gracilis.

Plate 14c. *"Pill-bug" isopod*, Gnorimosphaeroma oregonense.

Plate 14d. *Large barnacle*, Balanus nubilus.

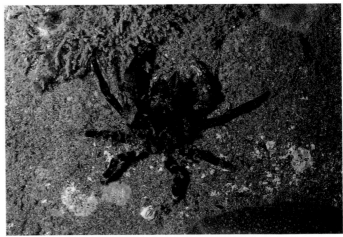

Plate 14e. *The very hairy crab*, Hapalogaster mertensii.

Plate 14f. Mimulus foliatus.

Plate 14

*Plate 15a. Purple sea urchins,
Strongylocentrotus purpuratus,
in tidepool.*

Plate 15b. The large red sea urchin, Strongylocentrotus franciscanus.

*Plate 15c. The green sea urchin,
Strongylocentrotus droebachiensis.*

Plate 15d. Common under-rock sea cucumber, Cucumaria
miniata.

Plate 15e. The daisy brittle star, Ophiopholis aculeata.

Plate 15

Plate 16a. *The sunflower sea star,* Pycnopodia helianthoides.

Plate 16b. *Two color forms of the Pacific sea star,* Pisaster ochraceus.

Plate 16c. *A short-spined pisaster,* Pisaster brevispinus, *investigates a clam,* Prototchaca staminea.

Plate 16d. *Rainbow sea star,* Orthasterias koehleri.

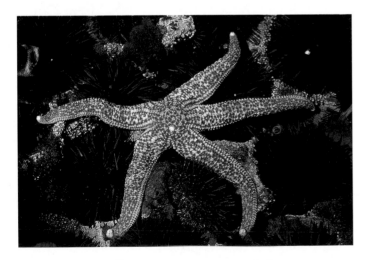

Plate 16e. *Troschel's sea star,* Evasterias troschelii.

Plate 16

Plate 16f. *A tidepool sculpin,* Clinocottus *sp.*

Figure 6-27. The omnivorous sea star, Asterina miniata, *commonly known as the sea bat.*

idence. I have also seen young of both species among rocks on muddy sand flats of coastal embayments.

The sea bat, *Asterina* (formerly *Patiria*) *miniata* (Figure 6-27), is another occasional tidepool inhabitant. The sea bat receives its name from its five stout, triangular arms that appear almost webbed, like the extended wing of a bat. This star reaches a diameter of eight inches, and varies in color, most commonly orange or light red, and is frequently mottled with other colors. Sea bats will eat almost anything. They are capable of everting (turning inside out) their large stomachs out of their mouths and over their plant or animal food, dead or alive. In addition to almost any animal food, sea bats feed on surfgrass (probably on the plants and animals growing on the surfgrass, called epiphytes) and algae, as well as the organic film on rock surfaces. Sea bats have a disjointed distribution, being common on the western coast of Vancouver Island, but rare in Puget Sound and the open coast of Oregon and Washington. They are common again along the northern and central coast of California.

The sunflower star, *Pycnopodia helianthoides* (Color Plate 16a), sometime seeks shelter in an upper pool when trapped by a receding tide. This beautiful star is the largest and fastest moving of all our sea stars, and individuals well over 40 inches have been described. Sunflower stars feed on a variety of prey but prefer purple sea urchins, *Strongylocentrotus purpuratus* (Color Plate

15a). These urchins occur occasionally in upper pools, but are much more common in tidepools in the low intertidal zone. In addition to urchins, this sea star will also take mussels, chitons, snails, and other sea stars such as the smaller *Leptasterias*. Sunflower stars have 20 or more arms, and they are usually purple in color, although an occasional yellow-orange individual is seen. Compared to the rigid-bodied Pacific sea star, *Pisaster ochraceus*, *Pycnopodia* is quite soft and flimsy. Improper or prolonged handling will cause this sea star to lose its arms, so it is best left at rest when found.

Under Tidepool Rocks

Under-Rock Crabs. If a mid-level pool is fairly deep and contains small boulders and a little sediment, another group of animals may occur. Remember to be careful when turning rocks over anywhere in the intertidal environment, and always carefully replace rocks the way you found them. Most prominent in this under-rock niche can be the red rock crab, *Cancer antennarius* (Figure 6-28). This crab may be quite large, over four inches across the carapace (back), although larger specimens are usually found in the low intertidal zone (see also Figure 7-7). The juvenile specimen illustrated here is more typical of the middle zone under rock habitat. It shows the prominent antennae that give this crab its scientific name *antennarius*. The rock crab has black-tipped claws that it uses for crushing the shells of its prey—mollusks and hermit crabs.

Figure 6-28. A juvenile rock crab, Cancer antennarius. *Note the long antennae and the black-tipped claws.*

Figure 6-29. *The black-clawed pebble crab,* Lophopanopeus bellus.

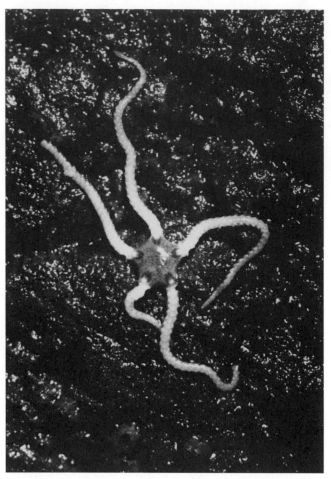

Figure 6-30. *The small, delicate brittle star,* Amphipholis squamata. *This echinoderm can be quite abundant under rocks.*

Specimens of the red rock crab are typically found under rocks, burrowed into the sediment with only a portion of their carapace showing. During nighttime high tides, they emerge and prowl the bottom.

Another crab in this under-rock hiding place is the small black-clawed pebble crab, *Lophopanopeus bellus* (Figure 6-29). The male black-clawed crab reaches a carapace width of one-and-a-third inches. Its body is usually tan to dun colored, although quite variable in color, and the carapace and walking legs are hairy. The male's claws are quite large in proportion to the walking legs, and are black at the tips. This crab scavenges for its food, eating a variety of plant and animal matter. They are usually found in mated pairs, the female being smaller with more slender claws. This crab is quite an actor. Like most crabs, it will raise up its claws and hold them outward menacingly in an attempt to appear big and ferocious. When this fails, the pebble crab will go rigid and play dead, sometimes remaining motionless for several minutes. The black-clawed pebble crab is found from Alaska to central California.

Brittle Stars. A small, delicate brittle star, *Amphipholis squamata* (Figure 6-30), and the similar-appearing, but much longer-armed *Amphiodia occidentalis,* are common under rocks that lie on top of sand and fine gravel in tidepools. They may also occur among the holdfasts of large algae. Typically, if one brittle star is discovered, careful inspection will turn up a number of these animals. Both species mentioned here feed on suspended and deposited organic material, and will autotomize (drop off) their arms if handled. They are best observed without being picked up. These brittle stars range in size from one-half to three inches in diameter.

In rocky tidepools lacking sediment, look for the beautiful daisy brittle star, *Ophiopholis aculeata* (Color Plate 15e), under and between rocks. This species can reach over three inches in diameter and is usually colored a mixture of buff or brown and bright or dark red. These colors are often mixed in bold display on the upper surface of the disk. The arms are typically banded in brown and bristle with fairly stout spines. The daisy brittle star feeds on detritus and diatoms. It is also known to trap suspended food in mucus secreted by its arms [2].

Under-Rock Fish. Common under-rock denizens of tidepools are the small fishes with elongate, eel body forms. There are several types of eel-like fishes that occur, including gunnels, snake eels, snailfishes, blennies, and pricklebacks [3]. These small, under-rock individuals are generally two to five inches in length. Shown here is a prickleback, *Xiphister* sp. (Figure 6-31). Larger specimens move downward in the intertidal and into the subtidal. Pricklebacks feed primarily on algae, with some animal material in their diets. They will also be found under exposed rocks throughout the middle and low intertidal zones, as will the majority of the other under-rock, tidepool fish species mentioned here.

Another interesting fish found occasionally under smooth tidepool rocks is the northern clingfish, *Gobieosox meandricus*. (Figure 6-32). This gentle-mannered fish reaches six inches long and is common in the Pacific Northwest and northern and central Cali-

Figure 6-31. A small (three inches long) prickleback eel, Xiphister *sp., viewed from above. Note the dark facial stripes and mottled body markings.*

Figure 6-32. A northern clingfish, Gobiesox meandricus, *three inches long. Note the large flat head and tapering body.*

fornia. It is mottled brown with white, and typically has a white band across the head joining the eyes. As the name implies, the clingfish clings to a rock with pelvic fins modified to function like a large suction cup. It will attach to the palm of your hand, and can support its own weight when inverted. Seen from above, the clingfish looks like a tadpole or frying pan with its broad, flat head and small, tapering body. Clingfish feed mainly on small crustaceans. Like the prickleback mentioned above, clingfish may also be found under exposed rocks in the mid and low intertidal zones.

Rock Undersides. When turning rocks in tidepools to discover what lurks on the substrate underneath, don't forget to look at the bottom of the rock itself. Here you will find a very interesting array of animals ranging from the juveniles of sea urchins and abalones, to a plethora of small mollusks and worms. They are too numerous to all be covered in this guide, but I will mention some of the more prominent ones. Again, be careful to replace the rock the same way you found it.

First, look closely at the bottom of the rock, and watch for movement. The most active animals will probably be small (half inch or less) amphipod crustaceans (Figure 6-33), which can occur in bewildering numbers of many species. The amphipods are primarily algae feeders. Also common can be isopods such as *Cirolana harfordi* (Figure 6-34), which is a scavenger on almost any animal tissue.

If decaying seaweed accumulates in the pool, check under rocks for the large isopod *Idotea wosnesenskii* (Color Plate 14b). This animal can be over an inch and a half long and quite robust. It is usually a solid color that ranges from brown through olive green to almost black. Specimens associated with coralline algae are often pink. A second isopod may also occur here, espe-

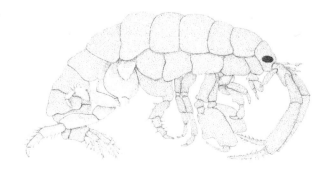

Figure 6-33. Common body form of an amphipod. Numerous species occur amongst intertidal rocks and algae.

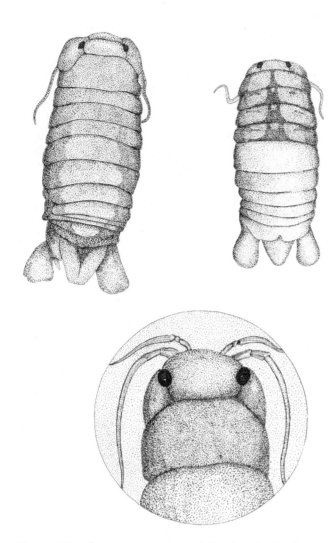

Figure 6-35. One-inch-long intertidal zone flatworm, Notoplana acticola.

Figure 6-34. The scavenging isopod, Cirolana harfordi, *common under intertidal rocks.*

cially if there is freshwater seepage into the pool. This is the stubby isopod, *Gnorimosphaeroma oregonense* (Color Plate 14c), which can be very abundant. This species resembles terrestrial isopods commonly called pill bugs in that it can roll into a tight ball. It is dull gray in color and less than a half-inch long. This pudgy fellow likes tight places and is also found underneath mussels and among barnacles.

A tan to pale gray, one- to two-inch-long flatworm, *Notoplana* spp. (Figure 6-35), is common here, and can be seen gliding along smoothly on a carpet of cilia. Look for a pair of eyespots near the front end of the worm. These very flat worms are perfectly suited to the tight quarters of the under-rock habitat. They feed on small mollusks and crustaceans, and range more widely

than the under-rock niche at night. Once you have discovered one flatworm, chances are excellent that there are several more close by. They are not limited to tidepools; virtually any rock resting on a slight bit of moist sediment in the upper, middle, or low intertidal zones may harbor flatworms underneath.

Occasionally, the beachcomber will uncover a veritable giant of a flatworm, either under a rock or on rocks exposed when other rocks are lifted off. This is *Kaburakia excelsa* (Color Plate 6b) which can reach over two inches in length. It is also quite broad and its multilobed gut shows through its thin gray to brown exterior. Black pigment spots are found all along the margin of the body, and close inspection will reveal a short pair of tentacles on the anterior of the worm.

The bottoms of rocks can also harbor a number of polychaete worms. Look closely for very small (a tenth of an inch or less), white, spiral shells (Figure 6-36). These are made by a worm in the genus *Spirorbis*. There are several species of these worms, and their identification is confusing. Not only do they attach to the undersides of rocks, but also to algae, shells, and even the skeletons of crabs. The worm itself protrudes a bright red ring of tentacles for filter feeding when submerged. One of the tentacles is modified into a stopper-like operculum to close off the shell. Once you have identified this worm, you will start seeing it everywhere.

Less abundant, but much larger, will be the thin, membranous, sand-encrusted tubes of the tentacle-feeding worms of the polychaete family Terebellidae. These worms are closely related to the large worm *Pista pacifica* (Figure 5-5) of the sand flat, introduced in Chapter 5.

Figure 6-36. Feeding tentacles and operculum emerge from the small (one-tenth of an inch diameter) spiral shell of the polychaete Spirorbis *sp.*

Figure 6-37. The polychaete worm, Thelepus crispus, *spreads its feeding tentacles. This worm has been removed from its heavy mucous tube.*

Shown here is *Thelepus crispus* (Figure 6-37), which can be almost a foot long although smaller individuals are usually seen. It remains in the safety of its semi-permanent tube and sends forth long, off-white, prehensile tentacles that creep along on cilia to scour the bottom of the tidepool for deposited organic material. These

Figure 6-38. The shield-back or kelp crab, Pugettia producta, *one-and-a-half inches across the back. Note the spidery, pointed legs.*

tentacles emerge from the worm's head region along with bright red gills used for breathing.

If there is a substantial amount of fleshy algae in a pool, searching through it will usually produce a swarm of small amphipod crustaceans and a number of small snails. A larger find (one to two inches across the back) may be the spidery-looking kelp crab, *Pugettia producta* (Figure 6-38). Also called the shield-backed crab, *Pugettia producta* ranges in color from green to dark brown and blends with its algal cover. The young kelp crab feeds on algae, and as it grows it moves downward in the intertidal zone and takes on a more carnivorous diet. Kelp crabs can also be found in several lower intertidal and subtidal habitats, and can reach a size of over three-and-a-half inches across the carapace (back).

While the kelp crab is probably the most common spider crab you'll see in these upper pools, the Pacific Northwest is rich in other spider crab species which also occasionally show up in tidepools. Be sure to check out the other members of this clan introduced in the middle and low intertidal zone sections of this book.

MIDDLE INTERTIDAL ZONE

The middle intertidal zone extends from 2.5 feet above MLLW to 0.0 feet MLLW along the Oregon coast, and from 3−4 feet above MLLW to 0.0 feet MLLW in the Puget Sound region. It is the part of the intertidal that is exposed by most low tides and covered by most high tides, so it spends about half the time submerged and half exposed. Unlike the upper and high intertidal zones that have relatively low diversity, the middle intertidal is awash with life. We have already discussed tidepools that occur in this zone, and there are several other fairly discrete habitats to consider. The exposed rock surface habitats of the middle intertidal zone will be discussed in the remainder of this chapter.

Exposed Rock Surface Habitats

Often portions of the rocky intertidal reef rise up above the flat bedrock of the reef face. These upraised areas are called outcroppings, and they provide rocky surfaces that are exposed to desiccation (drying out) more than adjacent flat reef areas (Figure 6-39). Similar-

ly, large boulders that remain relatively stationary also provide this elevated habitat. In unprotected intertidal areas that are exposed to considerable wave action, this upper exposed rock surface habitat grades into the mussel clump habitat as subtle changes in tidal height and the degree of wave exposure occur. Thus, many species occur in both habitats. In general, the exposed rock habitat is higher in tidal elevation and thus more subject to drying than is the mussel clump. The main line of demarcation between these two habitats represents the upper physiological limit of the California sea mussel, *Mytilus californianus,* which provides the superstructure of the mussel clump habitat discussed below.

Exposed Rock Seaweeds. The algae of the exposed rock habitat are similar to those found in the upper tidal zone. Tufts of brillo-pad alga, *Endocladia murica-ta,* are found on the tops of outcrops, and rockweeds, *Fucus* and *Pelvetiopsis,* hang down from the sides. Other algae include the thin sea lettuce, *Ulva* sp., and the red alga known as brown laver or nori, *Porphyra* spp. (Color Plate 2c), both of which can be quite abundant in the late spring and summer. On the lower, vertical surfaces of outcrops, several species of fleshy red algae, and a few large brown algae known as kelps, grow in profusion, especially in summer.

A final brown alga to look for is the tar spot alga, *Ralfsia* spp. (Figure 6-40). As the common name implies, *Ralfsia* looks like a dried tar spot on the rock. Beachcombers may think they've found the aftermath of an oil spill. The alga starts out as a circular, dark brown to black crust and then grows outward into patches up to eight inches in diameter. It may have

Figure 6-39. An exposed vertical rock face. Note the limpets in the upper zone, the mussel and barnacles at the mid zone, and algae beneath.

Figure 6-40. Small tar spot algae, Ralfsia *sp., growing on an exposed rock surface.*

slightly raised concentric ridges or it may be flat. *Ralfsia* is highly resistant to drying, and consists of short, erect, tightly packed plant filaments that grow so close together that they form a solid tissue. There are a number of other algal species that have this encrusting growth form, and these can be sorted out by the botanically oriented beachcomber using a good guide to marine algae [3, 4].

The Barnacles. The most abundant animal found on these exposed rocks often is the volcano-shaped, acorn barnacle. Barnacles are filter feeders and are active when they are covered with water. When seen at low tide, they are closed up and inconspicuous. The small barnacles found highest on the outcrop are *Balanus glandula* and *Chthamalus dalli* (Figure 6-10), the most desiccation-resistant of the common barnacles and introduced previously in the discussion of the upper tidal zone. From central California through the Pacific Northwest, a larger species, *Balanus* (*Semibalanus* in some treatments) *cariosus* (Figure 6-41), is found lower on the sides of the outcrop mixed with *Balanus glan-*

dula and *Chthamalus*. This barnacle is common on exposed rocks and on mussels. It grows to a larger size (to more than two inches in diameter) than the smaller, more abundant barnacles, has a thatched or ridged appearance, and is gray in color. *Balanus cariosus* usually occur as individuals rather than in large aggregations like *B. glandula* and *Chthamalus,* although they can be the dominant barnacle in some quiet-water situations such as is found at Rosario Head on Fidalgo Island, Washington. If *Balanus cariosus* escapes predation by carnivorous gastropods and sea stars, it can live up to 10 to 15 years.

A fourth barnacle species, the stalked barnacle *Pollicipes polymerus,* will also be found in sheltered cracks on the outcrop, but reaches its peak abundance in mussel clumps.

Exposed Rock Snails. In the lower, more shaded portion of the exposed rock habitat, the abundant, stationary acorn barnacles provide ready prey items for several carnivorous snails. In the Pacific Northwest, the most obvious predator is the snail known as the emarginate dogwinkle or whelk, *Nucella emarginata* (Figure 6-42). It occurs high up on these rocks and nestles among its prey during low tide. Like other snails that are barnacle predators, the dogwinkle is referred to as a "barnacle drill." It uses its radula to scrape or "drill" holes into the shell of its prey and get at the soft, edible parts. Careful inspection of the barnacles nearby these snails will reveal that many are the empty shells of past victims. *Nucella emarginata* has a compact, heavy shell with a low spire. It may have spiral ridges or be relatively smooth. The shell can reach over an inch and a half

Figure 6-41. Large acorn barnacle, Balanus cariosus, *of the middle intertidal zone. Smaller barnacles are* Chthamalus *sp.*

Figure 6-42. Two half-inch specimens of the emarginate dogwinkle, Nucella emarginata. *Shell pattern is highly variable in this snail.*

Figure 6-43. *Shells of the frilled dogwinkle,* Nucella lamellosa, *showing the variation in shape and sculpturing.*

Figure 6-44. *The channeled dogwinkle or dogwhelk,* Nucella canaliculata.

in height, but is usually smaller. The shell may be a solid color or stripped with colors varying from dark brown, gray, or black to an occasional orange individual. The interior of the shell is brown or purple. *Nucella emarginata* feeds mainly on barnacles and mussels, although it will also prey on *Tegula funebralis, Littorina scutulata,* and *Collisella scabra.*

From northern California to Alaska, another, larger dogwinkle species, *Nucella lamellosa* (Figure 6-43), can be found. This species is known as the frilled dogwinkle or wrinkled purple, and can reach up to two inches in height. As the common names imply, the shell of this species can be highly ornamented with frilled ridges and spiral bands. However, it can also be nearly smooth. The thinner, ornamented shells are found on snails in habitats where there are few predators, while the heavy, smooth shells occur on animals living in situations where predation, chiefly by large crabs, is common. The shell color varies from white to orange to brown, and can be a solid color or banded. Despite the large variation in shell shape, all *Nucella lamellosa* individuals have at least one row of tooth-like ridges, called denticles, on the inner face of the shell opening. These denticles are lacking in the other two *Nucella* spp. discussed here. The beachcomber is likely to find this snail somewhat below the level of the emarginate dogwinkle, and to see it more predictably in quiet, protected situations, like coastal embayments. Like the emarginate dogwinkle above, this species feeds chiefly on barnacles and mussels.

A third dogwinkle species is common in the Pacific Northwest, especially along the open Washington coast. This is the channeled dogwinkle or dogwhelk, *Nucella canaliculata* (Figure 6-44). It differs from

Nucella emarginata, in that the shell has a higher spire and a prominent shoulder on the body whorl (each revolution of the shell around its central axis is called a whorl; the last whorl secreted houses most of the snail's body and terminates in the shell opening—it is called the body whorl). There are evenly shaped and spaced spiral ridges encircling the shell. *Nucella canaliculata* is usually light colored, white to orange, and is sometimes banded. This snail can reach a height of one inch and shares a similar diet with its fellow *Nucella* spp.

All three of the *Nucella* species can occur in large numbers on a particular rocky shore. They have been extensively studied by marine ecologists at the University of Washington's Friday Harbor Marine Laboratory, and at the Bamfield Marine Station on Vancouver Island. During late spring and summer, the beachcomber can eavesdrop on the reproductive behavior of the frilled and channeled dogwinkles. Adults of these species come together in large mating aggregations, sometimes numbering in the hundreds. The snails mate and the females lay their fertilized eggs into vase-shaped egg cases. The yellow egg cases, sometimes called "sea oats," are deposited in communal nursery areas (Color Plate 10c), which are usually located in a shady area or under a rocky ledge. The snail embryos go through their entire development within these cases and emerge a few weeks later as small juvenile snails ready to enter the adult environment. The reproductive biology of the emarginate dogwinkle, *Nucella emar-*

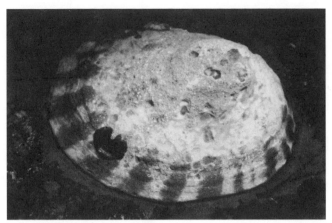

Figure 6-45. The shield limpet, Lottia pelta, *two inches long. Note the worn, robust shell.*

Figure 6-46. The file limpet, Lottia limatula, *showing the characteristic shell sculpturing of this species.*

ginata, is similar to other dogwinkle species, but it tends to lay eggs year-round rather than in a single mating season.

Nonpredatory snails found here include the ever-present black turban, *Tegula funebralis.* This snail sometimes aggregates in groups of hundreds on the protected, shoreward sides of outcrops. On outcroppings high in the intertidal, the periwinkles—*Littorina keenae, L. scutulata,* and *L. sitkana*—can be common.

Limpets. The ribbed and digit limpets, *Collisella scabra* and *Lottia digitalis,* will also be found on the outcropping, taking advantage of the microalgae growing there. The larger shield limpet, *Lottia* (formerly *Collisella*) *pelta* (Figure 6-45) can also occur here, usually under the protective covering of some overhanging algae. It is a robust limpet, reaching over an inch-and-a-half long, and highly variable in color, ranging from green to black and often with white checks or rays. The shell's apex is near the center of the shell, and the sides are all convex and frequently ribbed. As is the case with many larger limpet species, the top of the shell is often eroded. Shield limpets feed on a variety of fleshy brown and red algae including *Endocladia, Iridaea, Egregia,* and *Postelsia.* This limpet shows a marked escape response to a number of intertidal sea stars that are its chief predators. It lifts its shell well off the substrate and very quickly (for a limpet) crawls away.

From Newport, Oregon, south, a limpet that is frequently found near the shield limpet on semi-protected rocks is the file limpet, *Lottia* (formerly *Collisella*) *limatula* (Figure 6-46). The file limpet is so named for the strong, prickly radial ribs that grace its low-profile

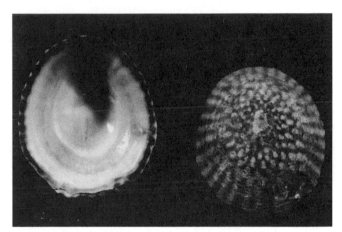

Figure 6-47. Top and bottom views of the large flat shell of the plate limpet, Tectura scutum.

shell. This limpet reaches over an inch and three-quarters long, and the shell is buff or yellowish or greenish brown in color, sometimes with dark mottling or white spots. It feeds primarily on microscopic algae, and algae that form sheets like the pinkish encrusting coralline algae.

From central California northward, a fifth limpet species, the plate limpet *Tectura* (formerly *Notoacmea*) *scutum* (Figure 6-47), may be found close to the base of the outcropping. This limpet is quite flat and broad and often sports tassels of attached algae. The plate limpet's shell reaches almost two-and-a-half inches in length, is low in profile, and the apex is round and near the center. These characteristics give the limpet a flat, plate-like appearance that distinguishes it from the other limpet species. Like the file limpet, plate limpets are grazers on microscopic algae and on encrusting coralline algae. They are preyed upon by the green-lined shore crab, *Pachygrapsus crassipes,* and by the sea stars *Leptasterias, Pisaster,* and *Pycnopodia.* The plate limpet has a running escape response that is elicited by these predatory sea stars. This response is similar to that described for *Lottia pelta.*

While we're on a roll, let's introduce the granddaddy limpet of them all, the owl limpet, *Lottia gigantea* (Figure 6-48). *L. gigantea* occurs on the most exposed middle intertidal rocks. This is the largest of our limpets, with a shell that can reach over three and a half inches in length. The shell is low in profile and the apex is near the anterior margin (front edge). The outer surface is rough and eroded, and brown with whitish spots. At low tide, large individuals of this species occupy "home scars" on the rocks that fit the margin of their shell. Interestingly enough, the shell of *L. gigantea* itself may be the location of the home scar of the smaller rough limpet, *Collisella scabra.*

Studies show that each owl limpet lives within a "territory" approximately the size of a dinner plate, grazing on the algal film that grows there. Striation marks in the center of the illustration are grazing scrapes left by *L. gigantea*'s large radula. Each owl limpet remains in its territory and keeps it free from other animals that may move in from adjacent areas. *L. gigantea* is preyed upon by shorebirds such as oyster catchers and occasionally by humans. The owl limpet ranges from southern California to as far north as Neah Bay, Washington, but is nowhere abundant along the open coast of Oregon and Washington.

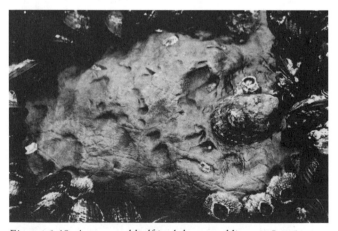

Figure 6-48. A two-and-half-inch-long owl limpet, Lottia gigantea, *rests on its home scar in a territory surrounded by mussels and barnacles.*

Figure 6-49. A male purple shore crab, Hemigrapsus nudus, *two inches across the carapace. Note the prominent dark (purple) dots on the chelipeds.*

Exposed Rock Crabs. The purple shore crab *Hemigrapsus nudus,* and from Ecola State Park, Oregon, the green-lined shore crab *Pachygrapsus crassipes* (Figure 6-9), can be found in this exposed rock subhabitat. These crabs can be seen holed up in cracks and crevices, and the green-lined shore crab is often seen scuttling all about the rock surface. The purple shore crab (Figure 6-49) is more abundant in undercut or overhanging areas of outcroppings that it shares with aggregating anemones. Large male purple shore crabs can reach two inches across the carapace (back), although most are smaller. The claws are marked with reddish-purple spots, and there may be some purple on the dark brown to red body. Shore crabs feed on low-growing algae that they crop with their claws, and scavenge for animal remains. The purple shore crab is known to occur from Alaska to Baja California, and is especially abundant in Puget Sound. Their chief predators are shorebirds and fish.

Mussel Clump Habitats

The Sea Mussel. Large beds or clumps of the California sea mussel, *Mytilus californianus* (Figure 6-50), are common all along the open coast of the Pacific Northwest. They range into the Strait of Juan de Fuca and the more exposed rocky intertidal sites in Puget Sound. The mussel thrives in areas of high wave energy and, indeed, its distribution corresponds to the most exposed, wave-tossed rocky intertidal habitat. Mussels reach five inches or longer in length in the intertidal zone, and up to ten inches in subtidal clumps. The shell is thick, pointed at the anterior end, and sculptured with radiating ribs and growth lines. The shell is often

Figure 6-50. A clump of the California sea mussel, Mytilus californianus, *an animal at home in the exposed middle intertidal zone.*

Figure 6-51. A large California sea mussel, Mytilus californianus, *serves as a host to barnacles and a limpet.*

eroded or worn from abrasion in the clump and frequently colonized by barnacles and limpets (Figure 6-51). Mussels are filter feeders, and the average mussel filters two to three quarts of seawater an hour when submerged. They filter mainly small particulate detritus and dinoflagellates.

One dinoflagellate commonly filtered is *Gonyaulax catanella,* which produces a toxin that can cause paralytic shellfish poisoning in humans. Mussels may accumulate large amounts of the toxin during summer months when the dinoflagellates can be most abundant. Therefore, it is always a good idea to check with local authorities when taking any shellfish in the Pacific Northwest, as sporadic plankton blooms of dinoflagellates can occur even during the "safe" season, and shellfish poisoning is a real possibility. See Chapter 2 for further information about clamming in the Pacific Northwest.

Mytilus californianus is able to settle and grow in wave-exposed situations because it attaches itself to the bedrock with stout fibers made of protein called byssal threads. In time, the mussel can monopolize the horizontal surfaces to the exclusion of other species that require attachment to the rocky substrate. However, mussels are not the only organisms that can live in this habitat successfully. First of all, the sea mussel is ultimately its own worst enemy. As the mussels grow and new larval mussels recruit into the mussel clump, the clump becomes more and more unstable. This occurs because the clump becomes several mussels deep, and fewer mussels are attached directly to the bedrock. Instead, they are attached to one another by their byssal threads. The growing clump offers more and more resistance to the pounding waves with less and less direct attachment, until large areas of the clump are torn away, leaving bare rock behind. This rock becomes available for new settlement, and a number of new organisms move in. Thus begins a cycle that may take seven or more years, and will end up with the mussel clump dominating only to grow and be torn away again.

Role of the Pacific Sea Star. The mussel's upper distribution is limited by its physiological tolerance to exposure. In areas of consistent wave action, the mussels can inhabit high intertidal zones successfully because of the wave splash; but in areas of periodic calm, their upper limit is the middle intertidal zone. Another control of the mussel is the Pacific sea star, *Pisaster ochraceus* (Color Plate 16b). *Pisaster*'s predation on the mussel is sufficient to preclude it from moving into and monopolizing the lower intertidal zone in the way it can dominate the middle intertidal zone. Thus, *Pisaster* keeps the lower substrate open for other species to colonize and inhabit, allowing for a much more diverse assemblage of organisms in the mussel clump habitat.

In addition to *Pisaster* and *Mytilus,* several other prominent organisms inhabit the mussel clump. The stalked barnacle, *Pollicipes polymerus* (Figure 6-52), occurs in round aggregations, sometimes surrounded by mussels. This filter feeder is capable of rotating its upper body on its muscular fleshy stalk. It can thus position its filtering mechanism, a series of modified legs with closely placed filtering hairs, into the current for the most favorable feeding on large particles of detritus and large zooplankton. The individual stalked barnacle may reach a length of three inches. Close inspection may reveal smaller barnacles attached to its stalk, because like the mussel, *Pollicipes'* larvae seek out and settle preferentially on the adult animals. Large barnacles are relatively immune to attack by most intertidal predators. Look closely at the photo of the *Pollicipes'* clump (Figure 6-53), and you may spot two cleverly disguised color variants of the digit limpet, *Lottia digitalis.* One is just to the right of center and the other is below center. Find them?

The solitary giant owl limpet, *Lottia gigantea* (Figure 6-48), is a conspicuous loner compared to the "togetherness" of *Mytilus* and *Pollicipes.* Occasionally, individual *L. gigantea* will actively maintain territories in the middle of a dense mussel clump. As discussed above, the territories consist of patches of closely cropped algae on which they graze. The owl limpet discourages intrusions onto its territory by other animals, including mussels and barnacles, through a series of very specific protective behav-

Figure 6-52. A stalked barnacle, Pollicipes polymerus, *with its filtering appendages in the normal feeding position.*

Figure 6-53. A colony of the stalked barnacle, Pollicipes polymerus, *with two camouflaged digit limpets,* Lottia digitalis.

Figure 6-54. Nuttall's chiton, Nuttallina californica, *two-and-a-half inches long. Chiton is nestled in a rocky depression amongst acorn barnacles.*

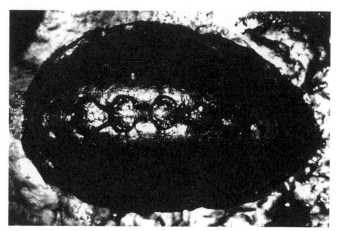

Figure 6-55. A four-inch-long katy chiton, Katharina tunicata. *Note how the shiny black girdle almost covers the shell plates.*

iors. Each *L. gigantea* retreats to a distinct home scar within its territory at low tide.

Another mollusk that lives on a home scar among the mussels or near the edge of the clump is Nuttall's chiton, *Nuttallina californica* (Figure 6-54). *Nuttallina* leaves its home scar at high tide to graze nearby algae and returns with the ebbing tide. It prefers erect coralline algae, but also eats *Endocladia* and *Cladophora*. The chiton's body is up to two inches long, and the shell plates are dark brown, although usually eroded or covered with algal growth. The fleshy girdle surrounding the shell plates is dull-colored and frequently overgrown by algae. The girdle is wide, coming up high on the shell plates, and is covered with short, rigid spines. This chiton's chief predator appears to be sea gulls.

The katy chiton, *Katharina tunicata* (Figure 6-55) is a second, larger (to five inches long) chiton also seen near mussel clumps. This chiton is robust and oval in shape. All the valves are deeply imbedded in a shiny black girdle. Only the very centers of the valves show, and these are often fouled with algae or animals. The bottom of the foot is a burnt orange color. Katy chitons feed on brown and red algae. They are especially common (Color Plate 8a) along the Strait of Juan de Fuca and in the San Juan Islands, where they appear to occupy the major herbivore role played on the open coast by *Tegula funebralis*.

The surface of the mussels' shells also serves as available habitat space (Figure 6-51). All three acorn barnacles mentioned in the exposed rock subhabitat section can be found on the mussels. *Balanus cariosus* is par-

ticularly abundant. Numerous small limpets of several species including *Collisella scabra, Lottia digitalis, L. pelta,* and young *L. gigantea* occur. Individuals of the aggregating anemone, *Anthopleura elegantissima,* and the proliferating anemone, *Epiactis prolifera,* can also be found on mussel shells.

With this abundance of small invertebrate prey, it is not surprising to find that the small, predatory six-rayed sea star, *Leptasterias hexactis,* and the barnacle-eating whelks, *Nucella emarginata* and *N. canaliculata,* are also common inhabitants of the mussel clump. These are only the larger, obvious animals of this habitat.

Organisms Within the Mussel Clump. Close scrutiny of the clump will reveal a myriad of smaller, motile animals and encrusting forms that combine to form one of the most diverse intertidal assemblages. In addition to the shells of the mussels, the webs created by their collective attachment (byssal) fibers provide a maze of nooks and crannies for marine invertebrates to inhabit. Young sea urchins less than an inch across find shelter at the base of the clump. Worms are especially able to maneuver here, and a wide variety of species occurs. Prominent are the polychaetes known as clam worms, pile worms, or mussel worms, *Nereis vexillosa* (Figure 6-56), and the very similar *N. grubei. Nereis vexillosa* is common among mussel clumps and a variety of other intertidal habitats. *N. grubei,* which is also common among mussel clumps, inhabits seaweed holdfasts as well. These nereid worms are omnivorous, feeding on a broad diet of animal and plant tissue. They possess an elaborate, jawed, eversible proboscis

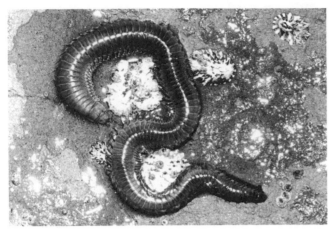

Figure 6-56. The clam worm, Nereis vexillosa, *common in mussel clumps.*

Figure 6-57. The scale worm, Halasydna brevisetosa, *a widely distributed errant polychaete.*

that is used to capture live prey as well as tear off bits of algae. *N. grubei* reaches a length of four inches and is tan to gray colored; *N. vexillosa* is larger (to six inches long) and darker, often with iridescent highlights. These worms fall prey to cancer crabs and fishes.

Another polychaete frequently seen in the mussel clump is the scale worm, *Halasydna brevisetosa* (Figure 6-57). This worm reaches two inches in length and has 18 pairs of flat scales along its back. This scale worm is a scavenger and detritus feeder. It also occurs in the tubes of other large polychaetes like *Thelepus crispus* (Figure 6-37), and *Pista pacifica* (Figure 5-5) of the sand flats.

The ribbon or rubber band worms (Phylum Nemertea—see Chapter 3) also thrive in the mussel clump. These elongated, predatory night-stalkers retreat into the protective maze of the mussel clump by day and actively forage through it and beyond at night. They are predators on a wide variety of invertebrates including polychaetes, and small crustaceans like amphipods and isopods. Several species occur here, and they vary more by color than shape.

The most obvious ribbon worm is the bright orange *Tubulanus polymorphus* (Color Plate 6c). As the specific name *polymorphus* implies, this worm comes in a variety of colors, including yellow, vermilion, and bright red, but orange is my favorite. It has a flattened, spade-like head and can reach a length of three yards when extended. It occurs from Alaska to San Luis Obispo County, California.

A second common species is *Emplectonema gracile* (Figure 6-58), which occurs in the mussel clumps, under rocks, in seaweed holdfasts, and in empty barnacle shells. This species is 4 to 6 inches when contracted, and can extend to 20 inches. It is yellowish green to dark green on the back, and pale greenish yellow to white on the bottom. *Emplectonema gracile* is often

Figure 6-58. The nemertean worm, Emplectonema gracile. *This semi-contracted specimen is six inches long. Note the dark upper and creamy lower surfaces.*

found huddled in tangled clusters. It also occurs in estuaries and on pier pilings.

One of the most common ribbon worms is *Paranemertes perengrina* (Color Plate 6e). It is frequently seen among mussels and coralline algae and under rocks. It is up to six inches long contracted, and purplish brown, dark brown, or orange-brown on the back. Underneath and on the sides of its head, it is deep yellow to white. This species stays hidden at high tide and ventures out in the early morning or at night at low tide. It is a predator of polychaetes, especially nereids, and can swallow a worm bigger around than itself.

A final mussel clump nemertean is the pink to pale white *Amphiporis imparispinosus* (Color Plate 6d). It is known to eat barnacles and small crustaceans. This ribbon worm reaches a length of three to four inches and is also found in algal holdfasts.

Crabs abound in the interstices of the mussel clump. Young of the familiar green-lined shore crab, *Pachygrapsus crassipes,* and the purple shore crab, *Hemigrapsus nudus,* are common. Other common crabs are the porcelain crabs, whose flat bodies allow them to move easily in tight quarters from which they seldom venture. Shown here is *Petrolisthes* sp. (Figure 6-59). Two species of this genus occur in the Pacific Northwest, and they both have this approximate shape. Porcelain crabs are so named because of their defensive behavior; when a leg or claw is grasped by a predator (or a human), they will cast off (autotomize) the appendage and run to safety. This drastic behavior led people to believe the crabs were delicate and easily damaged, thus the name "porcelain." Males reach about an inch or less

across the carapace and the females are smaller. These crabs are filter feeders, and use mouth parts (called maxillipeds) to set up filtering currents and strain plankton from the water. Porcelain crabs are preyed upon by other crabs, octopus, and fish.

The Sea Palm and Other Mussel Clump Algae. An alga that is a prominent seasonal member of the mussel clump association from Morro Bay, California, north is the sea palm, *Postelsia palmaeformis* (Figure 6-60). This lovely kelp plant is a brown alga (Division Phaeophyta) although its color is green. Sea palms have hollow, flexible stems (stipes) that allow them to bend with the force of the waves and backwash, then snap back into their upright posture. Almost all sea palms are torn away during fall and winter storms, but return, growing from microscopic germlings on the rocks, in the late spring.

Other, shorter-lived, seasonal algae of the mussel clump include the bright green sea lettuce, *Ulva* sp.

Figure 6-60. *The sea palm,* Postelsia palmaeformis, *a small kelp plant of the exposed middle intertidal zone.*

Figure 6-59. Smooth porcelain crab, Petrolisthes *sp., three quarters of an inch wide. Note the large chelipeds (claws) and flattened body.*

(Color Plate 1c), and the thin brown laver, *Porphyra* sp. (Color Plate 2c). Also common here is the by now familiar brillo-pad alga, *Endocladia muricata* (Color Plate 2e). Studies have shown that newly settled mussels will initially attach to *Endocladia* and then reattach to the rock as they grow. This is one of the first steps in the mussels' recolonization cycle.

Another large brown alga that shows up here, and throughout the rest to the middle and low intertidal zones, is the feather-boa kelp, *Egregia menziesii* (Figure 6-61). This plant is also known as Venus' girdle. It is a perennial plant that has a large, root-like holdfast. From the holdfast, strap-like stipes grow that can be several yards in length. The stipes consist of a stout,

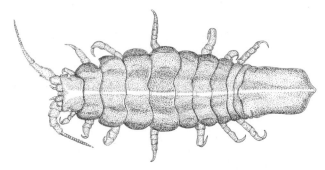

Figure 6-62. *The isopod,* Idotea stenops, *which lives attached to the midrib of the feather-boa kelp,* Egregia menziesii.

belt-like, midrib region from which grow short blades. Each blade has a small air bladder at its base that allows the kelp to float up off the bottom when submerged. During the winter the stipes break off, but the holdfast remains to produce more stipes in the spring.

Egregia harbors two very interesting hitchhiking invertebrates. The first hitchhiker is the large isopod, *Idotea stenops* (Figure 6-62), which co-occurs with the alga from Alaska to Point Conception, California. This animal reaches an inch-and-a-half long and matches the kelp's olive green to brown color perfectly. *Idotea stenops* feeds on the alga, and is always found tightly clutched to the middle of the stipe. The second animal is the kelp limpet, *Lottia* (formerly *Notoacmea*) *insessa* (Figure 6-63). The kelp limpet occurs from southern California to Alaska, but is not common north of Ore-

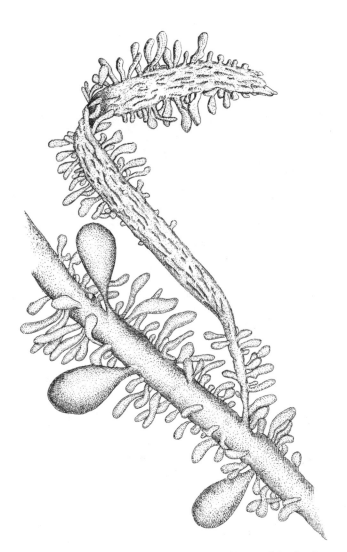

Figure 6-61. *Central midrib and lateral blade of the feather-boa kelp,* Egregia menziesii, *of the middle and low intertidal zones.*

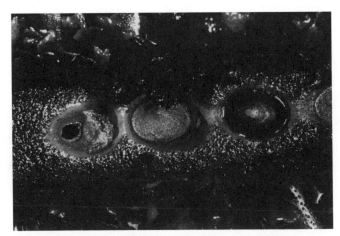

Figure 6-63. *The kelp limpet,* Lottia insessa, *residing in one of three depressions it has excavated along the midrib of* Egregia menziesii.

gon. Its thin, dark brown shell is less than an inch long, and the high sides are parallel and smooth. It also hugs the middle of the stipe from which it excavates depressions or scars with its radula. As can be seen in the illustration, the limpet can excavate a series of these scars. They eat the alga and nestle into the depressions to prevent drying out during low tide. The limpet can move from stipe to stipe.

REFERENCES

1. Ricketts, E., et al., *Between Pacific Tides,* 5th Ed. Stanford: Stanford University Press, 1985, 652 pp.

2. Kozloff, E. N., *Seashore Life of the Northern Pacific Coast.* Seattle: University of Washington Press, 1983, 370 pp.

3. Eschmeyer, W. N., et al., *A Field Guide to Pacific Coast Fishes of North America. The Petersen Field Guide Series.* Boston: Houghton Mifflin Company, 1983, 336 pp.

4. Abbott, I. A. and C. J. Hollenberg, *Marine Algae of California.* Stanford: Stanford University Press, 1976.

5. Scagel, R. F., *Guide to Common Seaweeds of British Columbia,* Handbook 27. British Columbia Provincial Museum, Victoria, 1971.

7

THE ROCKY INTERTIDAL ENVIRONMENT: MIDDLE AND LOW ZONES

In many rocky intertidal habitats with a gradual slope, the middle and low intertidal zones can be quite extensive. In addition to the upraised rocks and outcrops discussed in the previous chapter, the middle and low intertidal zones can contain extensive stretches of flat, open space, and areas where small boulders have accumulated, called boulder fields. Both of these habitats grade relatively seamlessly between the middle and low intertidal zones (below 0.0 MLLW), and I will include the entire sweep of middle and low intertidal in this treatment of reef flat habitats. Finally, two remaining habitats, the low tidepool and surge channel, will be covered briefly.

REEF FLAT HABITAT

Algal Turfs

The flat, open areas of the middle intertidal zone are usually characterized by lawns of short-growing (two to four inches) red algae and are sometimes referred to as red algal "turfs" (Figure 7-1). The flat reef has little relief to break up the sweeping surf, and consequently, the diversity of large invertebrates is relatively low here. The lush growth of red algae does provide ample fodder for herbivorous snails. The black turban snail, *Tegula funebralis,* is very common and is often found with the small hitchhiking snails—the black limpet, *Lottia asmi,* and the slipper limpet, *Crepidula adunca*—attached to its shell. Lower on the reef, the brown turban snail, *Tegula brunnea,* can be found and is distinguished from the more abundant *Tegula funebralis* by its dun to brown shell and an orange stripe along its foot. Hermit crabs, *Pagurus* spp., usually in *Tegula* shells, are also very abundant on these reef flats. The dire whelk, *Searlesia*

Figure 7-1. Flat, wave-washed middle rocky intertidal habitat. Dark plants are red algal "turfs"; lighter area is a patch of surfgrass, Phyllospadix sp.

dira, is occasionally found among the algae, although it is more common in tidepools.

The dense growth of algae and their holdfasts trap moisture and wave-borne materials. The trapped moisture makes a hospitable setting for clones of the aggregating sea anemone, *Anthopleura elegantissima,* which can be quite extensive. A layer of sand and small pebbles accumulates at the base of these plants, harboring many small animals including numerous worms, small snails, and a variety of crustaceans. Large numbers of amphipods ranging in size from a quarter-inch to a half-inch in length occur here, as do a number of small, (usually juvenile) specimens of crabs including *Pugettia producta* and *Cancer antennarius.* Interspersed among the algal turf are occasional large invertebrate predators. The Pacific sea star, *Pisaster ochraceus,* is on hand in low numbers to feed on *Tegula* spp. The leather star, *Dermasterias imbricata,* is found here feeding on the aggregating anemones.

Surfgrass Flats

The red of the algal turf is occasionally broken up by the bright green of the surfgrass *Phyllospadix* (Color Plate 3c). Unlike the algae, which attach to bare rock with their holdfasts, surfgrass is a flowering plant that must eventually sink its roots into soft sediments to flourish. Surfgrass takes up nutrients necessary for continued growth principally through the root system. This differs from the algae which absorb nutrients directly from the water across their entire surface. The root mass of the surfgrass traps suspended sediments and provides a habitat for many small animals, including peanut worms or sipunculids (Figure 7-2), polychaete worms of various types, and small crustaceans. As sediments accumulate, the surfgrass sends out rhizomes, trapping still more sediment and allowing it to increase its coverage.

Figure 7-2. Sipunculid worms. The larger specimen is four inches long and its introvert is fully extended, showing the feeding tentacles which surround the mouth.

On the individual blades of the surfgrass, a red alga, *Smithora naiadum,* grows epiphytically (i.e., on the plant). In summer, *Smithora* grows so densely that it may be difficult to see the green blades of surfgrass at all (Color Plate 3c). Also, during the summer, a group of seasonal algae appears. The salt sac, *Halosaccion glandiforme,* and the large, fleshy red algae like *Iridaea* spp. and *Gigartina* spp. (Color Plate 2d) are particularly abundant.

Surfgrass Beds

The lower intertidal zone remains submerged much longer than the middle intertidal, and surfgrass can grow quite lush here as a result. Extensive surfgrass beds that cover not only the solid rock substrate, but also small boulders and sandy areas as well, are common sights in many rocky intertidal areas. Surfgrass is a favorite low tide resting spot of large rock crabs, *Cancer* spp., and mated pairs can often be discovered in the spring (Color Plate 13c). Hermit crabs, *Pagurus* spp., and kelp crabs, *Pugettia producta,* are also common.

Octopus. Although they probably spend low tide under or among adjacent rocks, octopuses are occasionally seen during low tide seeking the refuge of the surfgrass bed, especially if it is still partially covered by water. Octopuses are such masters of camouflage that they are often overlooked, and thus are considered more rare than they actually are. My best advice to beachcombers is not to set out purposely to find an octopus. Instead, keep a ready eye when turning rocks or searching through algae and surfgrass. Octopuses are not only excellent mimics of their backgrounds, but also can move very quickly. When discovered, admire them from a distance, because some can give a good nip with their beaks and they do have a painful venom.

In the Pacific Northwest, most of the octopuses seen are the small (up to 18-inch-long arms) red octopus, *Octopus rubescens* (Color Plate 12c). Occasionally, small individuals of the much larger species, *O. dolfeini* (over 40 pounds, and 10-foot arm spread in Puget Sound specimens), are seen. Octopus species are difficult to identify because of their ability to vary the color and texture of their skin to match almost any background. They move about during high tide in search of prey that include crabs, shrimp, snails, and small fish. Octopuses feed by trapping prey in the web of their arms and biting them with their bird-like beaks and injecting a nerve-deadening toxin. They also feed on shelled mollusks by boring the shell with their radula. In turn, octopuses are preyed upon by bottom-feeding fishes.

Nudibranchs. The surfgrass beds and the standing pools of kelp like oar weed, *Laminaria* spp. (see Figure 7-35), and other kelp species, left by the lowest of the low tides, often harbor several nudibranch species among the vegetation. Nudibranch snails (sea slugs) apply the opposite color strategy compared to *Octopus*. These animals sport bright colors, often in elaborate patterns, supposedly to warn potential predators that they are unpalatable prey.

A word about nudibranchs: On a successful day, a trained observer may only discover eight or so species during a low tide foray, so don't be too discouraged if you only see one or two. Nudibranchs are somewhat enigmatic to beachcombers. Their appearance (and disappearance) is unpredictable, so be advised to enjoy them when you can. While I am placing nudibranchs here in the surfgrass section, realize that they will show up in a variety of rocky intertidal settings. Anywhere in the middle and low intertidal zones where there is standing water, nudibranchs may appear as bright specks of color against an algal backdrop. Many included here will also show up on floats and pilings that harbor their prey. I will mention only a few of the most common species. See more detailed references for coverage of all of the nudibranchs of the Pacific coast [1, 2].

One of the most common nudibranchs in the Pacific Northwest is *Hermissenda crassicornis* (Color Plate 10d). (Some place this species in the genus *Phidiana*.) It occurs on wharf pilings, in tidepools, on mud flats, and in eelgrass beds. *Hermissenda* is beautifully and variably colored, but always has areas of orange on its back outlined with bright blue or white lines. The dorsal protuberances, called cerata, are found in rows behind the stalked sensory tentacles. *Hermissenda* feeds on hydroids (small colonial cnidarians—see Figure 7-36), but also will eat small anemones, bryozoans, worms, crustaceans, carrion, and even other *Hermissenda*. This shell-less snail can reach over three inches in length, but is usually smaller.

Nudibranchs like *Hermissenda* that have dorsal cerata are known as aeolid nudibranchs. Aeolid is a reference to Aeolis, the Greek god of the wind, and it refers to the cerata that look like leaves blowing in the wind. A second common aeolid is the shag-rug nudibranch, *Aeolidia papillosa* (Color Plate 10e). This species occurs throughout the Pacific Northwest and is a specialist on sea anemones. How much of a specialist is it? Take a look at the color illustration. If you glanced at it in passing, you may have thought it was a sea anemone. Indeed, if this animal is in the middle of a clone of *Anthopleura elegantissima,* it is very hard to spot. The "shaggy" cerata on its back look just like a mass of anemone tentacles. The typical animal seen ranges from one-and-a-half to three inches long, although four-inch specimens occasionally occur. The basic color is white to brown, although it can take on the color of the anemones it's eating.

A second common nudibranch type is the dorid nudibranch, named after Doris, a sea goddess. These sea slugs lack the cerata found in the aeolids and instead have a pair of prominent anterior tentacles, called rhinophores, and a distinct circle of feather-like gills on the rear of the back. The dorid nudibranch can retract the gills and the rhinophores into special sheaths on its back.

One of the more conspicuous dorids, because of its size and bright color, is the sea lemon, *Anisodoris nobilis* (Color Plate 11c), which is bright yellow with black spots. The back is covered with small tubercles and the black pigment on the back occurs between, but not on, these tubercles. The circle of gills is white. This species can reach a size of over two-and-a-half inches in the intertidal zone, and much larger (up to six-inch) specimens occur in the subtidal. Sea lemon nudibranchs feed on sponges and are found from Baja California to Alaska.

A second "sea lemon" species often confused with *Anisodoris nobilis* is *Archidoris montereyensis*. This sea lemon is likewise yellow with black pigment spots and has tubercles covering its back. However, the yellow color is often dingy in this species whereas *Anisodoris nobilis* is always bright yellow or yellow-orange. *Archidoris montereyensis* also differs in having a circlet of pale yellow gills and the black pigment extending up onto the tubercles. *Archidoris montereyensis* is similar in size to *Anisodoris nobilis,* and also feeds on sponges.

A third dorid that looks like a bleached version of the sea lemons above is the white knight nudibranch, *Archidoris odhneri*. This sponge-eating nudibranch is seen less commonly than the sea lemons, but is unforgettable because of its pure white color and large size (a typical specimen is four inches long).

Another dorid nudibranch commonly seen is the yellow-edged cadlina, *Cadlina luteomarginata* (Color Plate 11a). It has a pale white color edged and dotted in lemon yellow. Like the sea lemons above, this species feeds on sponges. It reaches a length of two inches and is able to transfer the sponge's spicules (glass skeletal elements) into its own skin for defense.

The ring-spotted dorid, *Diaulula sandiegensis* (Color Plate 11b), is named after one of my favorite California cities, San Diego. A common, sponge-feeding nudibranch found throughout the Pacific Northwest, *Diaulula* is unmistakable with its dark rings on a gray to light brown background. Beachcombers will usually see small specimens one to three-and-a-half inches in length, although animals five inches long have been reported.

The sea-clown nudibranch, *Triopha catalinae* (Color Plate 11d), feeds on bryozoans. Bryozoans are found in most of the low intertidal habitats and can be recognized by the tiny reticulate (basketweave like) pattern on their surface (see Figure 7-5). The sea clown is usually one inch long, but can reach six inches, and is pale white to yellow with deep orange spots on the body, gills, and all appendages. A close relative, the spotted triopha, *Triopha maculata* (Color Plate 11d), is occasionally seen intertidally in its bright orange-red, juvenile form. It is usually less than a half-inch in length. Larger individuals are generally subtidal in distribution.

Laila cockerelli (Color Plate 11e) is easily mistaken for *Triopha catalinae*. Both nudibranchs are white with orange, but on *Laila* the orange spots are located on elongated papillae that superficially resemble the cerata of the aeolids. Closer inspection of *Laila*'s back will reveal retractable red-orange rhinophores and a white gill circlet that are characteristic of the dorids. This nudibranch reaches a little over an inch in length, and has been observed to feed on bryozoans.

Onchidoris bilamellata, a small but distinct dorid, feeds on bryozoans when small, but switches to acorn barnacles as an adult. This nudibranch reaches three-quarters of an inch in length, but is usually smaller. It has a pale background color with brown pigment splotches. *Onchidoris bilamellata*'s back is covered with rounded tubercles that give it a warty appearance.

The beachcomber will sometimes encounter a beautiful nudibranch with translucent dorsal appendages outlined in frost white. This is *Dirona albolineata* (Figure 7-3). *Dirona* is neither an aeloid nor a dorid, but belongs to a third nudibranch group known as arminaceans. The cerata are flat, sharp-tipped, and fall off easily. This nudibranch feeds primarily on small snails and can crack their shells with stout jaws. It is also known to eat a variety of other invertebrates including sponges, bryozoans, hydroids, and tunicates. Large specimens reach over two inches in length.

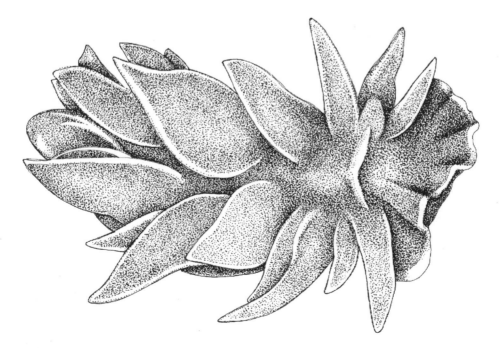

Figure 7-3. Frosted nudibranch, Dirona albolineata.

Another arminacean nudibranch seen throughout the Pacific Northwest is the jaunty *Janolus fuscus* (Color Plate 12b). This animal is sometimes mistaken for the ubiquitous *Hermissenda crassicornis* (Color Plate 10d), as the cerata of both often have yellow near the tip. However, *Janolus'* cerata have a white tip with a yellow band beneath, while *Hermissenda*'s cerata are tipped with yellow. *Janolus* also lacks the bright blue or white lines along the back typical of *Hermissenda* and has a yellowish-red streak between its rhinophores. It reaches one inch in length.

An unforgettable sight for any beachcomber is the rose-pink Hopkins rose nudibranch, *Hopkinsia rosacea* (Figure 7-4), with its tall papillae gently swaying as it moves across the bottom. Hopkins rose feeds on a rose-colored animal called a bryozoan, *Eurystomella bilabiata* (Figure 7-5), which forms encrusting colonies on rocks. Although its prey bryozoan occurs throughout the Pacific Northwest, *Hopkinsia* is seldom seen north of Coos Bay, Oregon. It is usually less than an inch in length.

BOULDER FIELDS

The Under-Rock Habitat

In low-lying regions of the middle and low rocky intertidal, small boulders will accumulate, forming boulder fields (Figure 7-6). In open, exposed rocky intertidal habitats, small boulders are frequently moved around and broken up or swept off the reef platform entirely by wave action. Therefore, boulder fields are more characteristic of rocky intertidal areas that are semi-protected from direct wave action. Here, rocks of dinner plate size and larger stand a good chance of staying in place. The under-rock habitat is available as a relatively protected, stable environment that supports a very rich and varied assemblage of plants and animals.

Look for rocks that have well-developed marine plant growth. This is an indication that they have remained in place for some time, and will constitute fruitful searching. The common seaweed species will include the flat-bladed *Gigartina* spp. and *Iridaea* spp. growing in profusion (Color Plate 2d). Also, you will often find a pair of kelp plants, the sea cabbage *Hedophyllum sessile* (Color Plate 2f), and smaller individuals of *Costaria costata*, distinguished by its five parallel

Figure 7-4. Hopkins rose nudibranch, Hopkinsia rosacea. *This inch-and-a-half-long sea slug matches its prey, the rosy bryozoan, in color.*

Figure 7-5. A three-inch diameter colony of the rosy bryozoan, Eurystomella bilabiata. *Note the basket-weave texture that is typical of bryozoans.*

Figure 7-6. A middle intertidal zone boulder field.

ribs and wrinkled texture. Larger *Costaria* occur in the lowest intertidal of wave-swept beaches and reach a length of over three feet.

Under-Rock Crabs. The under-rock habitat is prime crab-viewing territory for the beachcomber. Remember the difference between the true crabs and the other "crabs" discussed in Chapter 3. True crabs have five pairs of prominent walking legs visible, while the other "crabs" will have only four pairs visible. Among the most prominent true crabs are the purple shore crab, *Hemigrapsus nudus;* the large red rock crabs, *Cancer antennarius* and *Cancer productus;* and the small pygmy cancer crab, *Cancer oregonensis.* The spider crabs also make up a large group of true crabs found in the rocky intertidal zone of the Pacific Northwest.

Cancer antennarius (Figure 7-7), is the most abundant cancer crab found in the intertidal zone in southern and central Oregon. It becomes less common farther north and is replaced in prominence by *Cancer productus. Cancer antennarius* is brick red on its upper surface and is distinguished from the similarly colored *Cancer productus* by the presence of red speckling on its lower surface. *Cancer antennarius* feeds mainly at night on both live and dead animals. It preys on hermit crabs by chipping away their shells with its large claws until the crab is exposed. It also feeds on snails, other crabs, and carrion (dead animal tissue). Males grow larger than females and reach five inches across the carapace (back), like the animal illustrated. Females carrying eggs can be found in the winter months and during early spring. Beachcombers should be very careful with all of these large cancer crabs, as they can deliver a very painful pinch.

Cancer productus is found in the intertidal zone and also is commonly caught in crab traps with the Dungeness crab, *Cancer magister. Cancer productus* is brick red in color with black-tipped claws similar to the closely related *Cancer antennarius.* However *C. productus* does not have red speckles on its underside like *C. antennarius.* Young *C. productus* are frequently light colored with striped or mottled color patterns like the animal illustrated here (Figure 7-8). Occasionally, a gray to dark brown color variation of this crab is seen and looks very similar to *Cancer gracilis* (see Figure 4-17). The two can be distinguished by the color of the tips of their claws: *C. gracilis* has white-tipped claws, while *C. productus'* claws are tipped with black. Male *Cancer productus* can reach a carapace width of

Figure 7-7. Large male rock crab, Cancer antennarius. *The large size of the black-tipped claws are diagnostic of a sexually mature male.*

Figure 7-8. A juvenile rock crab, Cancer productus. *Note the prominent stripping on the three-inch-wide carapace of this male specimen.*

seven inches; females are smaller (Color Plate 13c). This crab is a nocturnal predator that feeds on barnacles, small crabs, and dead fish among a variety of other prey. This is the most common large cancer crab in the greater Puget Sound intertidal.

The pygmy cancer crab, *Cancer oregonensis* (Color Plate 13e), can be found under rocks in the intertidal zone from the Pribilof Islands in the Bering Sea to Palos Verdes, California. Look for this crab tightly ensconced in small holes or depressions in the rocks or in the empty shell of a large barnacle. As the name implies, the pygmy cancer crab only reaches a size of two inches across the carapace, but it has an attitude! Like its two larger cancer cousins above, it is usually colored orange or red, and the claws are tipped in black. However, white, mottled, and striped specimens are common in some areas [3]. The legs are usually quite hairy. The pygmy crab's carapace is nearly round in outline and is used like a stopper to block the opening of the hole it inhabits. *Cancer oregonensis* is a nocturnal predator like the other, larger intertidal zone cancers. It feeds primarily on small barnacles.

The under-rock habitat is home to the pebble crabs introduced in Chapter 6 in the tidepool section. Small (one inch across the carapace) *Lophopanopeus bellus* (see Figure 6-29) are often abundant, especially if the rocks rest on a bottom of mixed sediment and pebbles.

A number of spider crab species are found under rocks in the middle and/or low intertidal zone. Several of these spider crabs show a tendency to "decorate" or "mask" themselves with bits of living plant and animal material to provide camouflage. This behavior varies among the spider crab species. Young of the kelp crab, *Pugettia producta* (Figure 6-38), discussed in the tidepool section of Chapter 6, are often found with a small tuft of algae on the rostrum (front). Larger kelp crabs (three inches across the carapace) are usually clean. They rely on their solid carapace color which usually mimics their algal substrate. Kelp or shield back crabs, *Pugettia producta*, are the largest and most commonly seen of the spider crabs.

The graceful spider crab, *Pugettia gracilis* (Color Plate 14a), remains decorated throughout its life. However, like its cousin the kelp crab, it only decorates its rostrum. The graceful spider crab is commonly encountered in the low intertidal in association with rocks and algae. It reaches a carapace width of an inch and a quarter and its color varies considerably, especially in juveniles, ranging from white to bright red. As is common in most spider crab species, the males have proportionately larger claws than the females. This species is the second most common spider crab seen in the greater Puget Sound region. Both the graceful spider crab and the kelp crab also occur in eelgrass beds.

Scyra acutifrons (Figure 7-9), the sharp-nose spider crab, doesn't put much effort into decoration. Instead, the rough carapace is colonized by bryozoans and sponges which grow and break up the outline of the crab. Male *Scyra* have very long, large claws and relatively short legs. The "sharp-nose" common name is derived from the two short, flattened rostral horns that project anteriorly from the carapace. *Scyra acutifrons*

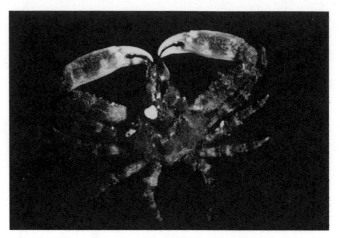

Figure 7-9. Sharp-nose spider crab, Scyra acutifrons.

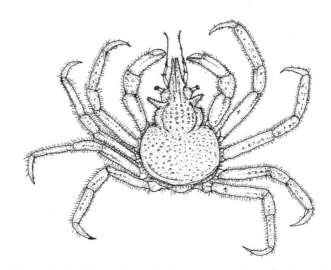

Figure 7-10. The spider crab, Oregonia gracilis, *often heavily decorated.*

reaches a little over an inch and a half in carapace width and feeds on detritus and sessile invertebrates.

The very spidery-looking *Oregonia gracilis* (Figure 7-10) goes all out and actively decorates its legs as well as its carapace, making it very difficult to see against an algal background. This crab is equipped with special hooked hairs on its carapace, legs, and claws, which it uses to lodge its decorative trappings. *Oregonia gracilis* grows to an inch and a half in carapace width and is probably an algal feeder. Both *Oregonia gracilis* and *Scyra acutifrons* discussed above are fairly common in the greater Puget Sound region and on the open coast of Washington and west coast of Vancouver Island. They are much less common in the rocky intertidal zone of Oregon.

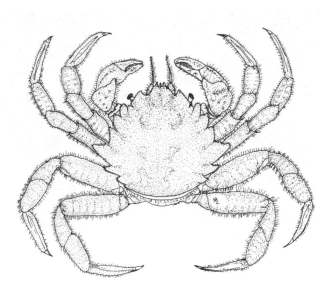

Figure 7-11. The helmet crab, Telmessus cheiragonus, *an occasional intertidal visitor.*

The foliate spider crab, *Mimulus foliatus* (Color Plate 14f), is found on the more exposed shore of the Strait of Juan de Fuca and all along the open coast of the Pacific Northwest. It is not seen in Puget Sound. The foliate spider crab rarely decorates and instead relies on its variable color pattern for camouflage. Colors vary from white or brown to yellow, orange, or red and are frequently beautifully mottled. *Mimulus* is the only intertidal spider crab the beachcomber will see that has a carapace wider than it is long. They reach a size of an inch and a half and feed primarily on drifting algae.

The helmet crab, *Telmessus cheiragonus* (Figure 7-11), is the final true crab I'll mention. The carapace of this crab has six jagged teeth on each side and is covered with stout hairs. The color is typically yellow-green and the claws are tipped in dark brown. Older crabs may have considerable orange, red, or brown color as well. The helmet crab reaches up to four inches in carapace width. It is common in the greater Puget Sound region and rarely seen on the open coast of Washington or Oregon. *Telmessus cheiragonus* is found among rocks with heavy algal cover and is also associated with eelgrass beds.

Hermit crabs (Figure 6-23) are commonly encountered in the under-rock habitat. Several species are found, and I'll let the beachcomber sort them out with more detailed references [3, 4]. Hordes of the flattened porcelain crab, *Petrolisthes* spp. (Figure 6-59) occur

under rocks in some places, and beachcombers must be diligent in replacing the overturned rocks.

Three lithode crabs are sometimes encountered in the under-rock habitat of the Pacific Northwest. Occasionally, while turning rocks in the low intertidal zone, the beachcomber is treated to an unusual animal known as the umbrella crab, *Crytolithodes sitchensis* (Color Plate 13a). The umbrella crab is also known as the turtle crab, both common names referring to the fact that the carapace extends out on the sides to hide the legs. This crab reaches almost three inches in carapace width, although usually smaller individuals are seen. It varies in color from the bright orange animal illustrated here to individuals with highly mottled color patterns. The underside is usually almost pure white. Very little is known about the biology of this strange-looking crab.

Speaking of strange, have a look at *Oedignathus inermis* (Figure 7-12). This lithode crab (note there are only four pairs of visible walking legs) has an outsized right claw covered with blue granules, a large, soft abdomen, and a carapace shaped like a pear. It reaches a carapace width of one inch and occurs from the middle intertidal downward in rocky crevices. It is reported to be quite adept at catching worms with its smaller left claw and crushing mussel shells with its monster right [3]. *Oedignathus inermis* occurs along the open coast from Alaska to Oregon. It is rarely seen in the San Juan Islands and never found in Puget Sound.

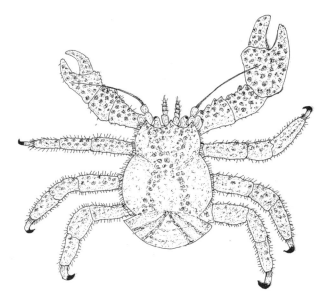

Figure 7-12. The large right claw identifies the crab Oedignathus inermis.

A third, unforgettable lithode crab that is seen occasionally under low intertidal rocks is the very hairy *Hapalogaster mertensii* (Color Plate 14e). Like *Oedignathus inermis* above, it also has a large right claw and a soft abdomen which it keeps folded loosely against its thorax. But the golden bristles and hairs that cover this crab's carapace, claws, and legs are what make it memorable. The color beneath the wreath of hair is brown or red and brown. *Hapalogaster* is an omnivore and reaches almost an inch and a half in carapace width. Its range is given from Alaska to Puget Sound [3], although it occasionally is seen farther south.

Under-Rock Serpent/Brittle Stars. If there is any sediment beneath the rock, the beachcomber should look for sipunculid worms, shallow-burrowed polychaete worms, and brittle or serpent stars. In addition to the three species mentioned in Chapter 6, one other species can be found. "Serpent" and "brittle" stars are closely related and belong to the echinoderm subclass Ophiuroidea (ophiuroids). The two common names roughly distinguish between those species that readily shed their arms when handled (thus, "brittle" stars) from those that don't. The common name "serpent" star refers to the jerky, snake-like movement of the animals' jointed arms.

The additional under-rock serpent star of the low intertidal zone of the open coast is the flat-spined *Ophiopteris papillosa* (Figure 7-13). *Ophiopteris* is a versatile feeder, employing mucus for suspension feeding as well as being an active carnivore. The disk is up to an inch and a half in diameter, with the arms three to

Figure 7-14. *The blood star,* Henricia leviuscula. *Adults of this star are bright orange red in color.*

four times the disk diameter in length. All the spines are thick and blunt, with the spines toward the tips of the arms being quite short. This serpent star is a deep chocolate brown in color, and although it occurs from Barkley Sound on Vancouver Island to Baja California, it is nowhere common.

Under-Rock Sea Stars. Several other echinoderms frequent the under-rock habitat. The small six-rayed sea star, *Leptasterias hexactis* (Figure 6-26) is common here as far south as the California Channel Islands. The blood star, *Henricia leviuscula* (Figure 7-14), shows up here under rocks. Large specimens (seven-inch diameter) are orange-red in color; smaller (two- to three-inch diameter) individuals are gray, tan, or purple, often banded with darker shades. The blood star feeds by trapping bacteria and other tiny particles in mucus on its arms, and transporting it to the mouth by way of ciliary tracts. It may also feed on sponges and bryozoans. The sea bat, *Asterina miniata* (Figure 6-27), can be occasionally seen on the tops and sides of rocks, but only under the rocks will you find small sea bats.

The Pacific sea star, *Pisaster ochraceus* (Color Plate 16b), can be common, and occasionally the giant pisaster, *Pisaster giganteus,* occurs. When found in the intertidal zone, *Pisaster giganteus* rarely exceeds a diameter of ten inches, although individuals two feet in diameter occur subtidally. In the intertidal zone, this species feeds mainly on mollusks, especially mussels and snails. Color varies in *P. giganteus,* but it can be distinguished by large, white, evenly spaced spines on its aboral (side opposite the mouth) surface that are surrounded by a zone of blue.

Figure 7-13. *The large, blunt spines of the serpent star,* Ophiopteris papillosa, *are unmistakable. This specimen is five inches in diameter.*

A third *Pisaster* species should be included here to complete the family portrait. This is *Pisaster brevispinus* (Color Plate 16c), introduced in Chapter 5. This robust sea star is light pink in color and not easily confused with any other star. It is primarily a predator found on soft bottoms, but individuals will show up in low rocky intertidal habitats as well as on pier pilings. In the rocky intertidal zone, bivalves are their primary prey, especially mussels.

Another sea star occasionally encountered among low intertidal rocks is the aptly named rainbow star, *Orthasterias koehleri* (Color Plate 16d). This sea star has long tapering arms festooned with prominent white spines and can exceed 20 inches in diameter. The color is variable, but usually consists of some combination of pinkish red, brick red, tan, gray, and dull yellow. *Orthasterias koehleri* has a broad diet that includes chitons, snails, bivalves, and barnacles. It is seen in the San Juan Islands and along the open coast from Alaska to southern California.

The beachcomber may come across two multi-rayed sea stars. The first is the sunflower star, *Pycnopodia helianthoides* (Color Plate 16a), discussed in Chapter 6. Sunflower stars are more at home subtidally, but they do forage into the intertidal zone and become stranded when the tide recedes, especially if it is a very low tide. The beachcomber can find Stimpson's sun star, *Solaster stimpsoni* (Figure 7-15), among low intertidal rocks. This sea star usually has ten arms and reaches a diameter of eight inches. Its color varies with red, orange, yellow, green, and blue individuals seen. However, it is readily recognized by a blue-gray spot on its central disk that continues as a distinct stripe onto the arms. *Solaster stimpsoni* is a fairly specialized feeder, preferring sea cucumbers.

Sea Cucumbers. Sea cucumbers are different from all the other echinoderm groups. Instead of being star-shaped or round, they are elongated and worm-like. Also, they are very flexible, not rigid like a sea star or sea urchin. These qualities make sea cucumbers very successful dwellers of tight quarters, like the under-rock habitat. Several sea cucumbers that occur in the rocky intertidal zone are filter feeders. They filter feed using highly branched feeding tentacles that surround the mouth. These tentacles are actually modified tube feet.

A relatively common sea cucumber under rocks in the Pacific Northwest is the creamy white to pale orange *Eupentacta quinquesemita* (Figure 7-16). This animal is two to three inches long, and all five rows of

Figure 7-15. The multi-rayed sea star, Solaster stimpsoni. *Note the prominent color pattern radiating from the disk onto the arms.*

Figure 7-16. The sea cucumber, Eupentacta quinquesemita, *with its anterior feeding tentacles extended.*

tube feet are still visible on its elongated body. *Eupentacta* only extends its branched feeding tentacles to filter feed at night when submerged. You may also find this animal on floats and pilings.

An unmistakable under-rock sea cucumber is the burnt-orange *Cucumaria miniata* (Color Plate 15d). Beachcombers turning rocks in the low intertidal zone will occasionally come across a mass of ten highly branched, bright orange feeding tentacles sticking out from a crevice or from a pile of tightly stacked rocks. The up to eight-inch-long body is usually concealed and held securely in place with the body's tube feet. Reddish brown and pinkish brown animals are also seen, but the bright orange tentacles are standard issue.

The most obvious sea cucumber that beachcombers will find is the warty character known as *Parastichopus californicus*. This animal can reach a length of at least 16 inches and is red, brown, or yellow in color. It has a series of blunt feeding tube feet around its mouth that are used to pick up deposited material from the bottom. The California sea cucumber moves on a "sole" of tube feet, and the rest of the body is adorned with stout conical papillae. This animal is found in the low rocky intertidal zone and also on subtidal soft bottoms. It is the source of a sea cucumber fishery in the Pacific Northwest, and there is some concern that the animal may be overfished [5].

Along the open coast in areas with substantial wave action, small (less than an inch in diameter) purple sea urchins, *Strongylocentrotus purpuratus* (Color Plate 15a), are found under the rocks. Although the common and scientific names of this species both include "purple," sometimes these small urchins have green rather than purple spines and may be mistaken for the green sea urchin, *Strongylocentrotus droebachiensis* (Color Plate 15c). However, the spines are blunter in *S. purpuratus* and there is almost always some purple coloration of the body of the animal, while the green urchin is green with brown. Small purple urchins are seldom seen among the larger individuals in other habitats, and it appears that they use the under-rock habitat along with the recesses of the mussel clump as nurseries.

Animals on the Undersides of Rocks. Attached to the bottom of the rocks will almost certainly be the agile, proliferating sea anemone, *Epiactis prolifera* (Color Plate 6a), in one or several of its variety of colors. You may also find the calcium carbonate tubes of two common filter-feeding polychaetes worms. The small, spiral tubes are made by *Spirorbis* spp. (Figure 6-36) already discussed above. The larger (three inches) coiled or meandering tubes are made by the fan worm, *Serpula vermicularis* (Color Plate 7d). *Serpula*'s tube is often partially concealed in a crack or abandoned burrow in the rock. When submerged, *Serpula* holds a bright-colored fan of red or orange filter-feeding tentacles into the water. Cilia on the tentacles trap plankton and other detritus and carry it to the mouth. One of the tentacles is modified into a knob-like stopper or operculum which *Serpula* pulls in last to seal off its tube.

Also seen attached to the under-rock surface are a variety of bivalve mollusks. By far, the largest (up to six inches in diameter) is the rock scallop, *Hinnites giganteus*. *Hinnites* lives freely as a yellow- or orange-shelled juvenile up to a size of almost two inches, and has a typical scallop appearance (Figure 7-17). At a size between one to two inches, the small scallop attaches by cementing its right valve to the rock. Once attached, the once beautifully symmetrical bivalve's growth conforms to the contours of the rocky surface, and it achieves a varied shape depending on the attachment site (Figure 7-17). The detached left valve is frequently found by beachcombers, and the remnant of the juvenile shell can still be seen near the hinge, along with a deep purple stain on the inside of the shell that identifies it as a *Hinnites'* shell. In life, the animal is quite spectacular, with bright orange flesh and silver-blue eyespots visible all along its outer margin when the shells gape. The upper shell is often riddled with the

Figure 7-17. Shells of the scallop Hinnites giganteus. *The lower shell is from a free-living juvenile; the upper shell is from an attached adult scallop.*

burrows of the boring sponge, *Cliona celata.* The sponge shows on the surface of the shell as small yellow dots.

In the quieter water of Puget Sound, a second scallop is occasionally seen, although it is much more common in deeper water. This is the pink scallop, *Chlamys hastata* (Color Plate 9a), whose shell reaches two inches in height. Unlike *Hinnites,* the pink scallop is not permanently attached to the substrate; it rests on its right valve and may be temporarily attached by a byssal thread secreted by a gland in its foot. If disturbed, *Chlamys* can detach, rapidly clap its shells together, and swim away.

Another flattened bivalve mollusk, the jingle shell, *Pododesmus cepio* (Figure 7-18), occurs under larger, smooth rocks. It is also common on floating docks and is occasionally found attached to the shell of red abalone, *Haliotis rufescens.* This distant relative of the scallop adheres to the rock with a large calcified attachment (byssus) that projects through a notch in the flat, lower (right) valve. The right valve is thin and conforms to the rock's surface, while the upper (left) valve is concave and can reach a diameter of three inches. Jingle shells are so named because when the thin left valve becomes detached, it bounces and "jingles" in the surf.

Two other attached bivalves should be noted here. These are known as jewel boxes or chamas. The first is the right-hand chama, *Chama arcana,* and the second is the reversed chama, *Pseudochama exogyra.* The jewel boxes are so named for their thick, deep, lower valves that are topped by the much thinner, flatter top valves like the lid on a box. The valves of most specimens are decorated with frilly or spiny projections, but can also be fouled with marine growth. Both these mollusks can reach two inches in diameter. They regularly

Figure 7-19. Two rock chamas, Chama arcana, *one-and-a-half inches in diameter. Note that the bottom (left) valve is deeply dished while the top valve is flat.*

co-occur all along the southern Oregon coast. They are distinguished by looking down onto the top valve. *Chama arcana* (Figure 7-19) illustrated here attaches by its left valve, and the top valve (the right valve) coils to the right. *Pseudochama exogyra* attaches by its right valve and the top valve (left valve) coils to the left. Like the scallop and jingle shell described above, the chamas are regularly found on a variety of hard substrates including breakwater rocks, harbor pilings, and the undersides of harbor floats.

Chitons. A variety of chitons is found on the rocks. The shells of these mollusks are divided into eight articulating plates that allow the chitons to conform and cling to irregular rock surfaces. The obvious mossy chiton, *Mopalia muscosa* (Figure 6-19), described in Chapter 6, also occurs here along with close relatives *Mopalia lignosa* (Color Plate 7d) and *Mopalia ciliata.* *M. lignosa* is fairly common on the sides and under large boulders from Alaska to Point Conception. Its valves are beautifully colored with greens and browns. *Mopalia ciliata* is common in well-protected crevices, but also under rocks and sometimes among mussels. It reaches three inches in length and the valves are highly sculptured with beads and prominent lateral ribs. *Mopalia ciliata* is an omnivore and can have as much as 45 percent of its diet made up of animal material [6]. It is found from the Aleutian Islands to Baja California.

Occasionally, the beachcomber will find what appears to be a small football or misplaced meatloaf among the rocks in the low intertidal zone. Congratulations, you just found the world's largest chiton, *Crypto-*

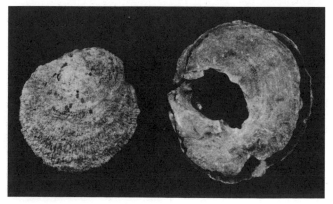

Figure 7-18. Views of the upper (on left) and lower valves of the rock jingle, Pododesmus cepio. *Note the deep notch in the intact shell on right.*

Figure 7-20. The gumboot chiton, Cryptochiton stelleri—*the world's largest chiton.*

chiton stelleri (Figure 7-20). Commonly called the gumboot chiton, this animal can reach a length of 14 inches and occurs from Alaska to as far south as California's Channel Islands. It is dark brown to brick red in color, and the stiff mantle completely covers the chiton's eight valves (shells). Look for the commensal polychaete worm *Arctonoe vittata* (Color Plate 7e) between the gumboot's foot and mantle. *Cryptochiton stelleri* feeds on fleshy red algae and certain coralline algae, and occasionally on brown and green algae. Unfortunately, the gumboot does not attach as firmly to the rocky substrate as other chitons, and frequently is washed out of the lower intertidal and stranded on the high beach during storms.

If there are any encrusting coralline algae on the rocks, you may discover one of the true marine jewels, the strikingly colored, lined chiton, *Tonicella lineata* (Color Plate 8b). This small (up to two inches long), beautiful chiton is common in low intertidal habitats that support its food—coralline algae. *Tonicella's* shells vary in color from purple to light red marked with zigzag lines of alternating colors in combinations of dark and light red, dark and light blue and red, or whitish and red. The stiff, fleshy girdle surrounding the shells is often alternately banded as well. The main predators of the lined chiton are the sea stars *Leptasterias hexactis* and *Pisaster ochraceus*.

The veiled chiton, *Placiphorella velata* (Color Plate 8d) is an interesting little chiton that sometimes turns up under a rock, but more often is positioned on the ceiling of an overhang or in the deep shade of a crevice. There's no mistaking this chiton's identity, for it has a fleshy extension of its girdle jutting out in front. This "veil" is held upright off the substrate and offers a safe, shady spot for a foraging crustacean or worm. It's not

safe for long, as the chiton lowers the veil in less than a second on the prey and maneuvers it into its mouth. *Placiphorella velata* can also feed by grazing algae with its radula like a more typical chiton. It reaches a length of about two inches and is found from Alaska to Baja California.

The Pacific Northwest has a very rich chiton fauna, and the list is too long to cover in this guide. I'll leave you with a pair of my favorites, *Lepidozona mertensii* (Color Plate 8c) and *Lepidozona cooperi* (Color Plate 8e), and refer you to more complete references for the rest [6, 7, 8]. *Lepidozona mertensii* reaches a length of two inches, and is orange-red to brick-red to crimson in color. It is sometimes marked with white blotches as is the handsome animal in the photograph. *Lepidozona cooperi* is often more abundant than its congener, but is less spectacularly colored. Its color ranges from dull olive to dull blackish-brown and is never red. The girdle is blotched in alternate light and dark gray. *Lepidozona cooperi* is conspicuous for its "big shoulders," high-peaked angular ridges running along the center of the chiton's valves. It reaches a length of two inches. *Lepidozona cooperi* is found on the open coast from Neah Bay, Washington, south to Baja California. *Lepidozona mertensii* is found from Alaska to Baja California and occurs in Puget Sound.

Under-Rock Snails. Among the rocks of the middle and low intertidal zones, a number of shelled gastropods occur. They are too numerous to include in this guide, so I'll stick with the largest, most conspicuous animals. The largest snails by far are the abalone.

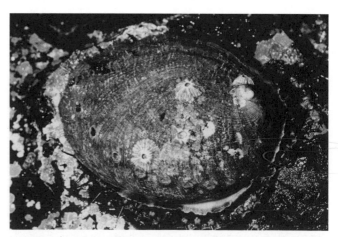

Figure 7-21. Five-inch red abalone, Haliotis rufescens, *showing prominent podial tentacles. Shell is encrusted with acorn barnacles and a bryozoan colony.*

From central California to Coos Bay, Oregon small (one to three inches long) red abalone, *Haliotis rufescens* (Figure 7-21), use the boulder fields as a nursery, with an occasional large (up to 12 inches) animal also appearing. However, because of human fishing pressure, the large red abalone are usually found only in the subtidal. The red abalone shell is usually brick red, and the surface uneven with three to four open holes. The holes are oval and slightly raised above the surface of the shell. These holes serve to allow the respiratory current to exit and to take with it wastes and reproductive products. The interior of the shell is dominated by a large muscle scar in its center where the abalone's massive foot is anchored to the shell. The color of the shell is influenced by diet, and it is frequently fouled and eroded by marine growth including boring sponges. In California, the red abalone is a favorite food of the sea otter. Sea stars, fishes, and cancer crabs are other predators. Red abalone are not abundant in Oregon. Attempts to introduce them to the northern Oregon and Washington coast appear to have failed.

Two smaller abalone species also occur in the Pacific Northwest. The flat abalone, *Haliotis walallensis* (Figure 7-22), is occasionally seen in the low intertidal zone along the open coast from British Columbia to La Jolla, California. It seems to be most common in Oregon. The shell of the flat abalone is sculpted with low ribs crossed by fine concentric ridges and reaches a length of seven inches. There are usually from four to eight open holes on the shell which is flatter and more elliptical than that of the other abalone species. The interior of the shell is pearly whitish-pink, and there is no prominent muscle scar like that seen in the red abalone.

The pinto or northern abalone, *Haliotis kamtschatkana* (Color Plate 9c), is occasionally found intertidally in Puget Sound and along the open coast from Sitka, Alaska, to Point Conception, California. It is mainly a subtidal species south of Washington. The shell of the pinto abalone is typically thinner than that of the other east Pacific species and has a wavy surface with three to six holes open. The outer shell color is reddish with white and blue markings. The interior of the shell is a dull pearl essence and it also lacks a muscle scar. Northern abalone reach a size of six inches and feed on attached and drift algae.

Another group of large snails closely related to the abalone are found among low intertidal boulders. These are the keyhole limpets. Keyhole limpets possess a respiratory opening at the apex of their shell that gives it a "keyhole" appearance. Water comes in over the limpet's head, passes through its gills and out this opening that serves the same function as the holes in an abalone shell.

Diodora aspera (Figure 7-23), the rough keyhole limpet, is common in Puget Sound and along the open coast from Alaska to southern California. The rough keyhole's shell can be over two-and-a-half inches long and gray in color, with coarse black and white radiating ribs. The "keyhole" opening is circular. It feeds on algae and encrusting animals such as bryozoans. Rough keyhole limpets are prey of sea stars and have a well-developed escape response that often foils their predators.

Figure 7-22. The flat abalone, Haliotis walallensis.

Figure 7-23. Two-inch-long rough keyhole limpet, Diodora aspera. *Note the strong pattern of radiating ribs.*

When touched by the tube feet of a sea star predator, they rapidly expand their fleshy mantle up over their shell, leaving no firm surface for the sea star to grab.

Almost all rough keyhole limpets harbor a commensal polychaete worm, *Arctonoe vittata,* between their foot and mantle cavity. The ivory color of the worm matches the color of the host's mantle remarkably well. *Arctonoe vittata* (Color Plate 7e) is also frequently found associated with gumboot chitons, *Cryptochiton stelleri* (Figure 7-20), and a number of other invertebrate hosts.

Megatebennus bimaculatus is a second keyhole limpet found intertidally along the open coast of the Pacific Northwest. It is also locally abundant along the Strait of Juan de Fuca. The mantle of this keyhole limpet is colored red to dingy orange to brown and often has dark spots or blotches. The mantle and body completely cover the shell and extend well beyond it. The shell itself has a relatively large "keyhole" with parallel sides and reaches slightly over a half-inch in length. *Megatebennus bimaculatus* is commonly associated with compound tunicates and sponges in the low intertidal zone and appears to feed on both [6].

Among the coralline algae-encrusted rocks, the dunce cap limpet, *Acmaea mitra* (Color Plate 9d), can be found. This limpet's steep, conical shell is white, although often covered with the same pink encrusting coralline algae on which it feeds. The shell can reach an inch-and-a-half long and over an inch high. This snail's relatively tall shell appears top heavy, and the hydrodynamic drag it creates would seem to be a liability in its wave-swept habitat. However, its foot is able to produce a remarkably strong attachment to the rocks, and it stays put.

The white slipper limpet, *Crepidula nummaria,* is more obvious in death than when alive, as its empty shell (Figure 7-24) is frequently found on the beach or in a tidepool. This snail is related to *Crepidula adunca* that rides around on *Tegula* shells, and like *C. adunca* it is a filter feeder. It lives under rocks or in the empty holes of burrowing animals or in empty shells. The white slipper limpet's shell is white and up to an inch-and-a-half long. The shape of the shell varies as it conforms to the contours of the animal's living space. The shell's exterior is often partially covered with a thick, dark brown, thatched material known as periostracum. The interior of the flat shell sports a prominent shelf, which gives the shell its slipper-like appearance. This shelf supports the limpet's large gills that are used in filter feeding.

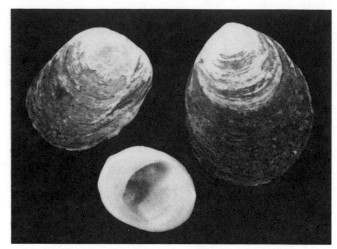

Figure 7-24. Shells of the slipper limpet, Crepidula nummaria, *often found empty on the beach.*

Figure 7-25. The leafy hornmouth, Ceratostoma foliatum.

The ornately shelled, carnivorous snail known as the leafy hornmouth, *Ceratostoma foliatum* (Figure 7-25), is found from Alaska to San Diego, California. This snail receives its common name from the elaborate "leafy" flanges on its shell and the sharp tooth that protrudes from the base of its aperture (shell opening). These flanges are more pronounced in subtidal and quiet water individuals, and their function is poorly understood. Leafy hornmouths can reach a length of four inches, although intertidal specimens are usually two inches or smaller. They can be found among the rocks of boulder fields, and on the sides of rocky outcroppings and surge channels. The chief prey items of this carnivorous snail are acorn barnacles (*Balanus* spp.) and bivalves.

The Oregon hairy triton, *Fusitriton oregonensis,* is another large snail occasionally seen among low intertidal rocks. The shell of this handsome snail, which can reach over four inches in length, is covered with a thick, brown epidermal layer (the periostracum) that sports stout hairs. The Oregon triton is a predator of sea urchins and bivalve mollusks. It is found from the Aleutian Islands to southern California.

A group of snails that specializes in feeding on sea anemones go by the curious name "wentletraps." This is a Danish word that means spiral staircase, and a glimpse at the tall, angular shell explains this common name. Shown here is Chace's wentletrap, *Opalia chacei* (Figure 7-26). It reaches well over an inch in length and is colored white to grayish white. Each of the shell's seven to eight turns (whorls) has six to seven axial ribs. This distinguishes Chace's wentletrap from the other common species, *Epitonium tinctum* (Color Plate 10b), which has nine to thirteen axial ribs per whorl. Wentletraps are always found associated with anemones such as *Anthopleura xanthogrammica* (Color Plate 4c) and *Urticina* spp. (Color Plates 5b and 5c). They feed by biting off tentacles and pieces of the anemone's column.

Another tall-spired snail commonly seen is the small *Bittium eschrictii* (Figure 7-27). The drill-shaped shell is less than a half-inch in length and is colored gray or brown. It is quite common under rocks and is frequently inhabited by a young hermit crab.

The top snails like *Tegula funebralis* and *T. brunnea* continue to be common in the middle and low intertidal. Remember a goodly number of these shells will house hermit crabs and not the original gastropod tenant. *Calliostoma ligatum* (Color Plate 9e) is a very common under-rock top snail throughout the Pacific Northwest. The shell reaches just under two inches in height and is ornamented with light-colored spiral ridges separated by brown furrows. These snails are omnivores, taking plant material and hydroids. There are several other genera of small top snails, and the beachcomber is referred to more extensive references to sort them out [6, 7, 8].

Amphissa columbiana (Color Plate 10a) is another very common under-rock snail. The shell of this very active scavenger reaches over an inch in height and is colored brown to pinkish brown. The shell is quite ornately sculptured with fine spiral lines crossed by strong axial ribs, but you have to get up close to it to appreciate it. *Amphissa columbiana* is quite adroit at finding dead animal matter from some distance. Place

Figure 7-26. Chace's wentletrap, Opalia chacei.

Figure 7-27. Small drill-shaped snail, Bittium eschrictii.

one in a plastic bag with some seawater, and it will quickly emerge and begin to explore. It holds its long siphon well forward, sweeping it back and forth to pick up the scent of a possible meal.

Ocenebra lurida (Figure 7-28) is somewhat similar in appearance to *Amphissa columbiana.* Its shell is likewise sculpted with spiral lines and axial ribs, but it is usually yellow-brown or orange-brown in color. The shell of *Ocenebra lurida* is also more inflated and has a more developed siphonal canal than *Amphissa.* This snail is primarily a barnacle predator of the open coast and reaches just over three quarters of an inch in height.

The Rock Borers

The rocks and boulders found in intertidal boulder fields are derived from a variety of sources. Some materi-

al may come from the weathering of cliffs that abut the intertidal zone. Much rocky debris may be thrown onto the reef from the subtidal zone by wave action. However, the majority of the rocks is usually composed of pieces broken from the solid reef substrate itself, especially if the reef is made up of soft, sedimentary rock like shale, sandstone, or siltstone. If the rocks of the boulder field are soft, the beachcomber might notice round holes in them. These are the burrows of the rock-boring bivalve mollusks. The burrows excavated by these unique clams appear round from the surface and conical when viewed from the side (Figure 7-29). These clams riddle the soft, rocky reef in the mid-and lower-intertidal zones until it becomes unstable, and pieces break away under the pounding surf.

There are several species of bivalve borers on the reefs of the Pacific Northwest, and the most abundant is the common piddock, *Penitella penita* (Figure 7-29). Occa-

Figure 7-28. The snail, Ocenebra lurida, *a predator of barnacles.*

Figure 7-29. A two-and a half inch-long rock piddock, Penitella penita, *shown next to a cutaway view of the burrow it has excavated in the soft rock.*

sionally, a detached piece of reef rock will contain a live specimen still in place in its burrow, but more often, only the elongated, augur-shaped shells remain. Piddocks or pholads, as they are also called, burrow by mechanical action. The anterior edges of their shells are laid down as a series of stout ridges which function as drill blades to cut into the soft reef rock. The clams anchor themselves by their foot with the anterior end of their shell pressed against the bottom of their burrow. They then rotate their shells around the foot by alternate contractions of the shell muscles, and a grinding, drilling action results. The worn shell ridges are replaced by the secretion of new shell. In this way, the clam excavates a conical burrow into the rock, which increases in diameter as the clam grows. Once the clam becomes sexually mature, the burrowing ceases. If enough clams have burrowed in proximity, the rock is severely weakened and subject to fracturing. This clam is found only on the open coast.

Another, less-common boring clam is the rough pea-pod borer, *Adula falcata* (Figure 7-30). Beachcombers will find the long, narrow, fragile shells of this clam in the same soft rocks with *Penitella* above. The pea-pod borer also uses its shell to excavate the rock, but it does not rotate the shell while it is boring, so it fits much more snugly in its burrow. Other rock-boring adulas are found in the Pacific Northwest and are recognizable by their thin, elongate shells covered by a tough, shiny, reddish-brown periostracum.

A final boring clam to consider is the robust rough piddock, *Zirfaea pilsbryi* (Color Plate 9b). The shells of this bivalve may reach five inches in length and are sometimes found on sandy beaches or the shores of embayments. At first, it would seem unusual to find the shells of a boring clam in a soft substrate habitat, but the mystery is solved when the substrate preferences of the piddock are examined more closely. In addition to boring into soft shale rock in the low intertidal zone and below, *Zirfaea* also bores into stiff clay substrates. These clay substrate deposits sometimes occur in embayments or offshore of sandy beaches. The rough piddock bores into substrates the same way as *Penitella penita* (Figure 7-29) described above, and when it dies, the shells are washed out of their burrow as the clay deposit is eroded and carried onshore.

When the boring clams die, the now vacant burrows become the home of a variety of other animals. Sipunculids, polychaetes, snails, small sea stars, nestling clams, and encrusting animals like sponges and bryozoans all can show up. Probably the most surprising

Figure 7-30. The rough pea-pod boring clam, Adula falcata, *shown next to its partially-exposed burrow. This clam is five inches long.*

animal to find here is the lumpy porcelain crab, *Pachycheles rudis* (Figure 7-31). This small (one inch across the carapace) crab often occurs in mated pairs, and sometimes grows too large to escape its tapered abode. It is also common in mussel clumps and in the holdfasts of large seaweeds. Like the smooth porcelain crabs, these animals are filter feeders, so they only need an open connection with the circulating water to feed successfully.

LOW INTERTIDAL POOLS AND SURGE CHANNELS

There are two remaining habitats that deserve mention: low intertidal pools and surge channels. Surge channels, technically, are not just a low intertidal habitat, as they can extend all the way to the highest intertidal zone; however, they have their origin in the low intertidal and will be treated from that perspective.

Figure 7-31. A lumpy porcelain crab, Pachycheles rudis, *three-quarters of an inch across the carapace, found in the empty burrow of a boring clam.*

Figure 7-32. Solitary purple sea urchin, Strongylocentrotus purpuratus, *two inches in diameter, residing in its rocky excavation in a low intertidal pool.*

Low Intertidal Pools

Low intertidal pools are unique habitats. The nature of the rocky substrate has to be such that dished-out areas occur in the low intertidal region, and the exposure to wave action plays an important role as well. So beachcombers won't find these habitats at every rocky area they visit, and of course, viewing them requires that the tide for the day be below the zero tidal level (a "minus tide"—see Chapter 2). However, they are easily recognized for the unique group of organisms they support.

The Purple Sea Urchin. The first and foremost inhabitant is the purple sea urchin, *Strongylocentrotus purpuratus* (Color Plate 15a). The purple urchin is one of the most common marine animals along the open coast. However, except for an occasionally stranded urchin tossed up by wave action or a hearty individual in an upper tidepool, it is often missed because it only occurs abundantly in the low intertidal zone and subtidally. This sea urchin cannot withstand long periods of exposure to warm air. Therefore, it inhabits the edge of the intertidal reef that is exposed only at extreme low tides, and low pools that are not exposed to the sun and air long enough for the water to heat up beyond the urchin's tolerance.

At very low tides (−1.0 feet MLLW or lower), large numbers of urchins can be found exposed on flat, seaward portions of the lower reef. In both this exposed, lowest intertidal region and in the low tidepools, the urchins occur in rounded depressions or pits (Figure 7-32). These pits are thought to be excavated by the urchins using their spines and their special five-jawed chewing apparatus called Aristotle's lantern. The urchin remains in its pit and feeds on any nearby attached fleshy algae or drifting plant material that is washed its way. As the urchin grows, it enlarges its pit, and if sufficient food is obtained, it will remain in place. The urchin sometimes becomes trapped in its pit, having grown too large to escape from the opening. The pit offers the round urchin a greater surface area for attachment of its anchoring tube feet and protection from rolling rocks and other wave-borne materials.

In Puget Sound, the conditions are apparently too calm for the purple sea urchin, which requires an area of considerable wave action. Only a few populations are found in the San Juan Islands and none in Puget Sound. However, a close relative, the green sea urchin, *Strongylocentrotus droebachiensis* (Color Plate 15c), is found. The green urchin has light green spines, and the body is green with reddish-brown blotches. It can reach a diameter of over three inches and does not excavate burrows like its purple kinsman. *Strongylocentrotus droebachiensis* feeds on attached and drifting algae. The green sea urchin also occurs in open coast tidepools along Vancouver Island and northern Washington, but is rarely seen in Oregon.

In the low tidepool, the dark purple of the urchin is contrasted against the lighter pastel purple and pinks of coralline algae (Color Plates 2a and 2b). Corallines, both the encrusting and erect types, are very abundant here because their calcium carbonate-impregnated tissues are too hard for the urchins to graze. Thus, the pools are dominated by substantial erect coralline growth on the pool margins, and encrusting corallines cover the bottom.

Low Tidepool Cnidarians. Other bright spots of color on the walls and floor of the low tidepool are provided by sponges of various shades of purple, red, yellow, and off-white, and by cnidarians. Located in shaded corners or under overhanging ledges are dime-sized polyps of the orange cup coral, *Balanophyllia elegans* (Color Plate 5a). These are close relatives of coral reef corals and each forms a rigid calcium carbonate cup into which it can retract.

Another cnidarian that shows up here is the strawberry anemone, *Corynactis californica* (Color Plate 5f). Like the aggregating anemone, *Anthopleura elegantissima,* of the upper zones, the strawberry anemone is a clone-forming species. Also like the aggregating anemone, *Corynactis'* clones battle for space. The colored illustration shows two different-colored clones in near proximity. Individual *Corynactis* polyps are about an inch across when open. The common colors are orange, pink, scarlet or red; however, purple, brown, yellow, and nearly white clones are also seen. The tentacles are tipped with white clubs. They are very common in the shallow subtidal as well.

The proliferating anemone, *Epiactis prolifera* (Color Plate 6a), is also common in the low tidepools, occurring in a range of vivid colors. Less varied in color, but nonetheless spectacular because of its size, is the giant green sea anemone, *Anthopleura xanthogrammica* (Color Plate 4c). Clones and large, solitary individuals of the aggregating sea anemone, *Anthopleura elegantissima* (Color Plate 4e), also inhabit these low pools. Finally, look for the large *Urticina* spp. (Color Plates 5b, and 5c), especially the striking green and red column of *U. coriacea.*

Polychaetes. Two polychaetes are common here. On the bottom and edges of the pool, especially under overhangs, colonies of the filter-feeding worm, *Dodecaceria fewkesi,* form off-white patches (Figure 7-33). This polychaete secretes a calcium carbonate tube. The colony resides in a smooth white matrix made up of these tubes. The surface of the tube matrix is dotted with small (one-tenth of an inch) openings through which the worm's head and tentacles protrude for filter feeding.

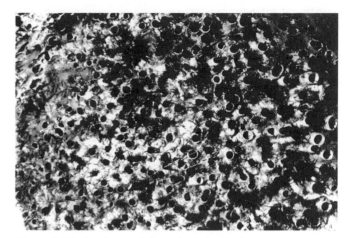

Figure 7-33. *A colony of the colonial polychaete,* Dodecaceria fewkesi. *Note the feeding tentacles projecting above the off-white tubes.*

Twin spirals of red or pink tentacles about the size of a dime, protruding from white, calcareous tubes, mark the presence of *Serpula vermicularis* (Color Plate 7b). This filter-feeding fan worm was introduced previously in the under-rock section.

Low Tidepool Mollusks. Several mollusks contribute to these colorful tidepools. The lined chiton, *Tonicella lineata* (Color Plate 8b), is thought to feed on coralline algae and is frequently found in these low tidepools, sometimes in empty urchin pits. Another coralline feeder found here is the dunce cap limpet, *Acmaea mitra* (Color Plate 9d). Other gastropods occur in the low tidepools, including *Tegula* spp. and limpets. Occasionally, *Ceratostoma foliatum* and *Searlesia dira* will be seen as well. A common snail here is the busy *Amphissa columbiana* (Color Plate 10a), seen moving actively about the surface of erect coralline algae. Often, this snail's shell has been appropriated by an equally active hermit crab, so look closely.

Another striking snail is the beaded top snail, *Calliostoma annulatum* (Color Plate 9e), with its half-inch-high shell gloriously wound with purple beads. The channeled top snail, *Calliostoma canaliculatum* (Color Plate 9e) is also seen here occasionally, distinguished by the vivid contrast of the brown and white spiral lines encircling its shell. Sporting these top snails' shells and various other gastropod shells are numerous hermit crabs, *Pagurus* spp. Occasionally, small clumps of mussels, *Mytilus californianus,* will appear in these low tidepools, probably dislodged from the rocks above. Another attached bivalve that shows up here is the rock scallop, *Hinnites giganteus* (Figure 7-17). It is distinguished by its bright orange mantle and blue eyes that are visible when the shell gapes open.

During the quiet morning minus low tides of spring and summer, the low tidepools feature the showiest of all the mollusks, the nudibranchs or sea slugs (see Color Plates 10–12). Nudibranchs were described above in the surfgrass section, but it is in the low tidepool, with its smaller area and beautiful background colors, that they can be most appreciated. Because the pools harbor sponges, cnidarians, and bryozoans that serve as food for many of the common nudibranchs, it is not unusual to find several species in a single pool. Look among the coralline algae and on the surface of the pool itself for nudibranchs crawling along upside down, using the surface tension created at the air-water interface as a foothold.

If there is any red sponge in the tidepool, look carefully for the camouflaged red sponge nudibranch, *Rostanga pulchra* (Color Plate 4a). *Rostanga* not only feeds on the red sponge, but also incorporates the sponge's pigment into its own body and that of its eggs that are attached to the sponge's surface. Look at the nudibranch photographed against a neutral surface (Color Plate 4b), and then try and find it on the host sponge (Color Plate 4a).

Sea Stars. Sea stars are seen in the low tidepools. The Pacific sea star, *Pisaster ochraceus,* the sea bat, *Asterina miniata,* the leather star, *Dermasterias imbricata,* and the sunflower star, *Pycnopodia helianthoides,* are all occasionally discovered here. *Pycnopodia* is a voracious feeder on purple sea urchins, and its mere presence in a low tidepool has been noted to cause the resident urchins to flee. Smaller species of sea stars more commonly seen in these pools include small blood stars, *Henricia leviuscula,* and six-rayed sea stars, *Leptasterias hexactis.* These two small stars often sport mottled colors that blend in with the coralline algae.

The other, urchin-dominated area of the reef, the low intertidal flat reef margin, is really somewhat different from the low tidepool, and might be considered a separate habitat. However, as this region receives considerable wave action and is exposed to air only at the lowest tides, it essentially supports a subset of the organisms described for the low tidepool.

Surge Channels

Physical Nature of the Surge Channel Environment. The last intertidal habitat to be described is the surge channel (Figure 7-34). Surge channels are formed by the differential weathering of the reef platform by the ocean. They are sometimes cut below the tidal level and thus never completely drain, even during the lowest tides. These submerged channels are typically at the very edge of the reef and support large stands of the oar weed kelp, *Laminaria* spp. (Figure 7-35), and other kelps on the bottom, and feather-boa kelp, *Egregia menziesii* (Figure 6-61), and wing kelp, *Alaria marginata* (Color Plate 3b) along the sides (Color Plate 3a).

Figure 7-34. Waves and a flooding tide enter the intertidal zone through a surge channel cut into an intertidal reef.

Figure 7-35. The strong, flexible stipes of the low intertidal kelp known as oar weed, Laminaria *sp., hold the exposed plants upright during a very low tide.*

Other surge channels extend well into the reef, in some cases reaching up into the mid-tidal level and above.

Besides tidal level, another variable in the surge channel habitat is orientation. Channels that extend directly into the reef, essentially perpendicular to the reef's edge, receive the direct force of the waves. Surge channels that turn to parallel the reef's edge are quieter and receive a somewhat less forceful flow of water. Finally, the shape of the surge channels must be considered. Channels with straight sides tend to harbor a more meager cast of organisms than do channels that have substantial undercutting and overhangs. Channels with dished-out bottoms tend to trap small boulders that bounce around and scour the walls, while channels with bottoms that slope continuously seaward are swept free of such material by wave action.

From this physical description, you can see that the surge channel habitat is a varied one. What you discover in a given channel depends on all the variables listed above and a number of others, including the time of year. One thing the beachcomber should remember about surge channels: They are high-energy environments. They require that organisms be able to attach and hold on against the movement of strong water currents. They are also food-rich environments in that the surging water contains many small organisms and organic materials swept from the reef and brought in from offshore. It is not surprising then that many surge channel animals are attached filter feeders that take advantage of this wave-borne bounty. A final note of caution: The same high energy that characterizes the surge channel can catch you off guard. Watch out for waves. These are fascinating areas to explore, and you are more often than not bent over or on your hands and knees. Have a lookout watch for incoming swells and unannounced surges of chilling seawater. Remember that the surge channels are the avenues through which the tide floods into the intertidal zone. Be alert.

Surge Channel Overhangs. The organisms occurring along the top of the surge channel walls reflect the general organismal association for the particular tidal height and exposure. Thus, some walls are relatively barren, others are cloaked in thick algal growth, and still others support the spill-over from a well-developed mussel clump. However, it is in the shade of deeply undercut or overhanging walls in the lowest intertidal

that the surge channel habitat reaches its zenith. (These strongly undercut niches are also found along the low intertidal, seaward edge of some semi-protected reefs.) When you first observe one of these well-developed, low intertidal surge channel overhangs, you will be taken by the variety of colors, shapes, and textures.

Because the overhang is in deep shade, only the heartiest encrusting coralline algae will occur, and these are in competition with a variety of space-monopolizing, encrusting animal forms. The top of the roof of the overhang typically harbors the proliferating sea anemone, *Epiactis prolifera,* and pale, individual aggregating anemones, *Anthopleura elegantissima.* To many observers, the oddest-appearing organism is the ostrich-plume hydroid, *Aglaophenia latirostris* (Figure 7-36), which hangs from the ceiling and sides of the overhang in feather-like colonies, up to three to four inches long. Look for the large (quarter-inch across) polyps of the hydroid *Tubularia* sp. also. Although this species is also a colony, the individual polyps are supported on stalks attached at their bases by rhizome-like connections. More delicate hydroids can be discovered commonly in the surge channel overhang, but are beyond the scope of this guide. The beachcomber is referred to more detailed sources [6, 7, 8].

Once you have identified a hydroid colony, take a close look at it to see an amazing inch-long or smaller crustacean known as a skeleton shrimp (Figure 7-37). These animals are highly modified amphipods, called

Figure 7-36. A colony of the ostrich-plume hydroid, Aglaophenia latirostris. *Each plume is two to three inches long and joined to the others by a common base.*

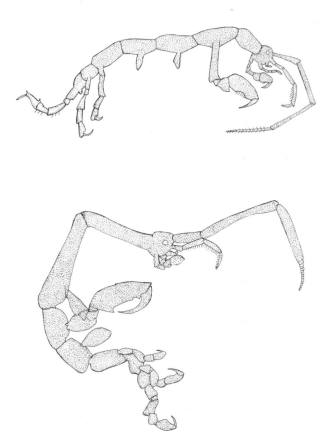

Figure 7-38. An eight-inch-square colony of the compound tunicate, Aplidium californicum, *commonly known as sea pork.*

Figure 7-37. *The amphipod crustaceans known as a skeleton shrimp,* Caprella *sp. Look for these animals wherever hydroids are found.*

Figure 7-39. Below: the Monterey sea squirt, Styela montereyensis. *Above: a related species,* Styela clava, *found in quiet water habitats.*

caprellid amphipods, and they co-occur with hydroids wherever you might find them. Compared to a more typical amphipod, caprellids have only a few appendages and use them to grasp the hydroid colony firmly and to reach out to catch passing zooplankton prey.

Sponges and Tunicates. The back wall of an overhang typically harbors several species of sponge growing in red, yellow, purple, brown, gray, and off-white sheets (Color Plates 4a and 6f). Sponges are discerned by their soft, pliable texture and the numerous tiny holes on their surface. Another group of encrusting animals typically found here are compound tunicates, with sea pork, *Aplidium californicum* (Figure 7-38), being one of the most common. Like the sponges, the compound tunicates are filter-feeding animals. However, they are much more highly organized than the sponges and are included in the same animal phylum (Phylum Chordata) as the backboned animals (vertebrates), which includes humans (see Chapter 3). Sea

pork occurs in soft, mushy sheets that are typically off-white to light yellow or pink in color. Compared to sponges, the outer texture of compound tunicates feels slicker to the touch.

You may find the Monterey tunicate, *Styela montereyensis* (Figure 7-39), hanging down from the roof of a surge channel overhang. *Styela* is classified as a solitary tunicate, which means it is a single individual and not a colony. It has a yellow to dark red-brown, woody tunic and two obvious siphons for filter feeding. *Styela* may reach ten inches in length, and although it frequently has hydroids or other marine organisms growing on its tunic when found in quiet habitats, it is clean here in the wave-swept surge channel. Look here also for clusters of the light-bulb tunicate, *Clavelina hunstmani* (Figure 7-40). As the common name implies, *Clavelina* has a clear tunic that allows the bright-white elements of the animal's filter basket to show through like the filament of a light bulb. The clusters of light-bulb tunicates are asexually produced clones. The two-inch-long tunicates are attached at their bases.

Scattered among the other encrusting animals, colonies of the rosy pink bryozoan, *Eurystomella bilabiata* (Figure 7-5), can be seen with their typical, basket-weave design. The solitary orange cup coral, *Balanophyllia elegans* (Color Plate 5a), is also common here, typically along the base of the back wall. Fan worms or feather-duster worms occur here. The most common is typically *Serpula vermicularis* (Color Plate 7b) with its white, calcareous tube sometimes partially concealed in the burrow left by a boring clam. Another large fan worm that can be found here is the beautiful

Figure 7-40. A colony of the light-bulb tunicate, Clavelina hunstmani. *Each sea squirt is connected to the colony via a common base.*

Eudistylia vancouveri (Color Plate 7c) which lives in a five-inch-long, parchment-like tube that hangs from the surge channel wall (Color Plate 7f). These large worms sometimes occur in large, round aggregations on exposed low intertidal rocks. I've seen them on Lighthouse Beach near Charleston, Oregon, on Beach #4 in Kalaloch, Washington, and at Tongue Point on the Strait of Juan de Fuca.

Surge Channel Floor. Animals on the bottom of the surge channel overhang include more sea pork, sponges, and patches of the colonial polychaete, *Dodecaceria fewkesi.* The giant green sea anemone, *Anthopleura xanthogrammica,* is frequently found on the bottom of surge channels. It waits here patiently for dislodged prey to be swept into its grasp. The principal food items for this anemone are sea mussels, *Mytilus californianus,* which are ripped loose from the clump by wave action. It must be a favorable feeding area for the anemone, and it reaches its largest intertidal size in the surge channels.

Occasionally, a large, rose-red anemone will be found in the surge channel. These are anemones in the genus *Urticina* (Color Plates 5b and 5c) discussed previously, and their colors are truly stunning.

Motile animals are also found in surge channels. Large cancer crabs, especially female *Cancer antennarius* brooding eggs, seek out cracks and crevices along the walls. Several echinoderms appear to use surge channels as avenues in and out of the intertidal zone and may be encountered here occasionally. The Pacific sea star, *Pisaster ochraceus,* and its more subtidal cousins, *Pisaster brevispinus* and *Pisaster giganteus,* show this movement pattern. The sunflower star, *Pycnopodia helianthoides,* and the leather star, *Dermasterias imbricata,* may also move in and out this way, as does *Solaster stimpsoni.* Six-rayed sea stars, *Leptasterias hexactis,* blood stars, *Henricia leviuscula,* and sea bats, *Asterina miniata,* appear to be more permanent residents. Occasionally, a very large (up to six inches in diameter) red to scarlet urchin is found in a surge channel. This is *Strongylocentrotus franciscanus* (Color Plate 15b), the purple urchin's subtidal relative, that sometimes is carried into the intertidal zone by strong wave action. Look for this large urchin in the very low intertidal of quiet-water areas as well. It is occasionally seen with the green urchin, *Strongylocentrotus droebachiensis* (Color Plate 15c) in Puget Sound and nearby inland waters.

Gastropods with tenacious grips occur in surge channels. *Tegula* spp., *Calliostoma annulatum, Ceratostoma foliatum,* and abalones, *Haliotis* spp., will be seen. Keyhole limpets will occur here occasionally, with the rough keyhole limpet, *Diodora aspera,* being the animal usually seen. Nudibranchs are seen here also. The sea lemon, *Anisodoris nobilis,* the ring-spotted dorid, *Diaulula sandiegensis,* and the red sponge nudibranch, *Rostanga pulchra,* are common species that occur. Chitons are sometimes seen in surge channels with the vividly colored lined chiton, *Tonicella lineata,* being the most common.

REFERENCES

1. Behrens, D. W., *Pacific Coast Nudibranchs.* Monterey: Sea Challengers, 1991, 107 pp.
2. McDonald, G. R. and J. W. Nybakken, *Guide to the Nudibranchs of California.* Milbourne: American Malacologists, 1980, 72 pp.
3. Jensen, G. C., *Pacific Coast Crabs and Shrimps.* Monterey: Sea Challengers, 1995, 87 pp.
4. Hart, J. F. L., *Crabs and Their Relatives of British Columbia.* British Columbia Provincial Museum Handbook No. 40, Victoria, 1982, 267 pp.
5. Gotshall, D. W., *Guide to Marine Invertebrates: Alaska to Baja California.* Monterey: Sea Challengers, 1994, 105 pp.
6. Morris, R. H., D. P. Abbott, and E. C. Haderlie, *Intertidal Invertebrates of California.* Stanford: Stanford University Press, 1980, 690 pp.
7. Kozloff, E. N., *Seashore Life of the Northern Pacific Coast.* Seattle: University of Washington Press, 1983, 370 pp.
8. Smith, R. I. and J. Carlton, *Light's Manual: Intertidal Invertebrates of the Central California Coast,* 3rd Ed. Berkeley: University of California Press, 1975, 716 pp.

8

MARINE MAMMALS OF THE PACIFIC NORTHWEST

Over the course of the year, more than 20 species of marine mammals occur off the coast of the Pacific Northwest. With luck, the beachcomber will probably only see a total of five or six. You may think it's pretty hard to miss a humpback whale, but even though they do occur in Pacific Northwest waters, they are normally found well offshore on the edge of the continental shelf [1]. In this chapter, I will introduce the most common marine mammals seen in the Pacific Northwest, and suggest where and when the beachcomber might find them.

Four very different groups of animals from the vertebrate class Mammalia have taken up life in the sea: (1) the order Cetacea—the whales—including the suborder Mysteceti (baleen or whalebone whales), and suborder Odontoceti (toothed whales); (2) the order Sirenia, including dugongs and manatees; and the order Carnivora, which includes (3) the suborder Pinnipedia, including walruses, seals, sea lions, and elephant seals, and (4) the sea otters in the family Mustelidae. As each of these groups adapted to the sea, they acquired a suite of similar adaptations. Their bodies became smooth and streamlined for ease of movement through the water, and the limbs became modified into flippers for swimming. All but the sea otters acquired a thick layer of fat or blubber for heat conservation and buoyancy.

In the United States, marine mammals are completely protected by the federal Marine Mammal Protection Act. It is illegal to take or possess any marine mammal or marine mammal part. Violation of this law carries a stiff penalty. The sea otters are further protected by the Endangered Species Act. In Canada, it is illegal to take, kill, molest, or be in the possession of an elephant seal, sea lion, sea otter, or killer whale without a permit [3]. Beachcombers should appreciate these animals in their wild state. If you come across a dead or injured marine mammal, don't intervene; instead, notify the appropriate state fish and game department and they'll take it from there.

THE SEA OTTER

Researchers believe the sea otter, *Enhydra lutris* (Figure 8-1) once occurred continuously along the West Coast from Alaska into Baja California. In the eighteenth and nineteenth centuries, American, Russian, French, and British fur traders eliminated the sea otter from the majority of its range. When a small colony was detected south of Monterey Bay off the Big Sur coast of California in 1938, people were caught by complete surprise as sea otters were thought to have been hunted to extinction everywhere on the West Coast except Alaska. From this original colony, the sea otter has multiplied and spread north and south along the California coast, and the annual aerial census conducted by the California Department of Fish and Game suggests the otter population has stabilized at between 1,500 and 2,000 animals.

No such remnant population remained in the otters' former range in Oregon, Washington, and British Columbia. In the early 1970s, the U.S. Fish and Wildlife Service (USFWS) transplanted several groups of otters from Alaska to the coasts of Oregon and Washington. Other groups of Alaskan otters were transplanted by Canada to the coast of British Columbia. The otter transplant was not successful in Oregon, but the Washington otter population did take hold and appears to be growing at the rate of 20 percent a year. The 1995 population estimate was approximately 350 animals. The otters are located along the Olympic Peninsula of northern Washington's open coast, mainly in the vicinity of Cape Alava, Cape Johnson, and Destruction Island [5].

The otters have not returned to Washington without controversy. As is their habit, the otters quickly remove

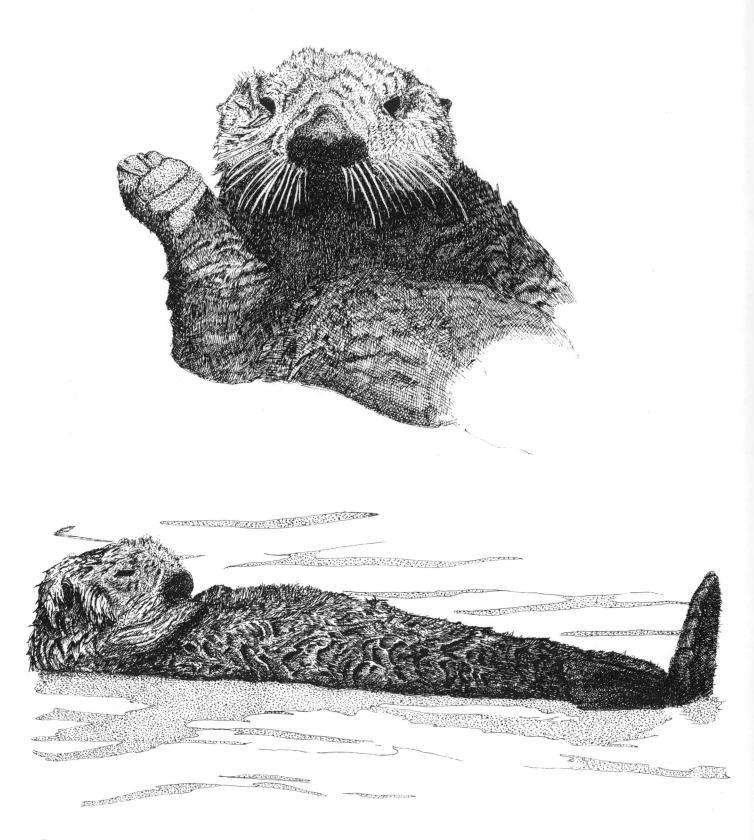

Figure 8-1. The sea otter, Enhydra lutris.

the large invertebrate prey, such as sea urchins, crabs, and shellfish, from an area and these are typically the same organisms sought by humans. As their numbers have increased, the otters have spread northward along the Olympic Peninsula. This northward spread of the otters' range places them in potential competition with the lucrative sea urchin fishery centered in Neah Bay and the Strait of Juan de Fuca.

The British Columbia otter population has reached approximately 650 animals and is also growing at a healthy rate of over 20 percent a year. They are found in the waters of Checleset Bay just north of Nootka Sound, and from Barkley Sound to Harvey Island [5].

Sea otters' closest relatives in the mammalian family Mustelidae are river otters. They are also related to badgers, wolverines, weasels, skunks, and minks. The male sea otter reaches five feet long including the tail, and can weigh upwards of 100 pounds. Females are smaller. The otter's large hind limbs are webbed and flipper-like, and along with their flat tail are used for swimming. Their forelimbs are short and stout, and their fingers stubby. However, otters are remarkable tool-users.

The sea otters' beautiful fur coat of fine, dense hair varies from reddish brown to black. Many older animals have silvery or white necks and faces. Because they lack a fat layer for insulation, the otter's coat is its only protection from the cold water. They spend much of their day grooming their fur, as it loses its insulating capacity when soiled. This is why otters are so vulnerable to oil spills. Otters will often roll vigorously in the water to trap air bubbles in their fur for added insulation.

Sea otters can still move on land, although they rarely come ashore. In the more northern part of their range, they do come ashore occasionally to dry their fur and to sleep. In the ocean, otters spend most of their time on their backs when on the surface. They swim, eat, rest, carry their young, and sleep on their backs. Otters feed by diving to the bottom and searching for food. Their most active feeding periods are early morning and late afternoon. They feed in kelp beds and on sandy bottoms.

Sea otters are notorious for their voracious appetites. The combination of a lack of a blubber layer for insulation and the cold Pacific water places a tremendous energy demand on them. A mature otter must eat an average of 25 percent of its body weight daily to maintain itself. It accomplishes this by eating the biggest, most energy-rich organisms it can catch. Abalones and sea urchins are the preferred prey when an otter first enters a kelp bed feeding area. The otter is known to use a rock to break the abalone's shell so it can be pulled off its rocky perch. Otters will also swim on their backs, cradling a rock on their chest that they use to crack open sea urchins. Otters will fairly quickly eliminate these large prey in a new feeding area. Along the open Washington coast where the otters occur, the only sea urchins you see underwater are in deep crevices, well out of the otter's reach. Many experts feel that the otter's fondness for sea urchins goes a long way toward maintaining the health and vigor of subtidal kelp beds. Sea urchins can reach high population densities and literally strip a kelp bed of vegetation, turning a lush vegetated environment into an "urchin barren." In the face of the otter's continued predation, sea urchins will be kept in check and the kelp can flourish.

Once established in an area, the otter's diet mainly includes large cancer crabs, shellfish, and whatever fish they can catch. Otters have been seen eating sea stars by biting off the tip of the arm and sucking out the innards. Sea cucumbers have also been noted as part of their diet along the Olympic Peninsula. In addition, sea otters are very effective foragers on sand bottoms, digging up clams and catching crabs.

The sea otter is truly a marine mammal. They mate in the water, and the female gives birth there as well. Female sea otters bear a pup about every one to two years between February and June. The female is a devoted mother, carrying her pup with her as she swims on the surface, and leaving it temporarily in the kelp as she dives after food. They are active during the day, and the normal behavior at night is to wrap themselves in the surface kelp canopy and sleep. The otters' chief natural predator appears to be the great white shark.

Viewing Sea Otters. The best places to see sea otters along the open Washington coast are Cape Alava, Point of Arches, seven miles to the north of Cape Alava, Cape Johnson, and Destruction Island. These waters are relatively protected with extensive kelp beds, and the otters are year-round residents. They sometimes ply the kelp beds immediately offshore, and can be viewed from some places along the shore with binoculars. Look for them during their active feeding periods in the early morning and late afternoon. Watch for sea gulls hovering over the kelp, waiting for the otters to surface so they can pick off the scraps of their meal.

Captive otters are featured at a number of marine aquaria in the Pacific Northwest including the Vancouver Public Aquarium, the Seattle Aquarium, and the Oregon Coastal Aquarium.

Friends of the Sea Otter. The concern for the sea otters' continued success and safety along the entire Pacific has led to the formation of a nonprofit citizens' group call the Friends of the Sea Otter. They provided me with the estimates for Pacific Northwest otter populations mentioned here. Beachcombers wishing for more information about these amazing mammals should contact this group at their Carmel, California, headquarters: Friends of the Sea Otter, P.O. Box 221220, Carmel, CA 93922; phone 408-625-3290.

A Note on River Otters. Although they may often be found in salt water, river otters are not classified as marine mammals and do not enjoy the protection of the Marine Mammal Protection Act [4]. River otters occur throughout the greater Puget Sound area, especially around the San Juan and Canadian Gulf Islands [4]. It is not unusual to encounter a river otter in salt water foraging around an island or nearby a river mouth. Here they feed on crabs, shrimps, fishes, and young seabirds [3]. Unlike sea otters, river otters spend a good deal of their time on land where they are much more nimble than their seagoing cousins. River otters are never far from a source of fresh water and always return to land to sleep. They also mate and raise their young on land.

River otters are smaller than sea otters, reaching about four feet in length with males weighing up to 30 pounds [3]. Sea otters are heavier bodied than river otters, their tail is shorter and flatter, their hind feet are webbed, and their cheek bristles (whiskers) are very long and mustache-like.

PINNIPEDS

The Latin term "pinniped" literally means "feather-foot," and is a reference to the seal and sea lions' flippers. Pinnipeds are thought to be most closely related to bears, and anyone who has gotten too close to a mature male Stellar sea lion can certainly attest to the similarity. There are two main types of pinnipeds: the family Phocidae and the family Otariidae [2]. Otariid pinnipeds are also known as the eared seals as they have visible earflaps on the sides of their heads. Otariids include the sea lions and the fur seals. These animals swim with their large fore flippers, and their rear

flippers can rotate under the body to support it on land. Otariids are quite agile on land and can move quite rapidly. The traditional "trained seal" of circus and marine animal parks is most likely a female California sea lion. In addition to the California sea lion, the Stellar sea lion is also commonly seen in the Pacific Northwest. A third otariid pinniped, the northern fur seal, occurs in the Pacific Northwest [5]. Female fur seals migrate south from their Bering Sea breeding grounds in the Pribilof Islands in the spring to feed; however, they remain offshore and will not be discussed in this guide.

Phocid pinnipeds lack a visible earflap, and have a simple ear opening on the sides of their heads. They swim by sculling with their rear flippers. They usually hold their fore flippers close to their bodies and use them to turn and maneuver in the water. The rear flippers point backward and cannot be rotated forward under the body to support the phocid on land. Their fore flippers are not positioned to hold the upper body erect. Consequently, these pinnipeds are much less adept at moving across open ground on land, and must scoot and bounce along on their bellies in inch-worm fashion. One phocid pinniped is common in the Pacific Northwest: the harbor or leopard seal. A second phocid, the northern elephant seal, is an occasional summer visitor to the coast of the Pacific Northwest.

Pinniped longevity varies among species, but in general, they live fairly long lives. California sea lions are known to live 15-plus years, and female Stellar sea lions can reach 30 years in age. In all the common pinniped species except the harbor seal, the males are larger and more aggressive than the females and tend to have shorter life spans.

The Harbor Seal

I'll start with the harbor or leopard seal, *Phoca vitulina* (Figure 8-2), as it is found year-round in the Pacific Northwest. The harbor seal is our smallest pinniped. Males may reach five to six feet in length and weigh up to 200 pounds. The females are somewhat smaller. The seals are silver-gray colored with dark brown to black spotting, which gives them the "leopard" common name. Some individuals are very dark, almost black, and the spots barely show through. Harbor seals have a broad geographic range. They are found from the Arctic to Baja California in the east Pacific, occur widely in the west Pacific, and are found on both sides of the

Figure 8-2. Four Pacific harbor seals, Phoca vitulina richardi, *hauled out on a middle intertidal rock. Note the rear-facing hind flippers and small fore flippers.*

Atlantic as well. Some experts recognize a unique subspecies, the Pacific harbor seal, *Phoca vitulina richardsi,* found only along the west coast of North America.

As the common name "harbor seal" implies, these animals can be found nearby humans. They haul out (come on shore to rest or sleep) on sand bars in river mouths and estuaries, and on rocky intertidal reefs at low tide. Harbor seals do not occur in large aggregations like the other pinnipeds. Usually six or a dozen at most will be seen, and occasionally up to 300 may gather on a large sand bar. The entire population of harbor seals in the eastern Pacific is estimated to be somewhere around 300,000 animals [3], with most living in Alaska. There is an estimated 5,000 harbor seals in Puget Sound year-round, with 2,000 in the San Juan Islands and 1,000 in Hood Canal [4].

On land, harbor seals are very skittish and will quickly return to the water when approached. However, in the water, they are often quite curious. Harbor seals float vertically with just their head above water. They don't dive to submerge like other pinnipeds; instead, they just sink and swim off horizontally. They also often swim with their head above water. It is not unusual to have a harbor seal follow you along a sandy beach, swimming at a safe distance. I have often had a curious harbor seal watch and follow my dog as we walk along the beach near our home. My most memorable experiences with harbor seals have occurred while SCUBA diving in Monterey Bay, California. Harbor seals frequently swim down and look over my shoulder while I work on the bottom. On a number of occasions, I have

also involuntarily "shared" fish I've speared for class with an aggressive harbor seal. The surprising thing about those encounters was I never felt threatened by the seal. It always seemed like a sporting proposition on both sides.

When they are not helping themselves to divers' catches, harbor seals catch their own fish, crabs, and cephalopods (squid and octopus) as their main diet. They eat primarily noncommercial fish species in shallow water, so they are generally not considered a nuisance by fishermen like some of their pinniped cousins.

Harbor seals mate promiscuously, that is, they don't form permanent pair bonds. They also don't come together in big mating aggregations and end up with a few males dominating the group like the other pinnipeds. Harbor seals give birth on land from May to July, and the pup is an adorable creature. The pups learn to swim fairly early, but initially are not strong enough swimmers to accompany their mother on feeding forays. The female will leave her pup unattended on a beach or rocky reef while she forages for food. This leads to an unfortunate scenario of concerned humans "rescuing" a supposedly abandoned pup from the beach. Meanwhile, the mother watches frantically from the water, too frightened to come ashore. LEAVE HARBOR SEAL PUPS ALONE. If they really appear in distress and no adult is in sight, or if they are entangled in something, call the state department of fish and game or the local animal shelter; don't attempt to take the pup in yourself.

Northern Elephant Seal

The second phocid seen in the Pacific Northwest is the northern elephant seal, *Mirounga angustirostris* (Figure 8-3). As can be seen from the illustration, this is not an animal you could cuddle up to. Males reach 16 feet in length and weigh up to 5,000 pounds. Females are considerably smaller, reaching over 9 feet and 2,000 pounds. The animals are brown to buff-colored when dry, and the sexes look very different. Females are very seal-like with big cow eyes, while the males always remind me of Jimmy Durante. Upon reaching sexual maturity at about 9 years of age, the male's snout becomes greatly enlarged into what is called a proboscis. The proboscis is inflatable, and serves as a resonating chamber for the male's deep-throated vocalizations made during mating season.

Figure 8-3. Male and female northern elephant seals, Mirounga angustirostris. *Note the male's large proboscis.*

Elephant seals are huge animals. They feed far out to sea and at incredible depths. Their prey includes squid and fish. Each year the adults reassemble on the rookery beach of their birth for the annual mating season. In California, the elephant seal rookery beaches are on the Farallon and Channel Islands, and at Ano Nuevo in southern San Mateo County. The males arrive first on the rookery in December and go through prolonged battles, both mock and real, to establish a hierarchy. As can be seen in the illustration, the bull elephant seal can raise his upper body upright. Bulls face each other and make slashing attacks to each other's chest area. They have an especially thick layer of skin in the chest and lower neck area, but it still can be a very bloody affair. The top males in the hierarchy are called beach-masters or alpha bulls. These animals don't defend specific territories like the sea lions, but instead position themselves on the rookery where the most females congregate.

Females do not arrive at the rookery all at once, but over a two- to three-month period. Shortly after their arrival, they give birth to a 60-pound pup. The female becomes sexually receptive a few days after her pup's birth and mates with the alpha bull. She will nurse the pup for four weeks. When she is through, the pup will weigh up to 300 or more pounds. After weaning her pup, the female leaves the rookery to return to the sea and replenish herself.

During the nonbreeding season, the elephant seals typically return to the rookery to go through an annual molt. They actually shed the outer thick layer of skin along with their hair, a process that takes three to four weeks. The males, females, and sexually immature animals come in to molt during different periods of the spring and summer.

Although their feeding forays will bring elephant seals into the deep waters of the passages in the Strait of Juan de Fuca and northern Puget Sound, it is the molting period when elephant seals can be seen by beachcombers in the Pacific Northwest. Male elephant seals who have traveled considerable distances from their rookery areas to feed are seen during the summer in the rocky intertidal zone of Cape Arago, Oregon, and on the beach along the Strait of Juan de Fuca where they come ashore to molt [4].

Viewing Elephant Seals. During the summer, elephant seals can be viewed by Oregon beachcombers from the Stimpson's Reef viewing area in Cape Arago State Park near Coos Bay. Stellar sea lions also use Stimpson's Reef as a rookery during the summer, as do a large contingent of harbor seals.

Elephant seals are a remarkable success story. Like the sea otters, they were hunted to near extinction by marine mammal hunters. Elephant seals were hunted for their oil, not their coarse, thick hides. In the early 1900s, they were reduced to an estimated population of fewer than a hundred animals on Guadalupe Island located off the west coast of Baja California [2, 6]. Once given protection by both the United States and Mexico, they have come back with a vengeance. They now number over 65,000 [4], and their population continues to grow. Beaches that are known to be the locations of historic rookeries are being reestablished on offshore islands and remote mainland California sites, and their appearance at Cape Arago and the Strait of Juan de Fuca in the 1990s is probably further evidence of their increasing numbers.

California Sea Lion

There is a beautiful place on the central California coast in Monterey County known as Point Lobos. Lobos means wolves in Spanish; however, the namesake wolves in question here were probably vocalizing California sea lions, *Zalophus californianus* (Figure 8-4). The barking of California sea lions is unforgettable once you've heard it. For many, these animals somehow characterize the happy-go-lucky, fun-loving image that

Figure 8-4. Two California sea lions, Zalophus californianus, *sun themselves. Note the wound in the flank of the upper animal.*

Californians are noted for. After watching them cavort around the rocks, body-surf choice waves, and steal salmon off anglers' hooks, it looks like the good life. However, it isn't all sun and siestas. Take a close look at the photograph of the sea lions. You'll notice an unmistakable wound on the right flank of the upper animal. This may have been caused by a large predatory shark or killer whale, or a dispute with a commercial fisherman. California sea lions live in an often hostile world.

The California sea lion is a seasonal visitor to the Pacific Northwest. Males migrate into the area during the winter months, while females remain south of the California-Oregon border. Mature males average seven feet or more in length. They usually weigh between 500 and 750 pounds, with an occasional 1,000-pounder observed. Adult males are readily distinguished by a thick neck and a pronounced ridge in the center of the head, called a saggital crest (Figure 8-5). The female lacks the crest and may reach six feet in length and 250 pounds. The animals appear black when wet, with the males drying to a dark brown and the females usually a lighter brown. The flippers are hairless and black in color.

In the Pacific Northwest, the California sea lion is found hauled out on the flat reefs of offshore islands, and at relatively inaccessible sites on the mainland including navigational buoys, mooring floats, barges, and occasional small vessels at anchor. Since 1979, California sea lions have become very common in the greater Puget Sound area. Nearly 1,000 animals have been seen at Port Gardner near Everett, Washington in recent winters [4].

During the late 1980s, a number of California sea lions found the pickings from the tourists so rich that they elected to hang around Monterey, California, at Fisherman's Wharf and the Coast Guard breakwater. Another batch has taken over Pier 39 in San Francisco, and driven the boat owners from their moorings. They have become quite a tourist attraction in California.

California sea lions are not quite as popular in the Pacific Northwest. In the Seattle area, several clever male sea lions have discovered large numbers of fish trapped at the entrance to the Lake Washington Ship Canal Locks [3, 4]. These fish include popular sport fish such as salmon and steelhead trout returning to run upriver and spawn. The sea lions feast on these fish, significantly reducing their number. Considerable effort has been made to deter the sea lions from this practice, including catching them and relocating them back to California. There was even an idea proposed of floating a giant fiberglass remote-controlled dummy of a killer whale in the waters around the locks. None of these attempts have been successful, and it may take more drastic measures to protect the migrating fish from these opportunistic Californians.

In the spring, male California sea lions move south to join the females on their chief California rookery sites on the San Miguel and San Nicholas Islands of the California Channel Island group. Similar to the elephant seals, a few dominant males monopolize the breeding that occurs from June through July. The female gives birth to a single pup and may nurse it for several months up to a year. After the breeding season, the males may travel as far north as British Columbia, with the females staying more to the south near the rookeries.

Pinnipeds are all very gregarious during their non-breeding seasons, and the beachcomber may encounter California sea lions mixed in with other pinniped species. In areas where they overlap, it is not unusual to find California sea lions hauled out together with Stellar sea lions and harbor seals.

Sea lions are exceptionally strong, graceful swimmers. With their long fore-flippers, they virtually fly through the water. When in a hurry, they sometimes "porpoise," leaping out of the water. They have been estimated to swim at speeds of up to 25 miles an hour. Sea lions can remained submerged for 10 to 15 minutes and have been known to dive to 800 feet. Sea lions eat

Figure 8-5. An adult male California sea lion readily distinguished by his thick neck and the pronounced ridge in the center of his head.

mainly fish and squid, and although they are known to take salmon and steelhead trout, most marine mammalogists believe their diet consists chiefly of noncommercial fish species.

Stellar Sea Lion

The Stellar sea lion, *Eumetopias jubatus* (Figure 8-6), is the largest of our eared seals. The males average nine-and-a-half feet in length and weigh up to 2,000 pounds. Females average six to seven feet and 600 pounds. Stellar sea lions are light yellowish in color, varying from almost cream color to yellowish brown, with black flippers. These animals are distinguished from the California sea lions by their larger size, lighter color, and the lack of the incessant, staccato-like bark of the California

sea lion. The male Stellar lacks the pronounced crest of the California, and has long, coarse hairs on his neck that resemble a mane. This mane, along with the Stellars' penchant for roaring at one another while defending territories on their breeding grounds, may be the sources for the common name "sea lion."

Stellar sea lions typically don't enter harbors or estuaries like the more adventuresome California sea lions. They are animals of the open coast, preferring offshore rocky reefs as haul-out sites. Stellar sea lions formerly bred in large numbers along the Oregon, Washington, and British Columbia coasts. Today, they are found in large numbers only off the coast of British Columbia. The most visible breeding rookeries are visible along the Oregon coast like that found at Stimpson's Reef at

Figure 8-6. Male and female Stellar sea lions, Eumetopias jubatus.

Cape Arago State Park in Oregon. You can also view Stellar sea lions at Sea Lion Caves, located a mile north of Heceta Head near Florence, Oregon. From 100 to 200 Stellars spend the winter in these caves, and during the summer, a number of male California sea lions can also be seen. An elevator carries people to viewing platforms in the cave, and there is an admission charge. Stellars can also be found at Sombroo Point and Race Rocks in the Strait of Juan de Fuca, in Plumer Sound in the Canadian Gulf Islands, and Sucia Sound in the San Juan Islands [4].

During the breeding season, the males begin to arrive in May. Like the California sea lions, an individual male may hold a harem of up to 30 or more cows, although it is usually smaller. The females arrive in June, give birth to a single pup, mate, and are gone by the late summer. Stellar sea lions head north after the breeding season. Males go to the rich feeding grounds in the Bering Sea.

Stellar sea lions once occurred commonly all along the coast from Alaska to California. However, the species has been in decline in the last two decades. The Alaska population was estimated at 140,000 in 1958, 68,000 in 1985 and 25,000 in 1989 [5]. In 1990, the Stellar sea lion was listed as a threatened species under the Endangered Species Act. One reason suggested for this animal's decline is the stiff competition they are facing for their once-plentiful food on their northern winter feeding grounds in the Bering Sea. Stellars feed mainly on fishes not used as food in the United States and Canada. However, foreign fishing fleets, in cooperation with the United States, have been taking wholesale amounts of these fish, especially the walleye pollack, and the loser appears to be the Stellar sea lion.

THE WHALES

Whales are divided into two categories: the baleen whales (suborder Mysticeti) and the toothed whales (suborder Odontoceti). The baleen whales lack teeth, and instead have horny, fibrous structures called baleen plates lining their upper jaws. These plates overlap one another and are smooth on their outer surface, while the fibrous bristles on the inner surface are frayed and cover the space between the plates. They feed by engulfing great quantities of water containing prey species. They force the water out between the plates with their enormous tongues, and trap their quarry on the frayed bristles on the inner side of the baleen plates. Prey varies from small fishes and squid in some species, to shrimp-like krill and other zooplankton. Baleen whales include the large, majestic whales like the blue and sei whales, the singing humpback whale, and the gray whale and minke whale that I will cover in this chapter.

Toothed whales include the sperm whale, killer whale, and the dolphins and porpoises, among others. As the name implies, these mammals have a jaw full of conical, pointed teeth. They feed by capturing fish and other large marine animals. On any given day on the water, a beachcomber may encounter Dall's porpoise, *Phocoenoides dalli*, a champion rider of the bow waves of ferries in the inland waterways of greater Puget Sound, or Pacific white-sided dolphins, *Lagenorhynchus obliquidens*, that often ride the bow wave of larger vessels offshore. I don't have room to cover all of these delightful animals, and recommend you consult the references at the end of the chapter [3, 4, 5] for more information. I will discuss only one toothed whale that has become somewhat of a symbol for the Pacific Northwest: the killer whale.

The Gray Whale

The most likely whale a beachcomber will see on the open coast of the Pacific Northwest is the gray whale. Gray whales undertake one of the longest annual migrations known for any mammal, a round-trip journey of over 13,000 miles. Each year, they move from their winter breeding grounds in the coastal lagoons of Baja California and mainland Mexico to their feeding grounds in the Bering Sea and north to the edge of the Arctic ice cap. During this northern migration from February to June, the gray whales remain close to shore, and are a frequent sight all along the open coast of the Pacific Northwest.

The gray whale, *Eschrichtius robustus* (Figure 8-7), is a medium-sized whale, ranging from 35 to 50 feet long and weighing up to 35 tons. The females tend to be slightly larger than the males for a given age. The animal is mottled gray with extensive white streaking, and has light-colored patches of barnacles all over its body, especially the back, head, and lower jaw. Gray whales lack a dorsal fin and instead have a midline ridge that extends from the head to a series of bumps or "knuckles" near the tail.

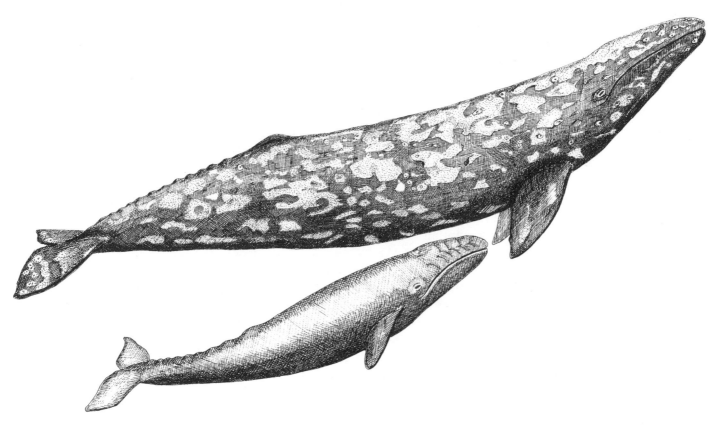

Figure 8-7. A female gray whale, Eschrichtius robustus, *and her calf.*

The life cycle of the gray whale is timed around the annual migration. Females give birth to a single calf in the warm breeding lagoons between December and April. The interval between calves is at least two years. The calf is born tail-first underwater and must surface to take its first breath. Gray whale calves are about 16 feet long at birth and weigh about a ton. The mother nurses them with a milk that is the richest known of any mammal, containing 40 percent fat and 40 percent protein with very little sugar. Females with calves don't begin their northern migration until late March, eight weeks after the rest of the pack. They are visible along the Pacific Northwest coast from April to July.

The gray whales spend from April to early November feeding in the Bering, Chukchi, and Beaufort Seas. The feeding of the gray whale is unique among all the baleen whales. On their northern feeding grounds, they eat almost entirely benthic amphipods that they obtain by stirring up the muddy bottom. They move their feeding northward as the ice pack melts in summer, and are driven southward as it reforms in the fall,

finally relenting and beginning their fall migration that lasts from October to January.

Gray whales don't migrate in large groups. As many as 20 have been sighted traveling together, but singles, duos, and trios are far more common. As the whales move along the coast, they can be observed jumping out of the water or breaching, or holding their heads vertically out of the water, a behavior known as "spyhopping." Some believe the whales spyhop to look for familiar coastal landmarks to guide them in their migration.

During the northern migration from late March to early April, gray whales can often be seen congregating near the mouths of rivers from northern California to Vancouver Island. It is believed that the whales are feeding on bottom organisms such as shellfish and burrowing mud shrimp during these periods. Gray whales are reported every year in the inner waters of Puget Sound and around Vancouver Island, apparently searching for shallow water rich in amphipods. They seem to prefer muddy bays and inlets to wide, open, deep channels. Some of these whales may remain the entire summer and do not undertake the trip to the Arctic. Individuals are known to have spent as long as four months in the inland waters of Washington and British Columbia, and up to three weeks in a single bay [5].

In addition to these seasonal visitors to the greater Puget Sound region, gray whales also occasionally come into coastal estuaries along their migration route. These whales usually stay a day or two and give the locals a thrill, and then swim back out to continue their journey. Often, these visitors are juveniles and it is not known if they are lost or just goofing off. Gray whales also frequently come into very shallow water along the open coast, especially near sandy beaches. Along the beaches, they are sometimes seen in the surf line, and researchers believe they may be attempting to scrape the barnacles off their skins.

Viewing Gray Whales. Most references suggest that the best time to view the gray whales in the Pacific Northwest is during their northern migration [5, 7]. While moving north, the whales swim at a more leisurely pace and tend to remain closer to shore than they do when they are returning south to breed. This is especially true for mothers with new calves that hug the surfline and edges of kelp beds. The northern migration also coincides with periods of more clement weather and calmer seas.

There are many shoreline sites in the Pacific Northwest where gray whales can be viewed quite successfully. The Oregon coast is replete with many capes and headlands, most all of which offer vantage points to watch gray whales pass at sea. The southern Washington coast is mostly low-lying terrain that does not lend itself to easy whale-watching. The northern Washington coast offers viewing access similar to Oregon. The Long Beach Unit of the Pacific Rim National Park is the place to view gray whales on Vancouver Island.

Unfortunately, I don't have room to list all the viewing sites by name. However, I can recommend the handy field guide to the gray whale prepared by the Oceanic Society [7] and offered by Sasquatch Books, 1008 Western Ave., Suite 300, Seattle, WA 98104. (phone 1-800-775-0817). This guide provides maps and directions to land and sea whale-watching sites from Alaska to Baja California as well as the best time to visit them. See also reference [8].

Beachcombers may wish to take advantage of whole- and half-day whale-watching cruises that are becoming widely available out of coastal ports throughout the Pacific Northwest. These can be hard on people prone to seasickness or very small children, so be mindful of the ocean conditions before such a venture. Sasquatch Books offers a generous service to anyone interested in whale-watching tours. Send a stamped, self-addressed envelope, and they will mail you a list of whale-watching tour and excursion operators, including addresses and phone numbers.

A final word on gray whales. They join the sea otters and elephant seals on the list of marine mammal survivors. There were once populations of gray whales in the Atlantic and in the west Pacific. These were hunted to extinction. The east Pacific population was likewise in trouble when the gray whales were protected by international treaty in 1946. Since then, the gray whale has bounced back, and is now estimated at a population size of about 15,000–20,000 [1, 5, 7]. In fact, the gray whale's recovery has been so solid that it was removed from the endangered species list in 1993. Gray whales are still taken for food in small numbers on their northern feeding grounds by indigenous tribes. However, their chief predator is thought to be the killer whale, especially on young whales during the migration.

The Minke Whale

A second baleen whale that occurs fairly commonly in the Pacific Northwest is the minke whale, *Balaenoptera acutorostrata* (Figure 8-8). Minke whales are small members of the rorqual whale group that includes the humpback and blue whales. Rorqual whales are distinguished from other baleen whales by the presence of expandable throat grooves that enable them to swallow large volumes of water. The grooves are collapsed and the water is forced out over the baleen plates which collect the small bait fish that are their main diet.

Minkes reach up to 30 feet in length and weigh from 6 to 10 tons. They appear regularly in the summer in the San Juan Islands and Canadian Gulf Islands, in northern Puget Sound, and off northern Vancouver Island [3]. They are also common in the summer a few miles offshore all along the open Pacific Northwest coast [1]. Little is known about their whereabouts the rest of the year.

Minkes are curious whales and will sometimes approach a boat within 20–30 yards. However, after one quick look, the minke will return to feeding, so the whale-watcher must be patient to catch a glimpse.

Figure 8-8. The minke whale, Balaenoptera acutorostrata.

Minkes are also very fast swimmers, able to maintain sustained speeds of 30 knots an hour. It is thought that they can outswim killer whales over long distances. Minkes apparently aren't bothered by killer whales in greater Puget Sound waters [5].

Researchers have been studying minke whales in the vicinity of the San Juan Islands for several years and have garnered some interesting insights into this whale's behavior. Individual whales show preference for both feeding location and method of feeding. Some minkes feed below the surface, while others lunge or breach out of the water scooping up prey. The most spectacular feeders are whales that use flocks of seabirds on the water as indicators of their favorite prey, herring. The birds feed on the herring by corralling them into a tight ball, and suddenly a minke will come up right in the middle of the school of fish, sending the birds scattering.

Minke whales have not had an easy time of it. Once the stocks of the great whales were depleted, whalers turned to the smaller, more numerous minkes, and their populations were severely reduced. Although now protected by the International Whaling Commission, a fairly large number of minke whales are still taken for "scientific" purposes by Japan and Norway. These "scientific" purposes are little more than a flimsy ruse to slaughter whales for human consumption.

The Killer Whale

There is no mistaking the killer whale, *Orcinas orca* (Figure 8-9), for any other marine mammal. Its striking

Figure 8-9. Two killer whales, Orcinas orca. *Note the large dorsal fin of the male in the foreground.*

black and white coloration, large, rounded flippers, and tall dorsal fin make it easily recognizable even far offshore. Once feared and loathed for their predatory activities, the performing orcas of marine theme parks have significantly changed the public's perception of these magnificent animals.

Mature male orcas may reach 30 feet long and weigh 8 tons or more. Females are smaller, reaching 23 feet and 4 tons. Killer whales have a small white patch immediately above and just behind the eye, and a large white ventral (bottom) patch that extends from their chins to their tails and extends up on either side of their rear flanks. They also have a gray saddle just behind the dorsal fin, and the pattern of this saddle is unique for each killer whale.

The dorsal fin of the female and immature males is curved (falcate). At sexual maturity, the male dorsal fin becomes steeply triangular, reaching six feet in height. The shape, pigmentation, and scarring of the dorsal fins and tail flukes are often unique. These characteristics, along with the distinctive saddle patch, have allowed researchers to identify and trace individuals over many years. The resident killer whale population in British Columbia and Washington waters numbers about 250 animals and is one of the most numerous in the world. Researchers have identified and named all of these whales and have studied their social structure and movements. In addition, modern genetic testing techniques have allowed scientists to trace the pedigrees of these whales and construct family trees that reach back several generations. What they have determined is truly remarkable.

In British Columbia and Washington waters, researchers recognize distinct northern and southern communities of resident killer whales, each of which has its own unique home range. The dividing line between the home ranges of the two communities is the tidal line near the mouth of the Campbell River in British Columbia, and the communities rarely cross over this line. Each community consists of several smaller groups called pods. A pod is basically an extended family of whales that numbers from a few to 50 animals. Each pod is divided into several subpods which are further separable into individual maternal lineages.

Killer whales don't leave their mothers. Sons and daughters congregate around their mothers when the pod sleeps. A female will seldom stray farther than a few hundred yards from her mother until her mid-teens when she has young herself. Females give birth to a 7-foot, 400-pound infant after a gestation period of 17 months. She will give birth at four to six-year intervals, and may have a total of four to six offspring in her lifetime. Females have an average life expectancy of 50 years, and a maximum longevity of 80 to 90 years. A female may live up to 20 years after she ceases giving birth. These older females take on roles similar to human grandmothers in their pods. Males have a much higher mortality rate in the wild [9], and their average life expectancy is about 30 years with a maximum longevity of 50 to 60 years.

Killer whales maintain their cohesive subpod structure and move, hunt, and play as a group. Whale researchers have identified a dialect of calls, shrieks, and whistles that is unique for each pod. They have also determined that each pod has a fairly well-defined feeding area as well as a predictable pattern of seasonal movement. Basically, these resident pods are following the seasonal runs of their main prey, salmon. In the summer months, resident pods come inshore to feed on the salmon that congregate in narrow coastal passages of Washington, British Columbia, and Alaska. Other prey of the resident orcas include herring, smelt, halibut, and rockfish.

The coordinated and independent behavior of the pods and the failure of the males to leave their mothers poses a potential problem for the resident killer whales. They run the risk of becoming too inbred and genetically weakened. Scientists believe this risk may be overcome by an annual "greeting ceremony" they have observed in the southern killer whale community. During late summer and early autumn, all the pods of the southern community gather and the adult whales are sexually active within and between pods. This may allow for mating to occur between pods and provide sufficient genetic mixing to keep the community healthy.

Besides the resident orca pods, other pods have been identified in the Pacific Northwest. These pods are known to be more nomadic and are referred to as "transients." Transient pods feed primarily on other marine mammals, including seals, sea lions, dolphins, and even the largest of all animals, the blue whale. These transient pods will move through the home ranges of the resident killer whale communities, but will have little or no contact with them. A transient pod does not have a unique dialect of calls, but instead shares a common dialect with the other transient pods from Alaska to Monterey Bay, California. This common dialect is much less sophisticated than those of the resident pods, consisting of four to seven calls, compared to up to fifteen call dialects known for resident pods. It is not unusual for transient pods to travel great distances, with some tracked over 900 miles of coastline. Killer whales have been reported from all seas at all latitudes, and these reports are most likely sightings of these nomadic transient pods [5].

Many whale biologists now believe that the resident and transient pods represent two unique races of killer whales. There are notable morphological differences between the two groups. The dorsal fin of the adult transient male is more sharply pointed compared to the more rounded dorsal fin of the resident adult male. Also, the pattern of the gray saddle on the backs of the two groups is distinctly different. Furthermore, DNA fingerprinting results reveal the two groups to be widely separated genetically. One estimate suggests the transient and resident groups have not interbred in the past 100,000 years.

It is the feeding behavior of the transient pods that has given the orca its image of a relentless killer. When attacking larger prey like gray whales, the transient killer whales have been observed to herd and attack their quarry in a very deliberate, coordinated fashion. They often take only the tongue of these large whales, leaving the rest for sharks. There is virtually no large marine organism that is safe from the killer whale.

Seasonal movements of transient pods seem to be tied to ice conditions in polar areas and the availability of food in other areas. One of the favorite haunts of these transient pods is the seasonally occupied rookery of pinnipeds. They are also seen near feeding areas or haul-out areas of pinnipeds, like the mouths of rivers or estuaries. Beachcombers wishing to view these transient killer whale pods should watch the local newspapers and news telecasts for reports of sightings. Usually, the pod will remain in an area for some time before moving on to the next food source

Viewing Killer Whales. The American Cetacean Society compares watching orcas from shore to watching sea gulls as they fly by the porthole of a boat [9]. Unless you happen to be looking just when the gull flies by, you could spend a lot of time staring out to sea. They recommend confining orca viewing efforts to a few special locations a few months of the year. The whales tend to stay closer to the shore in the summer and fall when the sea is calm and the hunting is best. They recommend Robson Bight, an outcropping of land jutting into Johnstone Strait in British Columbia. Another recommended site is Lime Kiln State Park on San Juan Island. Whale-watchers should dress warmly like beachcombers and be prepared for inclement weather. A good pair of binoculars or a spotting scope are required for any serious whale-watcher, as is the most essential quality, patience.

Another option is to look for orcas by boat. During the summer and early fall, whale-watching tours are available from a number of locations throughout the Pacific Northwest. Often, these tours are advertised as more generic "whale-watching" tours, but if an orca pod is nearby you can bet the skipper will take full advantage of it.

A note of caution for those striking out in their own boat on a whale-watching expedition. Despite their size and speed, whales are easily disturbed by boaters who come too close. There are very distinct guidelines in the Marine Mammal Protection Act that cover how a marine mammal is to be approached at sea. Failure to observe these guidelines carries a stiff fine, a prison term, or both.

The public's interest in killer whales has greatly increased with the popularity of the *Free Willy* movies.

The progress of Keiko (aka "Willy") the killer whale, currently undergoing rehabilitation at the Oregon Coastal Aquarium, is being documented by the Discovery Channel. If you wish more detail on the biology and behavior of these animals, there are several excellent references available [10, 11, 12].

REFERENCES

1. Leatherwood, S. and R. R. Reeves, *The Sierra Club Handbook of Whales and Dolphins.* San Francisco: Sierra Club Books, 1983, 302 pp.
2. Riedman, M., *The Pinnipeds, Seals, Sea Lions, and Walruses.* Berkeley: University of California Press, 1990, 439 pp.
3. Yates, S., *Marine Wildlife of Puget Sound, the San Juans, and the Strait of Georgia.* Chester: Globe Pequot Press, 1988, 262 pp.
4. Osbourne, R., J. Calambokidis, and E. M. Dorsey, *A Guide to Marine Mammals of Greater Puget Sound: A Naturalist's Field Guide.* Anacortes: Island Publications, 1988, 191 pp.
5. Flaherty, C. 1990, *Whales of the Northwest* (also includes pinnipeds). Seattle: Cherry Lane Press, 1990, 25 pp.
6. Orr, R. T., and R. C. Helm, *Marine Mammals of California.* Berkeley: University of California Press, 1989, 92 pp.
7. Anon., *The Oceanic Society Field Guide to the Gray Whale.* Seattle: Sasquatch Books, 1989, 50 pp.
8. Kreitman, R. C. and M. J. Schramm, *West Coast Whale Watching: The Complete Guide to Observing Marine Mammals.* HarperCollins West, 1995.
9. Gordan, D. G. and C. Flaherty, *American Cetacean Society Field Guide to the Orca.* Seattle: Sasquatch Books, 1990, 40 pp.
10. Bigg, M. A., et al., *Killer Whales: A Study of Their Identification, Genealogy, and Natural History in British Columbia and Washington State.* Nanaimo, B.C.: Phantom Press. 1987.
11. Gormley, G., *Orcas of the Gulf: A Natural History.* San Francisco: Sierra Club Books, 1990.
12. Ford, J. K. B., G. M. Ellis, and K. C. Balcomb, *Killer Whales.* Seattle: University of Washington Press, 1995.

9
DUNGENESS CRAB AND PACIFIC SALMON

Although this chapter heading reads like the main entrees at a seafood restaurant, it has a more serious purpose. Dungeness crab and Pacific salmon are the first thing most gourmets think of when the Pacific Northwest is mentioned. This widespread familiarity illustrates just how important these marine organisms are and have been to the economy and history of the Pacific Northwest.

Beachcombers may occasionally find Dungeness crabs in their explorations, and maybe won't see salmon at all. However, the life histories and welfare of these animals are intimately connected to many of the habitats the beachcomber will visit, and some information about them is considered essential. In this chapter, the biology of the Dungeness crab and Pacific salmon will be briefly introduced.

THE DUNGENESS CRAB

The Dungeness crab, *Cancer magister* (Figure 9-1), was first introduced in Chapter 4 as an animal often found on open beaches in the late winter. The crabs really aren't on the beach, but the molted outer skeleton (exoskeleton or "molt") of large male crabs are.

In the late winter, male Dungeness crabs molt offshore in close temporal synchrony in preparation for the spring and summer breeding season. They can be so abundant in some years that large windrows of cast male exoskeletons pile up on sandy beaches (Color Plate 13b). Because the crab molts its entire outer covering intact, a freshly molted exoskeleton can easily be mistaken for a live animal.

After the adult males molt and their new exoskeletons harden, they have love on their minds. The adult females do not molt all at the same time like the males, but instead spread their molting over the late spring and summer.

Like all true crabs, Dungeness crabs have internal fertilization. The male inserts specially modified abdominal appendages into the female's reproductive openings and transfers his sperm to the female. For this transfer to be successful, female Dungeness crabs must be recently molted (soft-shelled). Biologists believe that females advertise the fact that they are about to molt by releasing a special scent in their urine. A male, attracted by the scent, will grasp the female (Color Plate 13c), and hang onto her until she molts her old exoskeleton and the new one hardens sufficiently so she can be successfully mated. Once the male fertilizes the female, he continues to stay with her until her exoskeleton becomes firm enough to protect her from danger.

The female will carry the sperm internally for several months. She sets her fertilized eggs in the late fall or early winter and carries them attached to her abdomen over winter. By late winter or early spring, the embryos have developed and break through the egg membrane to enter the plankton. In the plankton, they go through

Figure 9-1. Male Dungeness crab, Cancer magister.

a series of progressive molts, growing and becoming more crab-like.

After about four months of feeding and growing in the plankton, the crab larvae finally reach a settling stage, sink, molt into recognizable crabs, and take up existence as bottom dwellers. At this point, the new crabs are about a quarter of an inch wide. They grow and molt frequently when young, up to ten times in their first year.

The juvenile Dungeness crabs (Color Plate 13d) seek out the protection of estuaries. They will move well up into an estuary where the salinity is low to avoid marine predators. As the crabs approach sexual maturity at three years of age, they move down the estuary and off-shore where the adults live on sandy bottoms. The males reach market size at about four years old.

The annual Dungeness crab population fluctuates dramatically. In especially good years, the late-stage larvae can be seen in the surface water of estuaries, buzzing around like a swarm of mad bees. The newly settled young turn up everywhere—on floats, in tide-pools, and under virtually every rock. Larger juveniles may be found in sandy-bottomed tidepools in the rocky intertidal zone. Be on the lookout for them during your summer beachcombing.

SALMON AND TROUT OF THE PACIFIC NORTHWEST

Although I found an adult coho salmon trapped in a tidepool once, the average beachcomber is not likely to encounter any of the salmonids (members of the family Salmonidae, the salmon and trout) on a foray into the marine rocky intertidal zone. (No, I didn't eat it, I caught it and released it into deep water.) However, exploration of flooded salt marsh and eelgrass bed habitats in estuaries and coastal embayments may reveal young salmonids sheltering and feeding, and beachcombers will surely be interested in the possibility of observing spawning salmonids in coastal streams and rivers. More about that in a while.

Salmonids are anadromous fishes. This means they spend time in both fresh and salt water, but return to fresh water to spawn. The typical life cycle begins (Figure 9-2) with the young fish hatching from nests excavated by the female in the gravel bottom of a stream or river. After hatching, the young salmon still have an external yolk sac and are called "alevin." The yolk sac is absorbed, and the young salmon, now known as

"parrs," are carried downstream into an estuary. Here they will spend some time feeding, growing, and gradually adjusting their physiology to live in salt water, a process known as smoltification. The juvenile salmon undergoing this adjustment in physiology are referred to as "smolts." Finally, the juvenile salmon leave the estuary and enter the ocean.

Salmon may stay at sea from one to four years, feeding off the rich oceanic pasture and attaining sexual maturity. They may range into the North Pacific a thousand or more miles from their home stream. The salmon finally begin a migration that will bring them to the estuary and back upstream to spawn at the site where they were hatched. How they are able to find their way back home is still not entirely understood. Scientists believe the salmon employ a number of cues to guide them in their journey, including the earth's magnetic field and the unique chemical makeup of the home stream which they are able to discern with their acute sense of smell.

Adult salmon stop eating after they reenter fresh water. Their entire upstream migration and spawning are fueled by energy stored in their tissues. The rich red muscle most of us associate with salmon turns pink or white. Their sea-run coloration is replaced by brilliant mating colors in many species. The snout of the male may become grotesquely hooked, and a large hump may form on its back. As the salmons' energy is depleted, their colors dim and their skin is often marred by blotchy white fungal infections. Yet they persist until every last calorie of energy in their bodies is expended, and their mission of procreation is completed.

Once the salmon arrive on the spawning grounds, the females select choice areas of gravel. Here she may dig a number of nests and deposit her eggs in them over a several-day period. These nesting territories are called "redds," and the females defend them from other females. Using their tails, the females excavate nest depressions in the gravel. The female's digging behavior attracts males who battle one another for access to the female. A victorious male courts the female, and they both hover over the nest depression she prepared and release their sperm and eggs. The female then moves just upstream of the nest and dislodges more gravel which falls into the nest, burying the fertilized eggs. The female repeats this process until she has spawned all her eggs, and then defends her redd until she dies. Males may court several females until they also exhaust themselves and die. Superim-

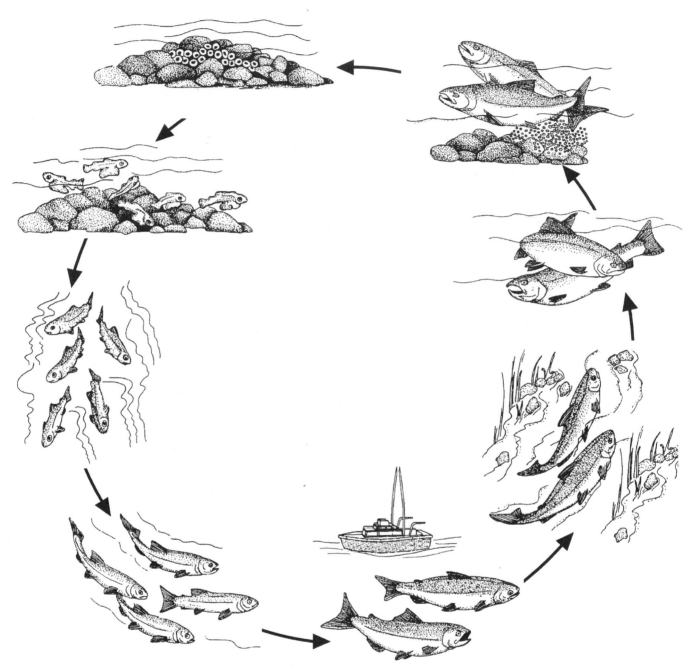

Figure 9-2. Generalized life cycle of salmonid fishes of the Pacific Northwest. Counter-clockwise from top: fertilized eggs develop in nest; alevin emerge from nest: young salmon move downstream; juveniles (smolts) adapt to salt water in estuary; young adults go to sea; mature adults begin spawning migration upstream; courtship; spawning.

posed on this generalized life cycle (Figure 9-2) are complex, species-specific patterns of behavior [1], which will be briefly discussed.

The fishes in the salmonid group include two trout species that have races that never leave fresh water as well as races that are commonly referred to as "sea run," meaning they spend part of their life cycle in the ocean. The two species are sea run rainbow trout known as steelhead, *Oncorhynchus mykiss*, and the sea run cutthroat trout, *Oncorhynchus clarkiii*.

Steelhead (Figure 9-3) have a metallic steel blue-black color on their back, silver along the sides, and

Figure 9-3. Common salmonids of the Pacific Northwest. From the top: chinook, coho, steelhead, and cutthroat trout.

Figure 9-4. Comparative sizes of salmonids of the Pacific Northwest. Smallest to largest: cutthroat trout, steelhead, coho, chinook.

round black spots on their back and tail. Males sport a pink to red band along their sides during spawning. They grow to 45 inches in length and can reach over 40 pounds in weight, with the average fish being 24 inches long and weighing 5–10 pounds (Figure 9-4). Steelhead are a highly favored sport fish and have been extensively cultivated in hatcheries to meet the sport demand. Steelhead spend from one to four years in fresh water and from one to four years in the ocean. Oregon and Washington steelhead average two years in each habitat [2]. Juvenile steelhead behave like resident trout, feeding on insects and fish. When they enter the ocean, they travel far out into the north Pacific. Unlike the salmon species which die after reproducing, steelhead can survive spawning and some may spawn two or three times. There are both winter and summer runs of steelhead entering coastal streams and rivers, and both runs spawn in spring, between February and June.

The cutthroat trout, *Oncorhynchus clarkiii* (Figure 9-3), receives its name from a vivid pink to red slash of color along its lower jaw. They are greenish-blue on the back, silver on the sides and belly, and speckled with

fine black dots on the head, back, sides, and tail. Sea run cutthroats may reach 25 inches in length and weigh 1–5 pounds. They spend from one to four years in fresh water and one year in seawater. In the ocean they stay close to shore and roam the edges of estuaries where they feed on small fishes. They are common in streams in the fall where they appear to follow other salmon to feed on dislodged eggs. Sea run cutthroats spawn from December through May, and like the steelhead, they are capable of spawning more than once [2].

There are five species of salmon in the Pacific Northwest. The chinook, *Oncorhynchus tshawttscha,* and the coho, *Oncorhynchus kisutch,* are considered to be the more primitive salmon species [2] and are the most popular sport fishes. The remaining three species are the sockeye, *Oncorhynchus nerka,* the pink, *Oncorhynchus gorbuscha,* and the chum, *Oncorhynchus keta.* These latter three species are the most numerous of the salmon, and constitute the majority of salmon taken by the commercial salmon fishery. These three species have more precise life cycles, tend to school more tightly, and follow a similar migration route once they enter the Pacific Ocean.

The largest and least abundant salmon of the Pacific Northwest is the chinook, *Oncorhynchus tshawttscha* (Figure 9-3). Chinooks are also known as king or spring salmon; fish over 30 pounds are known as "tyees." Chinooks grow to 58 inches long (Figure 9-4) and the unofficial weight record is 135 pounds [2]. The average fish weighs 15–25 pounds. In the sea, chinooks are greenish-blue to bronze on the back with numerous large irregular spots on their backs, upper sides, and the entire tail. They have black gums. When they return to fresh water, they become black with red blotches on their sides, and males may develop hooked snouts [3]. There are two types of chinooks, the stream type and the ocean type [2]. The stream type lives from one to four years in fresh water, goes to sea for two to four years, and then returns to fresh water several months before spawning. The ocean type leaves fresh water in its first year, spends two to four years relatively close to the coast, and returns to fresh water a few days or weeks before spawning. Often, male chinooks that remain close to their home streams will enter fresh water to attempt to spawn before fully mature; these are called "jacks." There is a major sport fishery in Puget Sound for winter blackmouths, a race of chinooks that appears to never leave the Sound [2].

Chinooks spawn from May through January, most often in large streams or rivers. Many chinook stocks travel far inland to spawn. These are the mighty salmon typically depicted scaling waterfalls with great leaps (they can jump 10 feet out of the water), and are the most vulnerable to hydroelectric dams that block access to the spawning habitat.

The coho salmon, *Oncorhynchus kisutch* (Figure 9-3), is also known as the silver salmon. It is the second least abundant salmon in the Pacific Northwest. At sea, cohos have a metallic green or blue back with silver sides and belly. They have black spots on the back and upper lobe of the tail, and white gums. In fresh water, the migrating adults turn dark green on the back and bright red on the sides. Mature males become deep red in color with a noticeably hooked snout. Cohos reach 38 inches in length (Figure 9-4) and average 6–12 pounds, with an unofficial record of 31 pounds [2]. Most cohos spend from one to two years in fresh water feeding on insects, and one to two years at sea where they may range one thousand miles from their home stream. They migrate back into fresh water between August and December and spawn between November and January. There is a race of coho known as "blue-backs" that never leaves the Strait of Georgia.

Chum, pink, and sockeye salmon are considered more advanced because of their greater specialization to oceanic life [1, 2]. These species are not typically caught by sport fishermen, but constitute the bulk of the commercial salmon catch. They have their main distribution from the Columbia River north, with many of the stocks found in Alaska. They are treated less extensively here.

Sockeye salmon, *Oncorhynchus nerka,* are the third most abundant of the Pacific Northwest salmon. Their backs are greenish blue with fine black speckles, with silver on the sides. Spawning adults develop dull green

heads with bright red bodies [3]. They grow to 33 inches in length and typically weigh 3–8 pounds. Sockeyes are unique in that they have adapted to lake environments where they show schooling behavior and feed on plankton. Juveniles may spend from one to three years in a lake, followed by one to four years in the ocean. Their migration back to fresh water begins in July, and they spawn from August through November [2]. Most sockeye stocks spawn in streams or rivers, although some use lakes. Some stocks have become landlocked and spend their whole life in fresh water. These landlocked sockeyes are known as "kokanees."

Chum salmon, *Oncorhynchus keta,* are the second most abundant salmon species in the Pacific Northwest. Chum salmon are metallic blue to blotchy purple on the back with no spots on the tail. They have yellow and pink streaks on the sides when spawning. They grow to 40 inches in length and weigh 9 pounds on average, with an unofficial record of over 33 pounds [2]. Chum salmon usually migrate downstream immediately after hatching, and spend three years at sea. They return to fresh water between July and December, and typically spawn in small coastal streams, close to seawater.

Pink salmon, *Oncorhynchus gorbuscha,* are the most abundant salmon species in the eastern Pacific. They are blue on the back, silver on the side, and have large oval black spots on the tail and back. During spawning, pink salmon are dark olive green on their backs. Mature males have irregular splotches of yellow and sometimes red on their sides. Pink salmon reach 30 inches in length and weigh 3–5 pounds [2, 3]. The life cycle of the pink salmon involves the least dependence on fresh water of all the salmonid species. The young salmon move quickly out of fresh water soon after hatching. They spend their first summer and winter relatively close to shore and migrate back to fresh water in their second summer. Pink salmon have precise two-year life cycles; pink stocks in Washington spawn in odd calendar years, while most stocks in Alaska spawn in even years.

These seven species of closely related salmonid fishes have evolved in the dynamic aquatic environment of the Pacific Northwest. Each species is made up of many separate stocks that are separated both physically and genetically. This separation occurs for two reasons. First, salmonids have an uncanny ability to return to the fresh water site of their birth to spawn, meaning all the members of a given stock spawn at the same time in the same place. Secondly, most of the many watersheds of the Pacific Northwest are unconnected. This physical separation and corresponding genetic isolation of the stocks has most likely allowed salmonids to fine-tune their life cycles to match the unique and changeable characteristics of their home waters. Furthermore, more than one species may share the same spawning habitat, separated by season. In fact, some watersheds have separate seasonal runs of the same species.

This same adaptive ability of salmonid species that has allowed them to be so successful over evolutionary time has made them vulnerable to living with human beings who have the capacity to disrupt or modify aquatic habitats abruptly. Logging practices modify streams, lumber and paper pulp mills pollute rivers and estuaries, and the erection of hydroelectric dams eliminates or seriously interferes with upstream migration. Thus, many of the traditional salmonid stocks have been lost or severely depleted along with their store of genetic variability. At one time, 10 million adult salmon returned to the Columbia River basin alone. Now, less than 10 percent of that number return to all the streams in the Pacific Northwest [4]. Chinook salmon, which migrate the greatest distances upstream to spawn, have been particularly vulnerable, and the depletion of the species has led the United States and Canada to enter into a long-term plan to close fisheries and attempt to revive the species.

Simply closing the fishery for a season or two, however, is not the answer. The management of salmon in the Pacific Northwest has relied heavily on replacing and/or supplementing endangered native stocks with hatchery-reared fish. Unfortunately, the hatcheries have traditionally focused on the short-term goal of providing more fish to catch without addressing the loss of genetic variability that keeps the species healthy over the long term. The young salmon reared by the hatcheries come from a limited number of spawning fish that return to the hatchery. This means that large numbers of fish of limited genetic variability are being released into streams to compete with native fish stocks. The result is a continued weakening of the native stocks along with a loss of their unique genetic properties.

In a report produced in 1995 by the National Research Council entitled "Upstream: Salmon and Society in the Pacific Northwest" [4], the depletion of wild salmon stocks is reviewed in great depth. The ultimate solutions recommended are far-reaching and sobering. The salmon of the Pacific Northwest are going to be saved only by a concerted joint effort of everyone that shares the aquatic habitat with the salmon. This includes the state and provincial fish and game departments, cities, industry, logging companies, sport and commercial fishermen, environmentalists, and everyday citizens.

There is an impressive grassroots effort to restore damaged salmon spawning habitat in local streams in the Pacific Northwest. Local schools are participating in programs in which the students rear salmon from the egg and release them into a locally restored stream habitat. Thus, the next generation is learning early that they can influence the success of the salmon and, at the same time preserve the unique environment of the Pacific Northwest for themselves and their children.

Beachcombers wishing to observe wild salmon in the act of spawning will have to do some homework. The timing of spawning and location of salmon spawning habitat varies from watershed to watershed [2]. Beachcombers should contact fishery biologists with state or provincial fish and wildlife agencies, or local officials who monitor water quality or habitat resources. Local fishing supply stores are also good sources of information. Ideally, the beachcomber should become a regular observer of a salmon stream and watch for the salmon's arrival.

REFERENCES:

1. Groot, C. and L. Margolis, eds., *Pacific Salmon Life Histories.* Vancouver, B.C.: University of British Columbia Press, 1991.
2. Steelquist, R., *Field Guide to the Pacific Salmon.* Seattle: Sasquatch Books, 1992, 64 pp.
3. Bond, C. E. and A. J. Beardsley, *Field Guide to Common Marine and Bay Fishes of Oregon.* Corvallis: Oregon State University Extension Service, Manual #4, 1984, 59 pp.
4. National Research Council. *Upstream: Salmon and Society in the Pacific Northwest.* Washington, D.C.: National Academy Press, 1995.

INDEX